EATING AND DRINKING IN FRANCE TODAY

Pamela Vandyke Price

CHARLES SCRIBNER'S SONS
NEW YORK

In memory
of the most loved of
travelling companions who taught me
about French food and wines
Alan
and Allan
Sans pareil

1 3 5 7 9 11 13 15 17 19 V/C 20 18 16 14 12 10 8 6 4 2

Printed in the United States of America
Library of Congress Catalog Card Number 73-19356
ISBN 0-684-13756-9

Contents

CONTENTS

CONTENTS

Acknowledgment

Throughout the preparation of this book and in the course of the revision made for the present edition, I have received help from very many people. The personal interest all have shown, as well as the information they have supplied, explains the length of this section.

Much of the book was written in the home of the late Allan and Mrs Sichel, who so often invited me to be their guest, both in London and in France, that I could never have undertaken to write anything about the country without their assistance. Mr and Mrs Peter Sichel, of Maison Sichel, Bordeaux, and Château d'Angludet have, likewise, been most helpful and hospitable, both there and at Château Palmer. Mr Alejandro Cassinello, my host at the Trois Glorieuses and on innumerable occasions in London, has also most generously put his knowledge and that of his many friends in France at my disposal. Miss Rosemary McRobert and Miss Helen Thomson, who accompanied me on some of the journeys involved, were benevolently critical, and Mrs Jean Robertson inadvertently sparked off the whole idea for this book when she asked for some recommendations and was nearly overwhelmed with a torrent of information.

I owe a great deal to Mr George Peploe, of Charrington Vintners, who first taught me about wine and has always encouraged me, and have especially to acknowledge the help received and the kindness demonstrated by: Mrs Elizabeth David, Madame Simone Prunier, Mr G. U. Salvi, The Honourable Moyra Campbell, Mr Patrick Forbes of Moët et Chandon, Messrs A. J. L. and B. Reuss of Dent & Reuss, Mr John Baker, founder of the Academy of Wine, Mr Frank Egan of G.E.V.S.O., Mr Hugh Mackay, Major Alan Rook of Skinner Rook & Chambers, Mr and Mrs Ronald Avery and Mr and Mrs John Avery of Averys of Bristol, Mr and Mrs John Sutton of J. J. Norman of Exeter, Mr and Mrs David Peppercorn and Mr and Mrs James Long of Gilbey Vintners and Mr Martin Bamford, M.W. of Château Loudenne, Messrs Edward Roche, R. E. H. Gunyon, and John Lipitch of Edouard Robinson, Mr John Davies, M.W. of Hedges & Butler, Mr Colin Fenton, M.W. and Mr John Lloyd of Sothebys, Mr Michael Broadbent, M.W. of Christie Manson & Woods, Messrs R. A. M. Morshead, Charles Whitfield, M.W. and R. Stowell of Stowells of Chelsea, Dr O. W. Loeb and Mr A. Goldthorp of O. W. Loeb, and Mr Edward

12

Bidwell, of Sichel & Co.

Special help with the detail of certain chapters has been provided through the good offices of Mr Gerald Asher, Mrs Nicole Oakley, Mrs Nan Keen, Mr and Mrs Michael Geare and Colonel and Mrs Geoffrey Portham. The help of the French Government Tourist Office in London, in particular that of Mr John East and, more recently, Mrs Pauline Hallam, and that of their colleagues in Bordeaux, Toulouse, Alsace and the Ardennes, was most generously given throughout; my admiration for their efficiency and patience is, I know, shared by many colleagues and visitors to France. The French Embassy, S.O.P.E.X.A., and Food From France have likewise been extremely helpful.

It was remarked that the acknowledgments in the original edition of this book were 'a directory of the British wine trade'. My gratitude to those named there is no less, but there have been changes in names of firms and, alas, a number of those who taught me and helped me are, now, only names. So I have decided to name only the firms and not the individuals for this edition; the traditions of hospitality and patience with someone who was trying to learn about food and wine are maintained even although others have been involved with the preparation of this book in its new form. But I owe thanks to: J. L. P. Lebègue, J. B. Reynier, Cock, Russell & Spedding, Christopher & Co., Lawlers of London, Corney & Barrow, Williams & Humbert, Mentzendorff, Deinhard, John Harvey, Hatch, Mansfield, Hedges & Butler, H. Sichel & Sons, French Wine Farmers, Morgan Furze, Heyman Brothers, G. F. Grant, Pimm's, Matthew Clark, George Idle Courtenay, C. H. Tapp, Charles Kinloch, Peter Dominic, Arthur Cooper of Reading, the Army & Navy Stores, Rutherford Osborne & Perkin and Percy Fox, in whose company I first drank a fine wine. Messrs. Ingram & Royle provided me with most interesting information about table waters.

In France I am particularly grateful to: M. Jean du Bouëtiez, who arranged for me to explore Brittany and to learn about Muscadet, M. Pierre Ligier of the Maison du Vin, Avignon, for a most comprehensive visit to the Rhône, M. Joseph d'Argent of the C.I.V.C. for an exemplary introduction to Champagne, and to Madame Rieffel, Délégué Régional au Tourisme for Alsace-Lorraine and her many colleagues who helped me in a return visit to that beautiful province. Friends who have been my especial hosts and helpers include: M. & Mme Robert Cointreau of Angers, M. and Mme Daniel Querre, of Château Monbousquet, in the Gironde, M. & Mme Pierre Viraut, M. and

Mme J. Saint-Martin, M. and Mme L. Séguin all of the Distillerie de la Côte Basque, Bayonne, MM. François and Robert Hine and their families of Jarnac, Mme and the late M. Guy Roullet of Cognac, M. and Mme Christian de Billy of Pol Roger, Epernay, and the establishments of Mercier, Taittinger, Ruinart, Perrier-Jouët and other hospitable friends in the Champagne region; M. Charles Déjean of Sète, M. Robert Debus of Schiltigheim. In Burgundy I would like to thank MM. Ernest and Jacques Breuillot, also the establishments of Louis Latour, Patriarche, Jules Belin, Bouchard Aîné, Lupé Cholet. In the Beaujolais I must thank MM. David & Foillard and their families, and M. Michel Gaidon of Château de Pizay, and M. Charles Piat. In Bordeaux I must thank M. Raymond Dupin of Château Grand Puy Lacoste, M. and Mme Jean Potesta, M. and Mme Henri Mahler-Besse, who gave me the chance to see Montaigne's estate and tower in sunshine and by moonlight, M. Gildas Bardinet and his colleagues, M. Nathaniel Johnson, MM. Jacques and Jean Calvet, the establishment of Marie Brizard et Roger, and that of Cruse, where M. Edouard Cruse has not only been my host on many occasions, but who has enabled me to drink some remarkable old wines; Baron Elie de Rothschild, my host at a Fête de la Fleur at Château Lafite, and the Baron and Baronne Philippe de Rothschild, who have enabled me to see the museum at Mouton Rothschild on several occasions. Great kindness has been shown to me by M. and Mme Hugel of Riquewihr, and, in Ammerschwihr, by M. Kuehn and MM. Schielé, in Gigondas by M. and Mme Meffre, and in Paris by the establishment of Géveor, who showed me round Paris-Bercy. Very useful information was provided by the houses of Kronenbourg, Noilly Prat, Lillet and Perrier.

Friends whose knowledge of living in France has been of great value to me include: Mr and Mrs Ronald Barton of Barton & Guestier and Châteaux Léoville and Langoa Barton, Mr and Mrs Nicholas Barrow of Château Courant and, perhaps above all, Mr and Mrs John Salvi of Maison Sichel, whose knowledge of French restaurants and of cooking equals their knowledge of wine.

It is not possible to thank all the restaurateurs who have patiently answered my questions, the curators of museums who have devoted much time to showing me their treasures, or the makers of wine who have most generously allowed me to taste ranges of wines throughout France. But I do owe a special debt to Mrs Vivienne Markham, who supervised my French and comments on French life, and Mr Daniel Salem who, in spite of being the head of an organisation in which I was for a while concerned, took the trouble to act as a more efficient sub-editor than any I ever had otherwise. My colleagues in the worlds of wine and food have given practical assistance by bringing additional information to my knowledge and helping me to update the text and I owe particular thanks to Mr Cyril Ray and Mr Edmund Penning-Rowsell, of whom it is true to say that I have never read anything written by them without learning a great deal.

Finally there are the readers who have found this book useful, the students who have said it has been helpful—their response and the enthusiasm of my publishers have made the work well worth while.

May all visitors to France have such friends.

London 1971

Since the first edition of this book, many people have asked me about the dedication. The two names are those of my husband, Alan Vandyke Price (1924–1955), and the man for whom he was named, Allan Sichel (1900–1965).

Introduction

For the past twenty-one years I have been spending holidays in France at seasons ranging from early March to late October and for varying lengths of time. But I have never remained there for more than three weeks at a stretch and although I have been fortunate enough to be invited by many friends to stay in their homes, I have never actually lived in the country and for much of my many visits I have been travelling about. Consequently I am a fairly experienced tourist rather than an authority on the country, and although my French is now fluent, it started by being rudimentary, especially as I was never lucky enough to be taught by a Frenchwoman. So what I know about France—a country in which I admit to finding nearly everything I want when on holiday—has been learned as an outsider, and if not exactly the hard way, then certainly by the necessity of making myself understood to people who cannot speak any English, travelling cross-country by various methods of transport, watching the budget, planning the route, looking after companions temporarily unwell and coping with myself and the various problems that arise for a woman older than twenty and younger than seventy travelling by herself.

Before I went to France I knew very little about food and nothing about wine. But the revelation of what food can be when handled by a master turned me, like many post-war travellers and self-made home cooks, into a fascinated amateur, and for the last nine years wine, especially the wine of France, has provided me with the same sort of interest and satisfaction as some people gain from music, painting or the contemplation of anything that is beautiful, living and expressive of the something beyond the stars that can, in various guises, touch most of us with its enchantment.

There is a lot of nonsense talked and written about both food and wine and also about France. In my opinion chef cooking is not at all to be confused with home cooking, any more than the music that one makes for one's personal pleasure and the diversion of friends is to be confounded with that of the masters of the concert hall. Nor are the little wines, some of which are perfect accompaniments to holiday or everyday meals, to be appraised in the same way as the great ones of the classic regions. All can be good but each has a place and a purpose. And, despite the ecstasies of some so-called gourmet travellers, my French friends will agree with me that it is perfectly possible to find indifferent food and bad cooking even in the gastronomic centre of the world.

Although, therefore, the scenery, the towns and the French character and way of life all play important parts in my holiday enjoyment, the food and drink of France share the star rôle; I think that I would prefer to be hungry than to endure real cold, but it is nevertheless possible to surmount the dreariness of an unattractive place, bad weather and low spirits if one can count on good fare. And an interest in food and drink is something that can triumph over differences in language, age and sex—a healthy appetite and a strong sense of curiosity are passports to goodwill in all places where goodwill exists. So it is sad to see a party of British travellers progressing across some of the richer provinces of France venturing only to order *apéritifs* of Dubonnet or 'le whisky', with omelettes and salad to follow—and being aware, vaguely, that they are missing something; the extroverts and those whose stomachs permit them to be adventurous may branch out with a change of fare, risking vast expense and possible disappointment, and those who are avid readers of cookery books may try to match up recipes with menus, but none of this is simple, especially if one has to depend on school French and a phrase book in which only the basic foods are included.

A book of the kind I have compiled would have saved ᵣne money, worry and embarrassment years ago, and would greatly have added to the enjoyment of my holidays. This is the test I have therefore applied when in doubt as to what to include. If it would have helped me, the information goes in. Of course, there is much, especially in the sections dealing with the different regions, where the knowledge of any one person must fall short of answering all requirements, but I have tried to pick out the things to see and try that will interest (even if they do not appeal to) anyone appreciative of good food and drink, not specifically the cook or specialised gastronome, but the family or group of friends wanting to get every scrap of enjoyment out of a journey through or holiday in France.

It must be admitted that, while I like value for money, I do not grudge spending on good fare, even lavishly on outstanding food, from time to time. So although I trust that this book will help many to get the best for their francs, it is not a guide to eating on the cheap in France—French food is expensive. Nor am I an advocate of stocking the boot of your car with tinned food so that you can economise, or of roughing it by way of a change. When I go on holiday I like other people to do the work for me which includes the cooking, and I want them to do it well. There are books dealing with camping, taking children abroad, inexpensive holidays and specialised pursuits, such as climbing, riding, winter and summer sports—all sorts of things that have no part in my kind of holiday, which consists of the sun, the countryside and sea, pleasant people, occasional interesting towns, comfort equivalent to that in my own home and food and drink that are at least good and different and at best an inspiration and a golden memory. There have been very few times when France has let me down.

How much difference can be accounted for between the two countries by the fact that French children are expected to eat like adults and English people to eat like their children?

The Sunday Times 1955

London 1971

Introduction to the American Edition

Many of my friends from the United States have found the earlier edition of this book helpful to them, and I trust that their number will now be augmented. The interest shown by Americans in French wines, and their willingness to increase their knowledge of different styles of cooking make me hope that increasing numbers will be encouraged to venture beyond the circuit of hotels offering 'international' dishes and the sort of wines about which one cynically comments that those who buy them are content merely to 'drink the label' rather than the contents of the bottle.

It is true that sometimes it appears that one's countrymen abroad are specifically bred for export, as one never sees them quite like that at home: the British demanding cups of tea and chips with everything, the Americans vociferously suspicious of the drinking water and plumbing and, as several French restaurants have sadly commented, unwilling to order anything except chicken or steak. We know these are unfair generalisations and perhaps all of us should be more assertive in counteracting the impressions made by this kind of behaviour.

The French are a proud people. They have had to be, to survive what their country has endured during the last century and a half. This gives them a toughness that can sometimes seem hostility to those who are both easier-going—because their lives have been easier—and who do not speak French. The French language is not only one of the most exquisitely precise tongues, it can be elegant as regards phrasing and beautiful to hear; the French cherish it and protect their language in a way that we who have inherited one of the richest vocabularies and most musical ways of speech have never done; our lack of words, repetition of meaningless phrases, sloppy diction, casual phrasing—and our assumption that none of this really matters—are something that they can never accept (and I think they are right).

So, in wishing you happy travelling—actual or armchair—with this book, may I also wish you the humility and ability to acquire even a few phrases of greeting or thanks in French, with an accent and intonation that does not offend the acute French ear. A correctly pronounced wine or food name, conduct that is reticent rather than ebullient at the outset, are passwords often more efficacious than lavish tipping and use of first names.

France is a woman—of infinite fascination and charm. She will yield little, if at all, to assault, much to adroit seduction. And as far as food and wine are concerned, she has still many treasures with which to welcome and delight the visitor.

London 1973

Part I Using this Book

If you are travelling through France or spending any time there I have assumed that you will be making use of a guide book. Even if one flashes through a town, it is somehow imprinted more on the memory if there is some kind of guide book tag as to what one could have seen, and what may be visited another time. There is a list of some current guide books at the end, with my own comments on them. But this book does not attempt to be a guide to anything except regional food and drink, plus such things as wine museums, medieval kitchens, cellars, cheese caves and places specialising in the manufacture of anything contributing to the enhancement of food and drink that may be of interest to the layman. Corsica is omitted from the regions simply because I have never been there, and Paris cannot be dealt with in detail, because that would need a separate book, and there are very many excellent and detailed guides to Paris anyway. Nor is there much about the great coastal resorts, as these tend to be rather like a certain type of luxury hotel, international rather than national or regional.

Just as the ideal way to learn about a town is to walk in it, so the ideal way to explore the provinces of France is to drive. But French buses and trains are good, also the internal air services, and although I hope that the majority of hungry travellers may have the use of a car, it is not essential to the enjoyment of regional food and drink at its best. Details of how to get about are not given because they are either included in other books or because even the non-French-speaking traveller really determined on achieving an objective will invariably do so by his or her personal initiative.

I would like to stress what I consider the importance of filling in a little of the background to the country before spending any time there. The list of books about France that I have enjoyed will, I hope, encourage travellers to brief themselves about some of the regions that form a background to their table and bottle of wine. There are, too, sections on keeping well while being greedy, coping with what I have roughly described as cloakroom problems and such things as securing a quiet bedroom, adapting to French home life and conversation when being entertained, and knowing what to take to France and what, in addition to happy memories, to bring home. I have been fortunate enough to meet a very wide range of French men and women; I cannot possibly comment, except in gratitude, on the difference between the kitchen and cellar of a two-room flat above a shop, a little house in a suburb of an industrial city, a country house and what was in all but name a palace; nor do I differentiate in my own mind between the café hôtel *avec chambres* that became like a friend's house to me, the Relais des Routiers where I was taught to cook sweetbreads in cream, the delightful pavilion in the country where one shared the witty conversation of the owners but to which one could never send the intolerant or conventionally strait-laced, or the splendid establishment where the owners were always friends but treated their visitors like royalty incognito. But, as it is always possible to learn, all these people and places, and many more, taught me things that have gone into this book: the advice of the outsider who learned it all the practical (never the hard) way.

The book is divided into two parts. At the beginning are the general counsels, which can be useful when you are planning a holiday or visit to France; then the different regions of the country are considered from the gourmet point of view, for reading on the spot. It is not possible to divide them sharply into either the modern French provinces or the older districts, because obviously food has no exact frontiers, so I have assumed in the reader my sort of approach: for example, a vaguely defined area that I term 'Loire' means the area along the river that this word signifies to the tourist, including the Indre and Cher, the châteaux country and up into the Sarthe. The ordinary guide book or map will give the exact boundaries.

Although one of the best ways of learning about a country is to take the advice of those on the spot, it must be admitted that, as far as the gastonomic traveller is concerned anyway, they are not always the best authorities. In our country we do not invariably and automatically take friends to certain well-known restaurants, popularised by their reputation for giving tourists something typically British, either in surroundings or in fare; often we consider this sort of thing overdone, or familiarity has made us hypercritical. But the visitor may be impressed precisely by the place or set of circumstances that we either do not rate very highly or else tend to ignore. So, although I have tried to take the traveller off the beaten track a little, I have not despised it, even though some French friends have assured me that this particular dish was only 'for the tourist', or that that tasting room was rather overdone—'for the tourist, you understand'. It is as tourists that we all gain our impressions, unless we are fortunate enough to live in a country for some time.

Similarly, my enthusiasm over certain French country houses and castles, in which I have found old kitchens, reconstructed dining-rooms, or even *musées folkloriques* have often surprised my friends; as a lover of food and drink, I am interested in collections of tasting cups, old wine presses and drinking glasses, or collections of kitchen utensils, even though these may be rather simply presented and not at all arranged to impress the tourist, but on many occasions I have had to insist that a particular place must be worth a visit in order to see such things, when my French friends were far keener on showing me something quite different.

This ruling may also be applied to choosing hotels and restaurants. The recommendation of a charming little place in the country by a French friend may lead one to finding oneself in a very simple hotel indeed, without the sort of comfort that many of us would consider essential to a holiday—though, by contrast, the standard of most French camping sites, with adjacent comforts, is far superior to many of our own. At the other end of the scale, many of the French luxury hotels in the country achieve a standard of excellence and costliness that only about a dozen establishments in the British Isles could equal, and the British tourist may be quite unprepared for the formality and expense of what superficially seems like a country house hotel.

Recipes are not included in this book because there are several excellent collections of them (see pp. 308–309) and because this is a guide to food and drink for the use of people who wish to enjoy rather than participate in the making of both. One is, after all, on holiday! The vocabularies at the end of most of the sections need a short explanation: they contain words that, because they may be technical or local, are not always to be found even in big dictionaries, and phrases that are useful but not included in most ordinary phrase books. For example, I have never found a phrase book that tells you how to explain to a waiter that you and your friends each want a separate bill, yet this is one of the commonest holiday requirements among groups of friends travelling together. Similarly, there are certain key words that used to baffle me when I was following an otherwise fascinating discussion on wine; to ask for an explanation may only release a torrent of comment that leaves one even more confused. I have arranged these vocabularies at the end of each section in which they may be required, as this seems less frightening to the beginner in French than to face a composite vocabulary like a small dictionary, and the way in which the words are given depends on the context: for example, in the section on wine regions, the French words and phrases are given first, because those are what the traveller will be hearing, but in the sections on hotel arrangements and cloakrooms the English words are given first, because it is the translations of these that the visitor will need, possibly in the course of a hurried conversation, when it is less convenient to scan a series of French words. Cooking terms are omitted, except when they concern the menu and ordering, as these will be found in the recommended cookery books, and the names of the kitchen utensils that travellers may wish to buy to take home are given, with descriptions, in Mrs Elizabeth David's *French Provincial Cooking*.

In the sections dealing with the different regions there are naturally omissions; the gastronomically rich districts get more space than those which, though they may be favourite resorts, are not markedly distinctive in this particular way. This does not mean that you cannot find good food and drink in them. Similarly, the author is human and cannot know each region equally well; lovers of one place may find favourite eating places and specialities left out, and I may have devoted too much detail to my best-loved districts. But the charm of food and gastronomy is like that of wine: no one can ever know everything and it is rewarding and fascinating for novice and old hands to exchange experiences and recommendations, for there is always the future in which one hopes to learn more.

*   *   *

'It is said that the English are conservative in matters of food. I have never agreed with this opinion. If English people appear conservative about their diet it is merely that nobody has ever taken the trouble to introduce them to something new . . . Few customers care to ask "What is this dish made from? What is it like?" This trait is conspicuously English; customers just will *not* ask, save in exceptional cases. Either they will take a chance and order it (with a subconscious feeling they won't enjoy it), or else they will give it a miss, and have something they do know about . . . So, if there is an unfamiliar dish on the menu and I am on friendly terms with the customer, I will recommend it, and tell them its ingredients, all about it, and any bit of history connected with it. Thus the dish becomes food for the mind as well as the body . . . With very few exceptions, most customers like to know about different foreign dishes, and quite rightly too. They miss a lot if they are not experimental with restaurant cuisine . . . On the whole I think that ladies experiment more than men. A lady likes to go to a restaurant because she can have dishes that can't be prepared at home.'

Joseph Vecchi *The Tavern is My Drum* (Odhams 1948)

How the French Eat

Food is of great importance to most French men and women although, as in the British Isles, the very wealthy and aristocratic tend to be less obviously concerned; a very large proportion of the average French income is spent on it—far more than in Britain. It is also in general more expensive, and although packaged and tinned foods, frozen food-stuffs, and all the conveniences of the supermarket have made some impression on French housekeeping, most people shop daily, so as to buy what is both fresh and at the best price, and, in addition to a conservative mixture of many so-called 'convenience foods', there is a current trend to opt for the natural and traditional. France is an agricultural country and the market is a feature of most towns and an important weekly event, or even a daily affair. The majority of people take their main meal of the day in their homes, and although it may be a surprise to see the enormous and expensive meals consumed in restaurants at weekends and on public holidays, it would be wrong to assume that the family eat on a similarly lavish scale at home; it may often be true, however, that even people in a fairly humble way will eat more elaborate and complicated food than their British counterparts. In many French homes one will look in vain for armchairs or a sofa. Conversation and good fare are such an integral part of French life that upright chairs, such as may be placed round a table, may be the only kind. Wit and profound talk seldom flourish when people lounge!

In general, breakfast in France is a very light meal—coffee with milk plus a roll or bread or rusks, with butter. Travellers or those who live alone and can afford to go out for this often do so. There is not a mid-morning coffee break, except for the very social or cosmopolitan, but at mid-day the principal meal is taken. The lunch-time lasts a couple of hours (except in Paris, where it is often only an hour), and people out at work go home if humanly possible, where they will have probably two courses or more, followed by cheese and fruit. There is no tea-break. The evening meal tends to be a light one, maybe soup, cold food and vegetables, followed by cheese and fruit, which may be taken around seven o'clock, although in the southern towns people usually eat a little later. An *apéritif* may be taken on the way home, or a family may go out to a café for coffee or drinks later. But it is as impossible to generalise about the details of French domestic catering as it would be to do the same about Britain; some French families live and eat very simply indeed, others in what might seem to many of us considerable style.

Sunday is the great family day; on Saturday marketing may be done, but on Sunday people often like to go out or entertain, especially for lunch. In the mornings, the pastry-shops are open so that *gâteaux* and cakes, *vol-au-vent* cases and elaborate tarts and cream confections may be bought by those who are receiving friends. Restaurants usually do their best trade and cafés and all places of refreshment may be crowded, although the evening is usually quieter. The same applies to the public holidays, which are rather more numerous than in Great Britain, and include the religious holidays of Christmas Day, Easter Monday, Ascension Day, Whit Monday, the Assumption (15 August), All Saints Day (1 November), and also New Year's Day, 1 May, Victory Day (8 May), Bastille Day (14 July) and Armistice Day (11 November).

These brief remarks do something to explain why there are certain differences in French hotel and restaurant ways from those to which most British visitors are accustomed. For example, the absence of a lounge or room in which to sit is not felt as a loss in small French hotels; people use the public rooms to eat and drink and otherwise go out when they are on holiday, or go to bed when a reasonable time has elapsed after their evening meal. There is seldom a writing-room, because pen and paper can always be supplied by a café. And as the French, when away from home, invariably take breakfast in their bedrooms—unless, of course, they go out to a café—visitors who wish to breakfast downstairs may find themselves the sole people in a dining-room that is being cleaned.

Types of catering establishment

Because French catering establishments are not quite the same as places bearing the same names in Britain, it may be helpful for the visitor to have a note of what can be got where. It took me some time to sort out the distinction between bar, café and buffet.

Un bar by itself is, essentially, a place where one goes for a rather quick drink, possibly standing up at the bar itself. *Un bar comptoir* is precisely this—a place for a stand-up drink. *Un bar dégustation* may have tables and chairs, and so may an ordinary bar. In large bars you may be able to get a sandwich or a snack, although a French bar is not really an eating place. It is perfectly correct for a woman to go into a bar, although, as in Britain, there are bars and bars. One assesses the establishment by the outside. But a bar is not a place to go for a cup of coffee, although sometimes large bars do have it available. One can always telephone from a bar. *Un buffet* is a type of restaurant for quick meals, both sitting at tables and the snack counter. The term is only used for eating places on stations and at airports, although the larger terminals may have a restaurant as well.

Une brasserie originally meant a brewery and hence the name implies somewhere in which beer is served, together with sandwiches and snacks. This is the place to find draught beer, which is seldom available in a small bar. But a *brasserie* may also serve light meals and other drinks, including coffee.

Un café is a family and social eating and drinking place, where one may go for a single drink, or, if it describes itself as a *café restaurant*, with menus posted outside, a full meal. According to its size and capacity it may serve ice-creams, snacks, sandwiches, and offer several menus of different prices, as well as an *à la carte*, in addition to alcoholic and soft drinks, tea and coffee. Families go to cafés to meet friends for special occasions or when on holiday, cards and other games may be played, and the waiter will always supply writing materials. Cafés range from the huge, smart and expensive kind, such as the Café de la Paix in Paris, serving first-class food, to the simplest sort. The solitary traveller need never be shy about ordering a meal or a drink in a café, and however busy the place may be, no one will hover over you implying that you should move; a soft drink or a coffee can be made to last hours if you wish. And the woman on her own need have no hesitation about taking meals or refreshments in a café; if she is so beautiful that she is bound to attract attention, she is also probably accustomed to disregarding it.

Un restaurant serves meals, not drinks by themselves, and usually only within the mid-day and evening meal times, whereas a *café restaurant* may have food, as well as snacks, available for most of the day and evening. *Casse-croûte* (snack) *à toutes heures*, or even *repas à toutes heures* imply this, and the words are often written on the outside of the establishment. *Repas rapide* is a sign sometimes seen on the side of main roads, where there are nowadays occasional *restauroutes*, which provide quick meals, often including the cold meat that visitors like when travelling and which can be difficult to get in an ordinary restaurant. In a town, I have occasionally seen the words *déjeuner homme d'affaires* (businessman's lunch) on a menu outside a restaurant, implying a meal that will be good value and not take much time, though, apart from the mere snack or sandwich, every French eating establishment considers it worth while taking more time than we allow for even a simple meal. After all, the lunch break does often consist of two hours. Although I have not encountered the minimum charge practice in France, a restaurant (even a humble one) will be reluctant to serve you with just one dish, unless it is fairly substantial and includes salad and other trimmings. This can cost as much as a small-scale *prix fixe* menu (see pp. 36–37). So if you do want just one thing, it is advisable to go to a café or snack bar instead of a restaurant, both for economy and convenience, or, if the restaurant has several sections, to inquire whether one of them may not be a quick meal or snack department.

As with cafés, the range of restaurants is very wide, but both cafés and restaurants offering meals almost always display a menu outside, both of the various set price meals and the *à la carte*, so that you can get an idea of the price before entering. Only the very exclusive and costly may not show their charges, though most do. *Un salon de thé* (unless it really is an English tea-room, kept by our countrymen or women) is rather more in the nature of what we should call a coffee house. It is often part of a *pâtissier*'s shop. Tea, coffee, cakes, ice-creams and sometimes sandwiches and little savoury snacks may be served, and sometimes alcoholic drinks, usually sweet ones, can be bought. A *salon de thé* may be in the nature of an elegant meeting place for fairly prosperous ladies and their families, so it can be expensive; tea and coffee can cost more than in a café, and cream cakes are seldom cheap.

Une buvette, which may be a kiosk or little hut out in the country, is a place where you can get a drink: mineral water, beer or *vin ordinaire*, and sometimes coffee and tea and ices as well. It is essentially somewhere for travellers to stop and refresh themselves. Sometimes sandwiches or very simple food may be served, and sometimes a *buvette* or bar or little country café may have the sign *Ici on peut apporter son manger*, or *On reçoit avec provisions* which signifies that you can bring your own picnic and eat it on their tables, sitting in chairs, with cutlery and tableware supplied, and only buy drinks as you wish. This is a great convenience for people who wish to be spared the major chores of a picnic but who want to take packed food out on excursions.

Un bistro(t) is a small restaurant where—at least in theory—you can get a meal fairly quickly. The word dates from the Allies' occupation of Paris after the Battle of Waterloo, when the Russian soldiers demanded quick service—for which the Russian word was *bistro*. Today, however, a bistro, especially in Paris, can be ultra smart and correspondingly expensive, despite the dictionary definition as *pub*.

Une guinguette is a refreshment pavilion, usually with music and possibly dancing, such as you may find on the side of a well-equipped swimming pool, or, as the dictionary rather meekly says, 'in the suburbs'. It is a type of snack eating place. In connection with dancing, it is worth noting that the word *bal* means a public dance, almost in the nature of a hop, rather than dance or ball as the terms are understood today. The name *guinguette* is supposed to derive from that of a type of grape, formerly grown in the outer suburbs of Paris, from which a rather sharpish wine was made, and sold in the taverns outside the city walls. *Estaminet* (which might be roughly translated as pub), *hostellerie* (now hotel), *taverne* (bar), and *auberge* (café-hotel) are all words that are on the archaic side now, and although they may be used in up-to-date establishment names, this may imply a certain olde worlde character, such as hostelry, or inn in English. But an *auberge* should not be taken to mean an old-fashioned place—some of the most luxurious and up-to-the-minute country hotels use the term and the same is sometimes true of *hostellerie*.

Un hôtel does not invariably have a restaurant, although, should there not be one, the establishment will be able to supply a continental breakfast. If there should be a restaurant, there will probably—but not invariably—be a bar, although this may be small, sometimes only a few chairs and tables.

Un cabaret means a small pub rather than a night club (for which the more usual phrase is '*boîte de nuit*'), but it can sometimes be a rather smart small eating place.

La terrasse, in connection with anywhere to eat or drink, means the tables and chairs that are set outside. Even although where they are placed is not raised or anything like the terrace that the term implies to British visitors, it is described as *sur la terrasse*, although it may consist either of two or three small tables, or up to a hundred. In this context, the term *volière*, which is sometimes seen listed among the attractions of a restaurant, means that there is an aviary or pen for ornamental birds, and not, as is easily imagined by associating the word with *voile* (sail), that there is an awning over the tables set out in the open.

French Hotels and How to Cope with Them

Even if your knowledge of the French language is very slight, you can be sure of getting both what you want and value for money if you shed some of your insular habits.

When booking or asking for hotel rooms, state exactly what is required and for how many people. It is cheaper for married couples, or for friends who share rooms, for the thrifty French tend to cram as many people as possible into a room so as to be sure of plenty of customers in their restaurant. This can be extremely annoying for friends travelling in company who nevertheless want rooms to themselves, and some hotels will refuse a single client for what is technically a double room, however willing he or she may be to pay for this; this is exasperating, although for those travelling with children, or for the young who do not mind going back to the dorm the practice can prove economical. It is, however, important to be definite as to how many people are going to occupy a stated number of rooms when you inquire about them.

As telephone bookings can be awkward, even for those with a fair knowledge of French, there is an alphabet appended to this chapter that will enable even the most hard of hearing receptionist to get the strange foreign name.

Especially in the country, a hotel will expect you to take dinner in the establishment where you are staying, and sometimes may refuse to give you a room if you are not going to dine. Therefore it is important, when you are inquiring about rooms, to state whether you will be arriving for dinner; if you are, space will usually be found for you unless the place is genuinely full. Should you, as may happen, be dining with friends, get them to do the telephoning and excusing, as the hotel will not wish to risk offending possible local customers and will accept the genuine excuse.

If you are staying for three days or more, it is usually well worth while asking for demi-pension or pension terms. But

28

remember that, except in a fairly large or town hotel, the main meal will be served at lunch-time, so that if you plan to go out midday with a picnic meal you may only get a light supper in the evening if you are a *pensionnaire*.

Special terms for children should also be arranged at the outset of any stay—French hotels are usually perfectly willing to provide these.

Always ask to see the room and inquire the price as a matter of course. You will be thought improvident if you do not and you will automatically be allocated the most expensive room in the house. The price should be given to you with the additional information as to whether the figure includes breakfast (continental, taken in the room), and the taxes and service. The phrase is *service et taxes compris (stc)*. These additions can make an appreciable difference to the total, so make sure whether or not they are quoted.

Rooms at the top of the house tend to be cheaper than those lower down, and if there is a lift, this need be no hardship. Should you want a cot or extra bed put in your room for a child this will mean a small extra charge, but it is something that can usually easily be arranged.

Although a room with a bath may sound like an extravagance, it can be the reverse, especially if you are staying in the south in the summer; to get a public bathroom unlocked can be a nuisance as well as an expense. Not all rooms with bathrooms, however, automatically have lavatories, so remember to ask about this if you want one to yourself. Rooms with showers are more frequently found than in British hotels and can be the perfect compromise if you cannot afford a bathroom. A *cabinet de toilette* usually consists of a basin and bidet and, possibly, a lavatory, but this is not invariable.

In the country you may come up against hotels that only provide double beds instead of two single ones in double rooms. Sometimes an extra bed can be moved in, but this again is something worth inquiring about when first making the booking.

Rather unexpectedly, it is often much cheaper to take a suite than two single rooms (one of them with bath), so for friends or a married couple with a teenage or older child, this is something worth asking for. Sometimes the main bedroom will have a very small one leading off it, or, if there is a sitting room, there may be a divan here for the third party. For people who like space in their rooms a suite can be a good idea, as some French hotel rooms are on the small side.

Many French hotels are built with a number of the rooms on the same floor communicating with each other. The timid traveller can be reassured that the communicating doors are nearly always double and will never be unlocked except by specific requests from the occupants of both the rooms concerned. But this too can be useful for a party travelling together, either with children, or else friends who may be sharing the bathroom attached to one of the rooms.

Peace and quiet   This is a problem that is often insoluble for the tourist. Personally, I do not think that the French mind traffic noises to the extent that most British travellers do, so that anyone who is easily disturbed must be really firm about trying to get a peaceful room if obliged to stay in any town. Not only should one avoid rooms on the main road, but equally those on corners, especially if there is a nearby hill where heavy lorries brake or change gear; a room that gives onto a market place, or a seemingly quiet square where there may be a café beloved by the late-night younger set may be equally unsatisfactory, and if you get the well of the hotel, then you may be disturbed by the conversations going on in every other room looking out onto it and the kitchen clatter coming up into the bargain—especially infuriating if there has been a big banquet at the weekend, after which the washing up seems to go on all night. One can also be over-clever in insisting on rooms at the back, as I once found when trying to avoid looking over a station (with public announcements starting at 6 a.m.), and got an apparently quiet room giving directly onto the town slaughterhouse.

It is only fair to say that, except on major routes nationales, most traffic declines from ten o'clock at night, but it tends to start bright and early soon after six in the morning.

If noise really upsets the traveller, it is also worth checking whether bells or clocks that chime are in the vicinity of the hotel. See that the room is not next to or very near the lavatory or any staff door or pantry, or over or adjacent to any banqueting suite or public room where other clients may sit late. As corridors may not always be carpeted, feet tend to thunder on wooden floors. Nor do I know of any French hotel room door that can be opened without a clatter or closed without a slam; the same tends to be true of windows as, even when these can be opened and closed without exercise of force, the shutters or exterior blinds seldom can, and as many of these last are made of metal, the sound they make, morning and evening, resembles the clanging of prison gates in a melodrama. French travellers generally rise earlier than

Les persiennes Venetian blinds
screens on the windows or in
country, do not fling open t
the room once it has been cl
the night)

Les volets The shutters (inside

Un oreiller A pillow (not inva
have to ask for one if you disli
But look in the wardrobe or c
kept there.)

Un saut de lit A bedside mat

Bathroom

Une salle de bain A bathroom

Un cabinet de toilette A small
lavatory, occasionally with a sh
basin and bidet. It may be par
that hasn't actually got a bathr

Une cuvette (de lavabo) A washbas

Une douche A shower

Une baignoire A bath

Une descente de bain A bath mat

Un robinet A tap

Un bouchon/Une bonde A bath plug

Un peignoir de bain A bath wrap (t

Une serviette A towel

La chasse d'eau The flush (of wate

Miscellaneous

En face Opposite

Un filet/Une moustiquaire A net (aga

Une fiche The plug of an electric ap

Une prise de courant An electric poir

Un insecticide An insecticide

Un vaporisateur A spray

Une bombe Insectiside

Fermer à clef To lock

Sur la grande route On the main road

Sur la cour On the yard or well

we do, and from 7 a.m. onwards breakfasts will be brought up-stairs and into rooms—with the concomitant door noises. If there are telephones in rooms, it is possible that these will be fixed by the beds backing on to each other, so that your neighbour's six o'clock call or eight o'clock long-distance conversation will be as loud to you as if it were in your room.

All this adds up to the advantage of staying in the country if you are on holiday. If, however, you have to stay in a town, I would advise either a first-class hotel, where precautions against noise will have been taken, or else a small, humbler one, that stands a chance of being out of the main stream of traffic and of being patronised by others in search of quiet. The middle type of hotel may be in the middle of a thoroughfare and often will be peopled by business travellers who must rise early. Frankly, this kind of hotel has seldom seemed to me to offer good value for the traveller for pleasure.

Tips If service is included (and the percentage can be as much as 15–20%), either in the terms agreed for your hotel room, or put as an additional percentage on your bill, it is not necessary to tip further, except for specific services rendered, such as to the porter who copes with your luggage.

Alphabet

To facilitate the spelling of names over the telephone

Anatole
Berthe
Célestin
Désirée
Eugène
Émile (for spelling any French word with an acute accent)
François
Gaston
Henri
Irma

Joseph
Kléber
Louis
Marcel
Nicolas
Oscar
Pierre
Quintal (if this is misunderstood as 'Cantal', try 'Quimper—comme en Bretagne')

Raoul
Suzanne
Thérèse
Ursule
Victor
William
Xavier
Yvonne
Zoé

The greatest trap, for the English-speaking, is the fact that in French 'i' is pronounced as 'e', and 'e' by itself as a sound approximating 'er'. 'Eugène' serves for most English 'e' sounds, but 'Émile' is given in case it is wished to spell any French word

containing a
French, and
name Xavier,
'Zavier'. But
than those giv
Robert for R-
do not gener
names, so th
simpler, when

Vocabulary

Hotel

Concierge The
keeper)
Une fiche policièr
Un passe-partou
Un appartement
Sur le même étag

Service

Régler To settl
Un chasseur A
La note The bi
Faire la chambre
the chamberm
she may draw
Petit déjeuner com
Enlever le plateau

Bedroom

Une chambre tranq
Chambre à côté A
Une chambre contig
Une chambre comm
Une chambre à part
Une chambre à deux
Un lit pour une pers
Un grand lit A d
Une lampe de chevet
Une couverture A

Making the Most of the Menu

Food is never cheap in France and unfortunately it is just as possible to get an indifferent meal there as anywhere else. But there are numerous ways of getting not only what you want but value for money. This chapter deals with meals in general. For specific food, see pp. 42–56. If you cannot adapt your usual eating habits to French ways during a holiday, then you will be advised either to budget for a lot of extras, or else to stay exclusively in international style hotels. But if you are that sort of traveller, you are unlikely to be reading this book.

Breakfast

This can vary more than is often supposed. In a hotel it is usually taken in the bedroom (at no extra charge), and if you come downstairs, you may be shown to a small salon, writing-room or even the bar in which to eat your breakfast, as the dining-room will probably be in the process of being cleaned. But there is nothing unusual about going out for breakfast, either to a café or a hotel. Should your hotel not have a restaurant, then only a simple meal can be served, of course.

Café complet, or, more accurately, *café au lait complet* means coffee with milk and lumps of sugar accompanied by bread or rolls and butter; sometimes jam is included, but it may be an extra for which you must ask, and marmalade will certainly be in this category unless you are staying in a very big hotel. Butter may come in pats or a small packed slab. In the country you will probably be lucky enough to get a large piece of farm butter, but in a smart hotel or resort the allowance tends to be on the meagre side for our tastes, the reason being that the French do not always use butter on the roll.

Even in the smallest hotel, you may order tea or hot chocolate instead of coffee if you wish, and the price is generally the same, though if you have a special sort of tea, this can be an addition to the bill. If you want a piece of fruit or fresh fruit juice, this is always possible but it can be quite expensive. The wrapped sugar lumps supplied are generally enough for most people, but if you take numerous lumps a personal supply is advisable.

Croissants, according to the Viennese who are said to have invented them after the Turks besieged the city, should be eaten within an hour of being made, otherwise they are doughy and dull. Certainly the average croissant is far from being the light, buttery delight often anticipated, and it can be dear. The majority of croissants are made with margarine, which also makes them heavy, and only the straight sort, available in Paris, have a dough made with butter. Rolls, however, can be very good, crisp and light, and slices of bread (when it is either *gros pain* or *pain de deux livres*, or slices of a *bâtard*, see p. 110) can be crusty and delicious. If you do not specify, you will usually get some bread or a roll and a croissant in a resort or large hotel, and perhaps just bread out in the country, where there may not be a nearby baker.

If you want toast, this will not cost extra, but there are two kinds: *pain grillé*, which is thickish slices of the delicious crusty bread (*gros pain*) brought into brief, fierce contact with a grill, and 'toast', which is toasted slices of either plain white bread or a type of semi-sweet *brioche*. *Pain grillé*, it should be mentioned, is very hard and crusty indeed. If you do not care for bread, there are usually rusks (*biscottes*) and, for the figure conscious, even starch-reduced rusks (*biscottes d'amidon réduit* or *biscottes de régime*).

Mention is made elsewhere of the rather disappointing quality of French jams—at least, as far as those served at breakfast are concerned. Gooseberry, raspberry, strawberry, plum and peach are the most usual, but one does get a jelly type of marmalade sometimes. Honey is not often served though it is usually available if you ask for it.

If you want a substantial breakfast, the simplest thing to order is a slice of cold ham, but bacon and eggs can generally be supplied, and also boiled eggs, though with these last the length of time necessary to bring them from the kitchen or pantry to where you are going to eat them makes it difficult to get the degree of hardness or softness exact.

Tea

Although tea, like coffee, is widely available, grown-ups in France who take it in a café or hotel (as opposed to a *salon de thé*) seldom make a meal of it, so that it may be difficult to get any accompaniments of the kind you are used to. China tea, with lemon, may be had as well as Ceylon or Indian tea.

You can usually get a few plain biscuits or, in a large hotel, pastries, at tea-time, but small sandwiches and bread and butter are not often found. It is simplest to have a croissant or a roll and butter if you want something rather plain to eat, or to buy a madeleine or little sponge cake or biscuit type pastry, such as a *palmier* or *sablé*, and keep it for tea-time if you like this kind of thing. Ice-creams, sundaes and fruit drinks are of course available. If you are offered 'cake', this will be a piece of fruit cake of the slab kind, which can usually be bought in cafés, wrapped in individual slices in a cellophane pack.

Lunch and dinner

As has been stated elsewhere, the main meal in France is generally taken at midday, but of course in a smart hotel or resort people will dine as they do elsewhere. Although, towards the south, both on the Riviera and near the Spanish border, people lunch and dine rather late, as in the south of England, the reverse applies in the north; for example, you may find a restaurant in a Brittany resort full by one o'clock, many of the customers having started their meal soon after 12.15 p.m. If you have lunch or dinner in your bedroom or suite, then an extra charge will be made, but for people with large families, who only want a light meal, this can be a good idea and not expensive if it spares you having to tip someone to keep an eye on any small children.

In the majority of restaurants there will be at least one *prix fixe*, a fixed price menu, offering several courses, with a possible choice of main course; often there will be more than than one menu of this kind, possibly a *menu touristique*, a little more elaborate, and a *menu gastronomique*, which is on banquet lines and correspondingly costly. It is always a good idea to take one of these menus if you want two dishes *à la carte*, for even without vegetables or extras you are sure to spend more than on the *prix fixe*. The shortest cheapest menu can be excellent value and provide a balanced meal, without the bother of choosing at length.

A *petit menu* will usually consist of either soup or a small *hors d'œuvres*, followed by a small portion of fish, then a meat dish with some kind of vegetable accompanying it, and possibly salad to follow. Then there will be cheese and a dessert—a fruit tart or ice —and fresh fruit, occasionally one or the other but often both.

Coffee may be included but is generally extra. There may not be a fish course, and occasionally a rather luxurious course, such as a lobster or special *pâté*, will have a note of a supplementary charge alongside it, but in such cases there will always be something else as part of the menu that does not mean paying extra. No false pride should deter the visitor from having the short menu anywhere—it is the mark of the greatest restaurants that their little menus are both excellent as regards value and gastronomic superiority.

If you do order *à la carte*, remember that many main dishes will come garnished—that is, accompanied by a small portion of vegetables, both to enhance the appearance and give better value. Unless you are a really dedicated vegetable eater, this should suffice you, but if you order separate vegetables, remember to specify whether you want to eat them with the main dish or, as the French do, by themselves afterwards. A single portion of vegetables is usually sufficient for two people. Usually a single portion of plain vegetables will come with butter on them, and salad will come with an oil and vinegar dressing, which will be put on at the table by the waiter. If you want a dressing made with lemon juice, ask for it in advance.

The French certainly do not eat as many potatoes as we do, but many grills are accompanied by chipped potatoes, so check as to whether the 'garniture' consists of these before you order any more. The water-cress or cress that comes on the dish when such things are served is also for eating if you wish, so do not hesitate to ask for it on your plate if you want a bit of greenstuff.

Soup of the *potage de jour* type is generally a vegetable soup and can be excellent, freshly made and comforting as well as nourishing, should travellers feel tired. *Consommé*, except in large establishments, may come out of a tin, though it can also be very good; remember when ordering to specify whether you want it hot, cold or in jelly form. A cold (as opposed to jellied) *consommé* made by a first-class chef is something to remember afterwards, as well as being delicious at the time.

Unless the restaurant is a moderately sophisticated one, or unless you are having an *hors d'œuvres*, butter may not be put on the table until the cheese course. If it is not, a charge will be made should you ask for it. The cover charge, however, does cover the cost of bread—within reason, as much as you wish to eat.

When cheese is served from the board, you may have several different kinds without an extra charge being made, but of course several large portions are charged up. The same applies to more than a single piece of fruit, although you can eat a fair-sized portion of grapes as a single helping.

Entremets can be a bit of a disappointment to visitors—there will probably be a *tarte maison* (often apples or apricots), possibly a *mille-feuille* or a creamy dessert of the trifle type, with ice-creams, but seldom much of a choice. A fruit salad, or *compote*, or fresh fruit such as strawberries in season may also be available. Any elaborate pudding, such as a *crêpe, soufflé* or similar concoction will almost certainly be quite expensive and have to be ordered a little in advance of when it is required.

Coffee is usually served by the cup, without milk or cream unless this is specially requested. Cona coffee will cost slightly more than a *filtre* or other kinds.

Plat du Jour This may be featured on the big *à la carte* menu, or form part of the middle course on one or more of the fixed price menus. It is usually something in season and at its best. Do not make a mistake I formerly did, thinking that, in a small restaurant in the Landes, the *plat du jour* of caneton Rouennais must be something left-over from a previous banquet; it turned out that the creation, worthy of the name, was what the chef had felt like making on that day, and as he had been a head chef under Escoffier at the Savoy and was now running his own little place virtually as a hobby, it was well worth eating the speciality of the day.

Specialities A restaurant proud of its cooking may list its special dishes separately, although at least one of them will usually be featured on one if not all of the fixed price menus. If, however, you are staying somewhere famous both for local raw materials and for the chef, it is only fair to try to give some notice of a particular dish that you wish to try, so that the establishment may do its best. Even if you are *en pension*, a friendly and understanding management will often arrange for your menus to be adjusted so as to include some of the specialities of the house and region.

It is important, however, to remember that in different parts of France certain items will be both cheaper and better than in others. Conversely, even on their home ground, some things, such as *foie gras* and caviare, will never be very cheap. In addition, sometimes the very best local produce goes either to the Paris markets or for export, so do not assume that, say, because you are in the early melon region, you will be able to enjoy these delicacies frequently and cheaply everywhere. Vegetables and salads tend to be more plentiful and varied in the south, trout in the mountains, dairy produce in the northern regions and shellfish round the coast, for obvious reasons.

Portions   For some travellers, and in some parts of France, these may be on the generous side. Burgundy, and even more Alsace, tend to overwhelm the Briton. But it is always possible to share a course, especially of something like *pâté* or a salad, that one may be taking as a first dish, and reference has already been made to ordering a single portion of a vegetable for two people. One could not, clearly, ask for something like a quail, a steak or a langouste to be halved, but otherwise it is a perfectly permissible practice to share a dish.

If you are a slow eater and dislike cold or lukewarm food, it is worth asking for a hotplate to be put on the table should you have anything served of which you do not take the entire portion at first go.

Hotels and, usually, restaurants are prepared to make up special menus for children, either half portions or two simple courses, and will only charge accordingly. It is, of course, sensible to try to make arrangements for family food of this kind in advance whenever possible. Soup, a little meat and a few vegetables, or potato *purée* are generally available.

If you or any member of your party should be on a special diet, this too can generally be catered for. The French are most understanding about this sort of thing and charges will be adjusted so that you only pay for what you actually consume. The abridgement of a menu in such a situation can usually be made if you ask the waiter. It must be said, however, that although the amount of interest and friendly inquiries that you may receive if you admit to being on a diet are most agreeable, you will be very surprised at what some French gourmets term a light meal. Not for them a little soup and a straightforward grill! Nor have I ever sorted out why it should be that sometimes a dish involving two sauces, truffles and a complication of delectable richnesses can qualify as light when a simple stew does not. But everyone on a diet has individual ideas—ourselves included—so I can only advise travellers who feel a little delicate or tired to stick firmly to their own ideas as to what will suit *them* and not be swayed by the expertise and experience of French friends.

Tips

If the service charge—which may be 12% or even 15%—is added to the bill, then it is not necessary to tip any more, although if there is some small change on the plate when the receipted bill is brought to you, and if you have enjoyed good food and pleasant service, it is a gesture to leave this as well. The cover charge has now been abolished, except in restaurants of three star category.

Vocabulary and useful phrases

Breakfast

A la chambre   In the bedroom
Confiture d'oranges   Marmalade
Un œuf à la coque   A boiled egg (stipulate time)
Un œuf dur   A hardboiled egg
Un œuf mollet   A soft-boiled egg
Un œuf sur le plat   A baked egg and the nearest you can usually get to a fried egg; *'au bacon'* means with fried bacon
Un petit pain   A roll
Une tranche de jambon blanc   A slice of ham (or *jambon de York*). If you don't stipulate this, you may get smoked ham (*jambon fumé*)
Un thé (café) simple   A cup of tea (coffee) by itself
Une cafetière   A coffee pot
Café noir/café nature   Black coffee (*café crème* is coffee with milk already added, such as you may order in a café)
Une orange (un citron) pressé(e)   Juice of a freshly squeezed orange (or lemon). If you ask for *jus d'orange* you will probably get either orange squash or something out of a tin

Tea

Thé de Chine   China tea
Au citron   With lemon
Une tartine   A slice of buttered bread, or bread and jam

Lunch and dinner

Je suis au régime   I am on a diet
Avec service   With service charge
L'addition   The bill
Un couvert   A place (setting)

Un coussin   A cushion. A restaurant will usually have one if you want to prop up a child at the table

D'abord   First

Désosser   To bone (meat)

Enlever les arêtes   To fillet (fish)

Ensuite   Next

Les entremets   The sweet course

Le garçon   The waiter

La garniture   The 'trimmings', signifying the accompaniments to a dish, such as potatoes, or a few vegetables

Le maître d'hotel   The head waiter, who takes the order in all but the largest restaurants, where there may be several head waiters in a room

La moitié   Half (used of portions)

Partager   To share

Un plat   A course

Un plat garni   A course accompanied by vegetables or salad

Un réchaud   A hotplate

Un rince-doigts   A finger bowl

La serveuse   The waitress

Une salade panachée   A mixed salad

Une salade anglaise   A mixed salad

Une salade verte   Green salad

La table d'hôte   This is the more conventional term for the *prix fixe*, or fixed price menu. In phrase books of the nineteenth century one notices travellers coping with the *table d'hôte*, which then meant whatever fare was available in the inn in which people sat down all at one table.

Un cadre soigné   Literally 'a well-kept setting'. Implies fairly luxurious décor—in other words, an expensive establishment

Le coin   The end of a long French loaf

Selon grosseur (often abbreviated to s.g.)   According to size— phrase used to indicate variation in prices of foods such as lobster on the menu

Eplucher   To peel (fruit, vegetables)

Prévenir   To forewarn. Used in the context of booking a table

Réserver   is generally used when booking a room. The phrase *nombre de couverts limité—prévenir* in a restaurant guide implies that, especially in the high season or at a weekend, you will not be able to get in without a reservation. And it should be further noted that, in establishments of this kind, your table will not be kept for you if you are more than a few minutes late—unless you telephone to advise accordingly.

French Food—general guidance for the visitor

France is so large and such a varied country that it is not surprising it includes several completely individual sorts of cooking within its boundaries. The cooking of a region depends on its natural resources: good pastureland, marshes and woods ideal for game, grassland suitable for rearing dairy cattle, country suitable for poultry, barren slopes that are the home of the greatest wines, or lush market garden country, and rivers or inlets of the sea for a variety of fish. Very often the actual deficiencies of a region result in its culinary assets, such as the slow, careful cooking of only fair quality meat which has produced some of the glorifications of the humble stew in France, or the scarcity of meat and poultry that has resulted in the use of all kinds of fish, flesh and fowl that richer people hardly considered worth eating until they became so delicious. As all cooking requires the use of some kind of fat, the availability of this characterises many dishes in regional cookery. There are three distinct regions of different fats in France: that of butter in the north, that of oil in the south, and that of animal fat, either goose dripping or pork lard, in the east and part of the south-west. The use of one of these instead of another will change the character of even a universal dish, just as the use of, say, a red Burgundy in a sauce will alter the flavour from that produced when a claret is used; the difference may be slight, but it will exist. French culinary traditions have also, since the time of the Crusades, received a multitude of foreign influences, from overseas as well as from adjacent countries, and the side-by-side growth of *haute cuisine* and *cuisine bourgeoise* (home cooking, for everyday, as quite distinct from chef or large-scale restaurant cooking) is most interesting to study. This is why the traveller should try to compare the two styles, by visiting both as fine a restaurant as he or she can afford, and also some of the humbler eating places, run by a family, who eat what they prepare for their clientele; some dishes are the prerogative of the one establishment and not the other, though it can be a revelation to see what a master chef or a real family cook will make of the sort of food that the visitors may often have reason to cook in their own homes.

There are certain foodstuffs that the traveller in France may not have encountered previously and it is the purpose of this section to describe them briefly, omitting items that will already be well known. Things that are purely the speciality of one region will be dealt with in the sections devoted to the different regions, and descriptions of the way in which a dish is prepared or presented are not included, simply because they will either be familiar to the majority of people interested in food or else so much an individual speciality of the house that an explanation should be asked for on the spot. Tags such as *Florentine, au gratin, sauce Melba*, have by now a general significance in menu language.

Shellfish are divided by the French into shellfish proper (*coquillages*) and crustaceans (*crustacés*), such as crabs and lobsters, which are further divided into *fruits de mer*, when they come from the sea, and *fruits d'eau douce* when they are from fresh water.

Oysters Although the majority of French—and, for that matter, most European oysters—start life in Brittany, a great difference is made to the adult creature (*huître*) by where it grows up. There are two different kinds of oyster, the *plate* (*Ostrea Edulis*), which is, as its name implies, flattish, and which is the type of high-class oyster that we might, properly enough, term a 'native' if it was brought up at Whitstable or Colchester or in the Helford River; then there is the Portuguese, or, in French, *Portugaise* (*Crassostrea Angulata*), with its bumpy, longish and deep shell, which is cheaper. Oysters are usually sold with the name of the place where they have been reared attached.

The *plate* most generally considered the best in flavour is the white-fleshed *belon*, which is also the dearest. This is a three-year-old oyster, and an *Appellation Contrôlée* governs its quality. The *Marenne* or *verte* is an oyster to which a greenish colouring, especially at what may be described as at the hinges of the creature, has been induced by contact with water in which certain sorts of seaweed and other marine substances are active. This gives it a special flavour. The oysters of Cancale, which are pinkish, are sometimes known as *pieds de cheval*, on account of their horseshoe shape. The term *claire* refers to the oyster park in which the creatures are reared, but sometimes it may be applied to the general product of whatever type of oyster is being cultivated in the neighbourhood oyster parks; in some areas this will be *Portugaise*, but occasionally one finds *plates* termed *claires* in markets.

43

There is no reason why oysters should not be eaten all the year round, but as they are at their best when fresh, which is a condition that cannot be long maintained if they are transported long distances in hot weather, it is usual for them not to be served outside the regions where they are produced in months that do not con-contain an 'r', just as in Great Britain. But on the coast and near any of the big oyster parks they will be on sale—and good to eat—at any time. They are graded according to size and numbered from, usually, 4 downwards, ending with o and oo; the lower the number, the larger the oyster, and a five-year-old oyster can occasionally be as big as a fried egg. It is entirely a matter of personal preference whether you choose large or small oysters.

Shrimps and prawns Shrimps are *crevettes grises*, and prawns *crevettes roses*, also sometimes called *bouquets*, a term which may confuse the menu reader into thinking that it refers to the presentation of the dish. Both are usually eaten with the fingers

Lobsters Lobster, as most people will know, is *homard* and the menu description in France that so often accompanies it will usually be *à l'Armoricaine* (in the fashion of Brittany—Armorica being the old name) and not *à l'Américaine*. The *langouste*, which is a smaller relation of the lobster, is translated variously as crawfish, rock lobster or spiny lobster in English. It does not have the lobster's big claws. The flesh of the langouste is both delicate and succulent and can, in my opinion, be more delicious than most lobsters. Although one can dig about with picks and crackers in the long legs of the langouste, it is the flesh of the body and tail that is really worth eating. The *langoustine* is like a giant prawn or little langouste, without claws, and is sometimes translated as Norway lobster or Dublin Bay Prawn, or even scampi.

Crayfish These are still to be found in British rivers, although they are seldom served in Britain. They are rather like a freshwater prawn, and range in size from prawn size to almost langoustine dimensions. The French name is *écrevisse*.

Scallops *Coquille Saint Jacques*, so named after the scallop shell worn by medieval pilgrims to the shrine of St James at Compostella in Spain. They wore them because, at the time St James's body was miraculously conveyed in a ship without oars or sails, from Joppa to Galicia, it passed a wedding procession. The bridegroom's horse plunged into the waves, but both horse and man were miraculously saved and the man became a Christian on learning he owed his life to the Saint, and his example was followed by all the wedding party. When the man emerged from the sea, his clothes were all covered with scallop shells, and the people of the neighbourhood henceforth took the shell as the sign of St James.

Clams The clam is not a wholly French mollusc though the name 'clam' is used; but the *praire* and the *palourde* (called *clovisse* in the south) are, as far as the general culinary significance is concerned, like small clams. They can be eaten raw, as part of an *hors d'œuvres*, or cooked, usually in the same way that mussels are cooked.

Cockles and winkles *Coques* (sometimes called *bucardes*) and *bigorneaux*, very popular at coastal resorts and in fish *hors d'œuvre*.

Mussels *Moules*, eaten raw as well as cooked in various ways.

Octopus, squid, inkfish, cuttlefish The French names respectively are *poulpe*, *seiches* (also *chiprones*), *calmars* and *encornets*. The hesitant should be reassured—when well prepared all can be delicious. They may, in so far as it is possible to describe a taste in general terms, be likened to a very slightly fishy version of a combination of good pasta and chicken. If served with the ink in the sauce, they can be succulently rich. These fish are found on the Atlantic as well as the Mediterranean coast of France.

Sea urchins *Oursins*, sometimes described as sea hedgehogs or sea chestnuts. They may be served poached, when they are sliced open and eaten with a spoon, or, especially in the south, raw. The flavour slightly resembles that of the *écrevisse*. In other words, they are well worth trying, in spite of the off-putting spiny appearance.

Snails

Escargots have been a table delicacy in France since Roman times. There are two main kinds, as far as the consumer is concerned: the *hélices vigneronnes*, or snails that fatten on the vines, especially in Burgundy, which are rather large and much esteemed, and the *petits gris*, which are gathered in the country everywhere. The best description of snails that I know was my husband's: 'Something of the texture and taste of grilled mushrooms and liver, plus garlic'. The most usual way of serving them is piping hot, in their shells (put back after they have been cooked), with a lot of garlic butter. They are eaten with a clamp-like snail holder, in which the shell is firmly held, while a thin-tined fork is used to extract the snail, and snail plates (*escargotières*) have little hollows in them so that the snails can be heated up immediately before being brought to table. Snails are served, like oysters, in sixes or dozens, although sometimes a menu will specify that nine constitutes a portion. Snails are neither slimy nor fishy and, if you can persuade someone to let you taste a single one you may well want to finish the portion.

Frogs

It is only the legs of the frogs—*cuisses de grenouilles*—that are eaten, and they are often served lightly fried or *sauté*-ed, though there are recipes involving sauces, cooking the frogs *au gratin* or *en brochette*, and *en beignets*. The flavour is very delicate, slightly like that of the little bits of sweet meat in between the leg and wing bones of a young chicken. It is almost impossible to eat *grenouilles* with anything except the fingers. The bones are not consumed.

Freshwater and saltwater fish

Poissons d'eau douce and *poissons de mer*, respectively, many of which will be known at least by name to British visitors to France, although it will probably be a matter of surprise to find what a variety of fish is available, even in small towns in the country.

Eel   *Anguille*, which is delicately flavoured when it comes out of a freshwater stream or river, rather than the muddy waters of a pond. Eels fished from the sea are also used in cooking. Methods of preparing eels are numerous. The flavour, depending greatly on the method of cooking, can resemble a combination of rabbit and herring, with a most agreeable something in addition.

The pike, or *brochet*, is possibly the most remarkable freshwater fish that may be unfamiliar to the visitor, and the *quenelles de brochet*, very delicate and complicated little skinless sausages of pounded, seasoned pike flesh are great delicacies. It must be admitted, however, that most people find the pike, even in *quenelle* form, a dish to eat only occasionally as, however good, it seems to have a boring quality if taken frequently.

The eel-pout, *barbot* or *lotte de rivière* is a fish for which I can find no adequate English translation. It is rather like an eel and may be prepared in the same sort of ways. There is a *lotte de mer*, or *baudroie*, a sea fish, which is monkfish.

Apart from the salmon and trout, other river fish that may be generally found on menus are tench (*tanche*), roach (*gardon*, which is often part of a mixed fry of fish and resembles whitebait), perch (*perche*), gudgeon (*goujon*), grayling (*ombre*, which is usually prepared like trout), carp (*carpe*, which is prepared in various ways, including with beer and with red butter), bream (*brème*), barbel (*barbeau*), and shad (*alose*), which is a seafish that like the salmon, goes up the river.

Sea fish include hake (*colin*), sea-bream (*daurade*), smelts (*éperlans*), whiting (*merlan*, which in France is not served with its tail in its mouth), red mullet (*rouget*), grey mullet (*mulet*), John Dory (*St-Pierre*), cod (*morue fraîche*, or *cabillaud*; salt cod is just *morue*), brill (*barbue*, which is a little like turbot), bass (*bar*, which is a very white, fattish fish, rather like salmon), gurnard (*grondin*), herring (*hareng*), haddock (*èglefin*), halibut (*flétan*), lemon sole (*limande*, always cheaper than sole), plaice (*plie franche* or *carrelet*), shad (*alose*, see above), skate (*raie*), tunny fish (*thon*, used in *hors d'œuvres* when preserved in oil, as well as being served hot) and swordfish (*espadon*, fleshy rather like tunny). Soft roes (*laitances*), are also sometimes served. The *loup de mer*, so often found grilled over fennel sticks all over the south, is a sort of sea-perch or sea-bass. Sole and turbot can, of course, be easily recognised, as the words are the same. One thing that is interesting about the sole and that applies to wherever you eat it, is that it is, in fishmongers' talk, the game of the sea. Therefore it should, ideally, not be eaten fresh from the salt water, but be allowed to stay in a cool place for 12–24 hours after being fished, when it will have both intensified and enhanced its natural flavour and be tender and succulent. A sole that is eaten immediately after being fished can be very good, but it tends to lack the flavour of a fish that has, so to speak, been hung, and may be stiff and tough.

Vegetables

There are a huge variety of vegetables available throughout France, as the size of the country means that different seasonal vegetables come to their best at varying times, and the markets are always colourful and interesting. Some of the names that can cause confusion are included here, as, for example, *céleri* (celery, usually given in the plural—*céleris*) and *céleri-rave* (celeriac), *chicorée* or *chicorée frisée* (endive), and *endive* or *Witloof* (chicory); in the chicory department, too, there is *barbe de Capucin*, which is a bitter chicory, long and rather like feathery-topped chives in appearance, and *chicorée scarole* or *maraîchère*, which is a bunchy vegetable rather like ordinary endive, with fatter, flatter, toothed leaves.

47

Different kinds of lettuce (*laitue*) include *laitue romaine* (cos), and *laitue batavia Beaujolaise*, which is similar to a Webb's Wonder, crisp and curly.

Peas (*petits pois*) are nearly always gently stewed in butter, so that, while being very tender and succulent, they differ in flavour and colour—more of an olive green—from the bright green garden peas of Britain as well as being much smaller in size. *Pois chiches* are chick peas, which are sometimes served in salads.

Beans are: *haricots verts* (French beans), *fèves* (broad beans), and *haricots* or *haricots blancs secs* (dried white beans, butter beans), of which the type called *soissons* (which is of medium size) are often listed on menus under this name; these are the beans most frequently used for *cassoulet*.

Asparagus (*asperges*) are usually fatter than in Britain; the most highly esteemed is the very pale type, called *Argenteuil*, of which only the very tips are at all green, then there is the *Lauris*, greener but still very fat. *Cavaillon* is another type with a high reputation; it too has green tips, and there are various kinds of completely pale yellow *asperges blanches*, all of which are served both hot and cold.

Artichokes are either *topinambours* (Jerusalem artichokes), or *artichauts* (globe artichokes).

Here is a list of other vegetables, spices and herbs with English translations:

Chervil   *Cerfeuil* (often found, together with chives, in an omelette fines herbes)

Chives   *Ciboulette*

Cloves   *Girofle*; a single clove *Un clou de girofle* (not to be confused with *giroflé*—gilly flower)

Garlic   *Ail*; a clove of garlic is *une gousse d'ail*

Gherkin   *Cornichon*, invariably served to accompany *pâté* and cold cuts

Horseradish   *Raifort*

Juniper   *Genièvre*

Leeks   *Poireaux*

Lemon Balm   *Mélisse*

Marjoram   *Marjolaine* (but a marjolaine in the entremets section of a menu is a flat, layered concoction, somewhere between cake and pastry)

Nasturtium seeds   *Graines de capucine*, which are rather like capers (*câpres*) and are often used in salads.

Nutmeg   *Muscade*

Orange bigarrade The type of bitter orange used in the famous
  duck recipe
Parsnip *Panais*
Pearl barley *Orge perlé*
Rosemary *Romarin*
Shallot *Échalote*
Sorrel *Oseille*
Sweet peppers *Piments doux,* or *poivrons*
Tarragon *Estragon*
Turnip *Navet* (usually only tiny ones are served)

Some vegetables that may not be familiar are sorrel (*oseille*)
which is cooked rather like spinach and also makes delicious soups,
dandelion leaves, which have the extraordinary name of *pissenlit*
and which are both cooked and used raw in salads; salsify (*salsifis*)
which is a curious vegetable, looking rather like braised celery in
appearance; *rocambole*, which is rather like a shallot, and savory or
sarriette, a slightly bitter herb.

Potatoes There is a greater variety generally available in France
than in Britain, and the special waxy potatoes used in salads are
well worth trying. The British are said to refuse them at home,
on account of their yellow colour. As well as these, and various
red-skinned varieties, there is a violet-skinned potato which looks
like quite an exotic vegetable if you see it in a market. In addition
to the ubiquitous *frites* (fried potatoes or chips), it is perhaps worth
mentioning that *purée de pommes de terre* in France is a very different
thing from mashed potatoes, being creamy, light and usually of
the consistency of an unbaked sponge mixture—excellent for
children or for anyone wanting a light, comforting vegetable
course. Any good restaurant will, if given the necessary time, also
cooked a baked potato in its jacket, and it is perhaps of interest to
know that whereas originally the name for this was, logically
enough, *pomme de terre en robe de champ* (in its field-coat), the refinements of menu language have changed this to *pomme de terre en robe
de chambre* (in its dressing-gown).

Aubergine, courgette, oignon, tomate, carotte, choux- and *chou-fleur* are
probably all easily identifiable without explanations. *Gourdes* and
courges (pumpkin) appear in the south.

Meat

The big joint is seldom seen in France. Indeed, it is the thing to offer to any visitor from that country coming to Britain. But a few of the cuts of meat available do require a little explanation, as French butchers have a different system from our own and indeed, although meat in France is expensive, it is so economically prepared by the butcher that there is virtually no wastage in anything bought. The cuts described are the nearest to the familiar English ones, but they may be differing in shape and appearance due to the different methods of butchering.

Beef A *contrefilet* or *faux filet* is virtually equivalent to the end of the rib, or boneless uppercut of the loin, the larger part of the T bone or porterhouse steak. The *aloyau* is the entire sirloin and the *filet* the fillet. A *tournedos* (see p. 129 for how it got its name) is a thick cut from the fillet. An *entrecôte* is either a piece of the rib meat or a cut from the fillet, and it is worth noting that it is usually very much larger in size in France than in Britain; if you want a small *entrecôte*, it is worth asking for an *entrecôte minute*, which even so will be thicker and more substantial than the British minute steak. A *Chateaubriand*, usually served for two people, is a thick double fillet. There are of course many types of stew—*pot-au-feu, daube* and *bœuf à la Bourguignonne* (by no means only to be found in Burgundy) being some of the best known. The most famous French beef comes from the white Charollais cattle of Burgundy. Beef of this kind will be named on the menu.

When ordering a steak, the waiter will ask how it should be cooked. Remember that the cut will usually be thicker than a steak in Britain and calculate accordingly. The descriptions to remember are:

bien cuit well done
à point medium done
saignant literally bloody, but what most people would consider definitely underdone—certainly bright pink in the middle.
bleu blue, or very underdone. Although this is the way I like my steaks, it is far too raw for most people and should indeed be actually raw or blue in the middle.

Lamb and mutton Best end of lamb is *carré d'agneau*, leg of lamb *gigot*, and shoulder and saddle are respectively *épaule* and *selle*, which makes things easy. *Côtelette* is, as you would expect, a cutlet, and *chope* a chop. For special occasions, a *baron* of lamb—the whole of the hind-quarters, like a baron of beef—is sometimes served. The most vaunted type of lamb comes from flocks that feed on pastures by the sea, which gives the meat a special delicacy; this type is known as *pré salé* (salty meadow) and has an *Appellation Contrôlée*.

Travellers should be warned that the French like to cook their lamb only until it is just pink, very underdone by British standards, so it is necessary to stipulate that a cutlet or chop should be *bien cuit* if you do not like this meat in what many people consider a half-raw state.

Pork Apart from ham, sausages and various types of pudding (*boudin noir* is rather like a blood pudding and *boudin blanc* is a type of white sausage in haggis shape), *carré de porc* (loin), *filet de porc* and *côte de porc* (pork chop) are found on most menus all over France, with certain pork specialities in many districts. There is no prejudice against eating pork even in the height of summer and it is usually very good in quality, though the lover of crackling will not find any in France.

Veal Although travellers in Europe sometimes admit to getting very tired of eating a lot of veal, French veal is usually of high quality and at least different from that available in Britain because of the method of feeding. *Escalope de veau* and *côte de veau* will probably already be familiar to everyone, but *ris de veau* once confused me into thinking that it had something to do with rice; in fact it is veal sweetbreads, which are a great delicacy, light, tender and capable of being prepared in many ways.

Tête de veau vinaigrette, calf's head, often featured on the French menu, is a very specialised taste; to me it is horrid, a combination of flavours and textures that do not appeal, and people who do not care for fatty things should beware of it, though for those who like it, it tends to be a favourite dish—so one can only try for oneself.

Variety meats (offal) include brains (*cervelles*), kidneys (*rognons*), and liver (*foie*) which appear in many different ways and are generally referred to as *les abats*. If you do not like these things in Britain, it is at least worth trying a portion, from a friend's plate if possible, when they are recommended in a really good restaurant, as, unless you have a real revulsion from offal, a good chef's version of it in some of the classic recipes can be a delightful surprise. As I like all these things, I may be prejudiced, but it is possibly worth mentioning that such things, together with veal sweetbreads, plainly cooked, make excellent choices for people whose digestions are on the tired side.

Poultry

The most reputed type of chicken in France is the *poulet de Bresse*, which has an *Appellation Contrôlée* (see p. 300), but, good though this can be, an ordinary *poulet de grain* (grain fed) can be excellent and will certainly be cheaper. Different regions have certain special types of birds that are dealt with in the sections on regional specialities. A *poularde* is a large hen, *chapon* a capon.

Pigeon, *oie* (goose), *dindonneau* (young turkey), or *dinde* (young hen turkey), *caneton* (duckling), *col vert* (a type of wild duck), and *pintade* or *pintadeau* (guinea-fowl) need little explanation. *Palombe* is a wood-pigeon.

Game

In a country such as France rough shooting is a popular sport and *la chasse* something that engages even humble people; licences and the equipment involved are comparatively cheaper than in Britain and, of course, the size of the country makes many forests and rough land available for shooting. Visitors may be surprised and sometimes genuinely shocked by the sort of things served as food on French tables, but many French countryfolk might retort that the price of meat in France is so high that the utilisation of even song-birds for food is often an economic necessity. Unless one has very strong feelings about this matter, it seems fair to suggest that something recommended as a delicacy should at least be sampled before a decision is made for or against its use. Game (*gibier*) is divided into what is *à poil* and *à plume*, which mean respectively 'with hair' and 'with feathers'.

The wild boar (*sanglier*) is generally wild but sometimes reared in captivity. Up to the age of six months it is known as *marcassin*, up to a year, *bête rousse*, and these are the two names under which it appears on the menu. As might be expected, it is a gamey meat.

Venaison is virtually the same thing as in Britain, especially if it has not been marinaded first, and *chevreuil* (roe-deer) can be a very delicate form of venison, but the phrase *basse venaison* signifies hare (*lièvre*) and *lapin de garenne*, which is wild rabbit, as compared with *lapin de clapier*, the domestic rabbit, reared both for its flesh and its skin throughout the country. *Râble de lièvre* (saddle of hare), and *civet de lièvre* (which is the sort of stew that might be translated as jugged hare *in excelsis*) can be excellent; the idea that hare and rabbit are not highly acceptable table delicacies (except, of course, for those whose religion forbids their consumption) is strange to the average Frenchman.

Game birds such as *faisan* and *perdreau* (partridge) appear in various forms of stews as well as being roasted; other game birds are: *coq de bruyère* (capercailzie), *bécasse* (woodcock), *bécassine* (snipe), *pluvier* (plover), *caille* (quail), *sarcelle* (teal).

The *ortolan* (wheatear) is noted on p. 173, and the *becquefigue* or *becfigue* on p. 283. Larks (*alouettes*) are on the menu throughout a large part of France, either in *pâtés*, or, under the name of *mauviettes*, in both *pâtés* and various recipes. Lark *pâté*, I must admit, is usually both delicate and rich and I have often enjoyed it, although it is certainly not one of those things that one would wish to eat, however unsqueamish, constantly. *Grives* (thrushes) are often prepared and served in a *pâté* or like quails, and so are blackbirds (*merles*), especially those from Corsica, which have a very slightly herby flavour. Whether or not you approve of eating song-birds, it must be admitted that all of them are fiddly things to manage, and there is very little meat on a single bird (one crunches the bones), each of which will be quite expensive. Personally I think that they are all interesting to try—once.

The French are great admirers of 'le grouse', but do not let anyone tell you that it is the same as either the *bécasse* or the *coq de bruyère*—an alternative name for the latter being great grouse. The grouse is peculiar to the British Isles and strangely enough even when attempts have been made to transplant and rear British grouse in France, the bird has either not thriven or else, in an odd way, has somehow lost its special character and almost turned into another type of game bird.

Another thing about game in France is that it is frequently eaten while fresh, although often it may be rendered more gamey by being put in a marinade. But people in Britain who dislike birds hung until they are really high should try the same birds in France before making up their minds never to eat, say, pheasant or woodcock. One can appreciate both the extreme highness and comparative freshness, just as it is possible to enjoy the pinkish lamb in France and well-cooked lamb in Britain, providing that the product and the cooking are both good.

Cheese

Although the different regional cheeses are dealt with in the relevant sections, it is worth noting that the term *persillé*, as applied to a cheese, has nothing to do with real parsley. It means the tracing of blue-green veining which can look like parsley.

Fruit

This forms part of most luncheon and dinner menus. It is sometimes termed *la corbeille des fruits*, which simply means fresh fruit from the basket. *Fruits rafraîchis* or *compote de fruits* are what we should call fruit salad, which usually has a syrup and some liqueur —often kirsch—added. The names of most fruits such as pear, apple, banana, apricot and orange are easy to recognise, but *pamplemousse* (grapefruit), which is often at the beginning of the menu, always sounds rather more glamorous than it is, and *ananas* (pineapple), and *grenade* (pomegranate) are sufficiently unlike their English names to warrant giving the translations.

A *prune* is a plum, a *pruneau* is a prune, a *prune de damas* a damson, and a *reine-Claude* a greengage, supposedly named after Queen Claude, wife of François I, who, after horticulturalists evolved the greengage, became specially partial to them; there are many varieties of plums including one named after Monsieur, the pervert brother of Louis XIV, but two that may be met with in open tarts or similar pastry cases are *mirabelles*, rosy-yellow little plums, and *quetsches* which are purplish ones. *Une groseille* is a gooseberry, though French gooseberries tend to be small compared with the larger, pinkish ones that are delicious to eat raw in Britain; *une groseille rouge* is a redcurrant, and *une groseille noire* or *un cassis* a blackcurrant (though *un cassis* can also refer to the syrup or liqueur); *un raisin de Corinthe* is a currant, and *un raisin sec de Smyrne* a sultana. The two main types of melon are the *melons brodés*, of which the Cavaillon is probably the best-known, and the *melons cantaloups*, of which there are also many kinds; the water melon—*melon d'eau*—does not appear so often, except, of course, in the south where it is known as *pastèque*.

Both cultivated strawberries and wild strawberries (*fraises des bois*) are served throughout the summer, the latter being found far more frequently and usually being more succulent than in Britain. The French sometimes eat strawberries with sugar and cream, but also with just a sprinkle of lemon—which brings out the flavour very well—and sugar, or else they pour a little red wine over them, which can be deliciously refreshing.

Ices

Une glace is a cream ice and *un sorbet* a water-ice. *Une cassate*, now standard in France, is what it sounds like, and there are a whole range of ice-puddings, ices containing fruit, and ice-cream *gâteaux*. Without trying to describe these in detail, it may be useful to state that the following are made with ice-cream, in different forms and with different ingredients: *biscuits glacés, bombes, mousses, parfaits, poudings glacés* and *soufflés glacés*; the following are made with water-ice: *granités, marquises* and *spooms*. An *omelette Norvégienne* and a *soufflé en surprise* are both slightly different and superlative versions of baked Alaska, and a *vacherin* an equally superlative transformation of the humble meringue and ice-cream.

When the waiter asks *Quel parfum?* relating to an ice, he means What flavour? and nothing to do with the smell. The most usual are: *vanille, chocolat, fraise* (strawberry), *framboise* (raspberry), *café* or *moka*, and *praliné* (caramelised nuts). *Une glace panachée* is a mixed ice-cream.

Sweets

Les entremets, are not always of as varied a range as some people, who are accustomed to the huge sweet trolleys of large restaurants, expect. The term dates from the time of Louis XIV when sweet things—rather like *sorbets*—were served in the middle of important banquets. The King, however, liked them so much that they were served at his private dinners and suppers but because the ordinary guests, lacking the royal appetite, could seldom eat anything after them, they came to be the last course of the meal instead of the 'between courses' their name implies. But there will always be ices, fresh fruit and usually one tart or slice of pastry. You can usually see what any large-sized pudding is likely to be like, and *soufflés* and *crêpes* (pancakes), whether *flambé* or not, are usually to be ordered in advance, so that it is generally possible to find out if they are different in any special way from that expected.

Finally, a few general menu terms:

Une assiette anglaise is a plate of assorted cold meat, often ham and chicken.

Les crudités are raw vegetables by way of *hors d'œuvres*, excellent when the palate is tired of rich dishes.

Une salade verte is a green salad; *une salade panachée* a mixed salad; *une salade Niçoise* may vary slightly, but usually comprises lettuce, hard-boiled eggs, tomatoes, tunny fish, black olives and fillets of anchovy, in a *vinaigrette* dressing. Mayonnaise is seldom served with a green salad in France and, as far as *hors d'œuvres* are concerned, most usually with eggs.

Un hachis is 'chopped up' and *un hochepot* the nearest the French can get to hotpot.

Le jus The juice or gravy from the meat (different from *un peu de sauce*).

Un salmis is a stew of game, as is *un ragoût* of meat.

For everything else the interested traveller who cannot remember menu terms should ask the waiter. In any restaurant where food is considered a serious matter the barriers of language can usually be overcome. It is worth bearing in mind that certain names of dishes are often expressed in slightly shortened and even ungrammatical terms, e.g. *Pommes Lyonnaise*, instead of *à la Lyonnaise*.

*   *   *

'We might have dined at the *table d'hôte*, but preferred the restaurant connected with and within the hotel. All the dishes were very delicate, and a vast change from the simple English system, with its joints, shoulders, beefsteaks and chops; but I doubt whether English cookery, for the very reason that it is so simple, is not better for men's moral and spiritual nature than the French. In the former case, you know that you are gratifying your animal needs and propensities, and are duly ashamed of it; but, in dealing with these French delicacies you delude yourself into the idea that you are cultivating your taste while satisfying your appetite . . . In my opinion it would require less time to cultivate our gastronomic taste than taste of any other kind; and, on the whole, I am not sure that a man would not be wise to afford himself a little discipline in this line. It is certainly throwing away the bounties of Providence to treat them as the English do, producing from better materials than the French have to work upon nothing but sirloins, joints, steaks, steaks, steaks, chops, chops, chops, chops! We had a soup today, in which twenty kinds of vegetables were represented, and manifested each its own aroma; a fillet of stewed beef, and a fowl, in some sort of delicate fricassee. We had a bottle of Chablis, and renewed ourselves, at the close of the banquet, with a plate of Châteaubriand ice. It was all very good, and we respected ourselves far more than if we had eaten a quantity of red roast beef; but I am not quite sure that we were right.'

Nathaniel Hawthorne, *French Note Books 1858*

The French Wine List

Wine is treated far more casually in France than in the British Isles, and although most French people are interested in it, as they are in food, the majority are no more expert on the subject than we, as a nation, are authorities on tea or beer. This does not apply, of course, to the wine-growing areas, where the livelihood of so many people is involved with wine that most are informed to some extent about the local product.

The wine lists of all but the largest and smartest French restaurants tend to be short, featuring the local wines first or, if this is not a wine-producing area, giving three or four wines from Burgundy, Bordeaux, the Rhône, the Beaujolais, Alsace, the Loire and Champagne, plus liqueurs. The carafe wine, which is invariably available, red, white and *rosé*, may not be listed separately; it will usually be cheaper than the cheapest wine on the list and sometimes better, so that one need not hesitate to order it. In the main wine areas there will, in the better restaurants, be a very long list of the wines of the region, but, to our eyes, surprisingly few from many others; for example, a first-class restaurant in Bordeaux might list over a hundred fine clarets and up to thirty or fifty white wines, but only include three or four Burgundies. It must be remembered that this sort of establishment caters for a regular clientele of the businessmen and the social gatherings of the area and not the tourist trade in particular, so that a very catholic list would be unsatisfactory. As far as wines from other countries are concerned, there may be a few German wines on lists in Paris restaurants and also some Italian wines, especially in the south, and sherry and port are usually to be had, though they may not be listed; otherwise, the lists seldom include outsiders.

Carafe wines and ordinaires The carafe wine may be an ordinaire, of the sort that you could buy from a grocer, or it may be a personal purchase by the owner of the restaurant from the vineyard or area concerned. If the latter, then you may get something unexpectedly good; but even if only the former, it will usually be a palatable drink at low cost. If these wines are listed on the tariff of 'consommations' above the bar, or if there is any choice apart from the colour, the question of degree of strength may be quoted or mentioned: a wine that is, for example, 12·5° (% of alcohol by volume) in which the strength will be quoted, will not, as is emphasised elsewhere, taste 'stronger' but it will probably be a slightly more enjoyable wine, in the inexpensive class, than one at 11·5° or one for which no strength is given. It may, because of both these things, cost very slightly more.

Wine may always be ordered by the glass, and often the small restaurant or café will put a bottle on the table and merely charge for what has been consumed by the end of the meal. A small carafe or little jug of wine may also be ordered; there is no standard measure, as far as I can make out, but in many hotels and restaurants the capacity of an ordinary carafe is six glasses (as compared with eight glasses to a bottle), and a small carafe or jug may give about three generous glasses.

Regional wines Leaving out the really great classic wines, which will not be cheap, the small-scale wines of the region are usually both good value and of special interest to the wine-loving traveller. Many of these, for example, Muscadet and the Anjou wines, may be bottled at the properties where they have been made, and as the ordinary wine drinker is unlikely to encounter many of these estate-bottled 'little' wines in Britain, it is an excellent opportunity to try them in local restaurants. There seldom will be an appreciably higher price put on them because of this estate bottling. With white wines in particular it is usually possible to note an additional definiteness in quality.

With small-scale wines slight importance is attached to the vintage, which may not be indicated at all. In any eating place worthy of a reputation the wine waiter or head waiter will be able to recommend local wines likely to appeal to the visitor, and as these are probably what he drinks regularly himself, his advice is usually good. There are, however, two French preferences that may not invariably coincide with those of British visitors: the first, prevalent everywhere but lately in the north of France and Paris especially, is the growing popularity of *vin rosé*, which is drunk in enormous quantities and at all kinds of meal. It is, of course, an easy, undemanding drink and can be very pleasant, though when considered as an accompaniment to all but the simplest food I personally do not think there are many *rosés* that can make more than a very slight contribution to the meal. There are some exceptions, which are mentioned in the sections dealing with the different regions of the country, but in general I think the traveller seeking a drink that is both interesting and unlike the sort of thing he can get easily at home would be advised to choose a red or white wine to go with a meal that is at all special. There are, after all, many first-rate *rosé* wines available in Britain.

The second French preference, the result of much publicity and now an established taste, is for drinking wines while they are very young. Economic necessity after the war was originally respons- ible, and of course there are many little wines that gain nothing by being kept long in bottle, but the stress on the enjoyment of the fine and middle-grade wines while they are still, to our mind in Britain, maturing and improving themselves is something that may come as a surprise to many visitors. The fine wines are dealt with later in this chapter, but it is worth pointing out that, certainly as far as white wines in the little category are concerned, many of these may well seem acid and unpleasantly sharp to the British visitor if they have been bottled very early and appear on the table within a year of being made. If you like wine like this, of course there is nothing to prevent your enjoying it, but the visitor who prefers a little 'bottle age' and a slight mellowness in even the driest of wines may be well advised to moderate his intake of young, dry wines in the inexpensive ranges, as for the unaccus- tomed they can be taxing to drink.

Many of the regional wines in the cheap ranges on wine lists may be V.D.Q.S. wines (see p. 138 for the significance of this). Some wines in this class are now available in Great Britain but, in general, it may be said that, if they are not, there is some good reason. Either supplies are not enough for both the home and export market, or else the wines are such that no adequate market exists for them outside their home area. The wine that tastes so delicious when quaffed on holiday while you are sitting on a terrace in the sun may be a shadow of itself when poured into a glass in a pub on a foggy evening at home. It is not necessarily true that, with modern methods, such wines do not travel, but rather that tastes change according to environment. Hence, although the wine-loving tourist should take full advantage of all chances to enlarge his or her experience of wines, it is often a great disappointment to bring home quantities of a loved holiday wine, or to make a wine merchant import it specially.

Fine wines Something that may surprise the traveller is that, in very smart restaurants, the prices of the classic wines may be even higher than those of the same wines at retail wine merchants in Britain. It is to the credit of the British wine trade that they do not up their prices with every hitch given to the cost of living, but because of this it may well be that certain of the classic wines still available may be even better bargains at home. Certain Champagnes and well-advertised names in the wine world can be just as expensive in smart eating places as they would be in the West End of London. And in the ordinarily good but not outstanding French restaurant it is unlikely that the traveller will find as many older vintages—by which I mean those of ten to twelve years old, not necessarily beyond that time—as in the fortunate establishments in Britain who have built up and established cellars in even fairly modest circumstances. If a stock of old wines is held in a fairly remote country restaurant, it may well be that these will be at advantageous prices, simply because the local customers prefer the 'young and fresh' wines, and then is the chance for the wine lover to gain valuable experience at low cost. The practice of drinking fine wines young, however, does have one advantage for the British wine lover: it provides him with the opportunity of tasting, at an early stage, wines which may not yet be on restaurant lists at home for a year or more, and which his wine merchant may not think of offering for several years—the 1961 clarets being a case in point at the time of writing (1971), as these enormous wines of the finest classed growths have years to go before they will be even approaching what British wine drinkers consider their peak, though you will find them on French wine lists right now.

With both very old and very young fine wines, however, you have to depend on the wine waiter for their service if they are to be enjoyable. This too poses many problems.

Decanting and serving   In general, the French do not bother very much about having their wines decanted or even opened ahead of time. A fine red wine will almost always be served from a basket. It may indeed have just been removed from the bin, but any deposit will be much stirred up in the process of pouring it out. And white and *rosé* wines tend sometimes to be chilled to a lower temperature, even before they arrive at the table with the ice-bucket, than many British wine lovers find acceptable. Beaujolais of the year—that is, within a year of its vintage—is now traditionally served cool and may even be put into an ice bucket as well. However, I have at least never encountered the horror of the warmed-up red wine in France! In fact, wine is usually served correctly if without very much attention to its individual character, except in the restaurants that enjoy the services of a *sommelier* who is an informed and knowledgeable enthusiast, who cannot only guide the customer to wines that may be new and interesting—and not always more expensive—but who will serve them with the consideration that will bring them up to the peak of their excellence.

Usually, a French wine waiter will only consider decanting a wine that has thrown a heavy deposit. Even then he may, out of a wish not to deprive the customer of even a tablespoonful of a precious beverage, allow some of this deposit to get into the decanter. The idea of airing a wine by pouring it into another decanter is usually regarded as strange and part of *le goût anglais*, which is accepted to be a preference for old wines—often for wines that the Frenchman would consider well past the time when they are worth drinking. The decanter is seldom seen in Burgundy or the Rhône, though, possibly due to British insistence, it is more common in the Bordeaux region and even, rather unusually, occasionally in restaurants along the Loire when and where the older red wines of that area are stocked.

As far as glasses are concerned, there is a tendency to use very large glasses for the fine red Burgundies and Rhône wines, and for these to be larger in accordance with the quality of the wines, so that, for example, some of the Romanée Conti wines are poured into glasses that, if filled to the brim, would actually take the contents of a whole bottle. For myself, I find it exasperating to get distant whiffs of the bouquet of a fine wine far down in the glass, and the additional aeration involved by the wine having to flow over such a comparatively vast area of glass in a too-capacious container can, for me, detract from the delicacy of certain fine old wines that do not need much airing, and it adds nothing to the charm of a wine that is young and vigorous. A glass of this exaggerated type draws the attention away from the wine and makes the whole enjoyment of drinking a performance. But you will not often get the detestable Champagne saucer, as the French do usually serve sparkling wines in tall tulip glasses, and in general the tulip glass or rounder 'Paris' goblet, both in rather larger sizes than commonly used by British restaurants, are those that will be found, unless a particular wine region has its own tradition for a certain type of glass. Liqueurs, too, are usually served in larger glasses than in Britain and, if they come into the category of being *alcools blancs*, such as the fruit brandies, the balloon or tulip glasses will have ice put into them first, to be swirled round and cool the glass so as to bring out the fragrance and taste of the liqueur when it is poured after the ice has been tipped away. In some supposedly smart restaurants the enormous brandy balloon

(*a*)   (*b*)

(*a*) Beaujolais 'pot', containing half a litre.

(*b*) Flûte d' Alsace, also used for Tavel. The same shaped bottle, of an imperceptible difference in contenance, is also used for *rosé* and some white wines.

(*a*)   (*b*)

(*a*) Burgundy bottle, also used for Rhône red and white wines and some wines from the Loire and elsewhere. The true Loire bottle is in fact very slightly fatter and shorter, but no difference is perceptible to the eye unless the two are actually side by side.

(*b*) Bordeaux bottle.

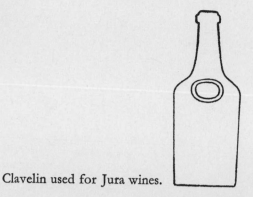

Clavelin used for Jura wines.

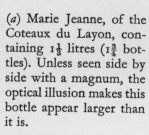

(a) Marie Jeanne, of the Coteaux du Layon, containing $1\frac{1}{3}$ litres ($1\frac{3}{4}$ bottles). Unless seen side by side with a magnum, the optical illusion makes this bottle appear larger than it is.

(b) Champagne magnum holding two bottles.

(a)   (b)

63

Standard wine glasses, as used throughout the country. They may be a little larger in Burgundy than Bordeaux and those used for white wines may be slightly smaller than those used for red.

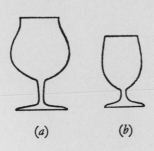

(*a*)   (*b*)

(*a*) Brandy glass—and, on a larger scale, the shape of glass often used for fine red Burgundies. The same shaped glass, of middling size, may be used for the service of *alcools blancs*.

(*b*) Glass of a type used for liqueurs or brandy.

(*a*) Anjou glass.

(*b*) Alsace glass, usually with green stem.

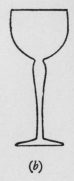

(*a*)   (*b*)

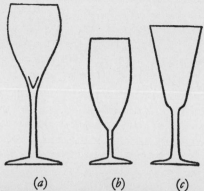

(a)   (b)   (c)

Three forms of Champagne glass for champagne or sparkling wine.

(a) tulip;
(b) elongated tulip;
(c) a modern version of the flûte.

Any of these glasses might also be used for white wine.

(a) Old style Champagne glass with hollow stem.

(b) Champagne flûte, such as is sometimes seen in old pictures.

(a)   (b)

and even the absurd brandy glass warmer are to be seen, but the lover of good brandy will know how to refuse both.

Wine not consumed at a meal If you are staying in a hotel and do not finish the bottle you order at one meal, it will, unless you give orders to the contrary, be re-corked and brought out at the next meal with scrupulous care. This can be a convenience, especially if a particular wine is not available in a half bottle; for example, a bottle of white wine can always be half consumed at lunch and be the accompaniment to the first course at dinner. Although a very fine wine will not gain by being left open for a day or more, the everyday sort of wine will take no harm by this treatment.

The way to get general good value with the wine list should the *sommelier* be worthy of his calling, is to allow him to choose for you, once you have indicated your tastes and, naturally, what you are eating. It is unlikely that you will then be recommended any-thing very expensive. But if you see something listed in the higher price ranges that looks worth trying and within your budget, mention it; if the wine waiter plays safe and suggests something you already know, or that is widely advertised, you can always say that you want to be more adventurous, and there are few good *sommeliers* who are not delighted of the chance to hear the opinions of customers found to be true lovers of wine. The British have earned a reputation for being knowledgeable and critical in recent years, and the discriminating traveller may be sure of encounter-ing far more happy surprises than disappointments during his encounters with the wine list in France.

Vocabulary and useful phrases

Comme boisson? What (will you have) to drink?

Le bouchon The cork; *bouchonnée*—corked (but there are far more bottles sent back as corked than deserve this fate, so be very sure before you do it. A corked bottle is usually distinctive in its unpleasant smell, but a wine that disappoints may simply be an indifferent bottle, not necessarily one that has anything the matter with it)

Un broc A jug, generally of pottery or even wood and metal

La carte des vins The wine list

La cave The cellar (used to signify stock of wine as well as the place)

66

Le casier à bouteilles   The bin or bottle rack
Chambré   At room temperature
Déboucher   To draw the cork of a bottle
Décanter   To decant
Le dépôt   Deposit (in wine)
Étampé   Stamped (used frequently to describe wines that have branded corks)
Frais   Cool
Un panier verseur   A wine basket
Un pichet   Also a jug (usually of glass or china)
Un seau à glace   An ice bucket
Une serviette   A napkin

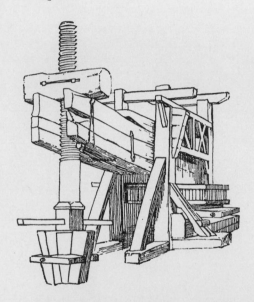

A medieval wooden wine-press, still able to be used, such as is often seen in Burgundy. The spiral shaft is sometimes used decoratively in tasting rooms or restaurants.

Aperitifs and Between Times Drinks

Anyone sitting at a café table in France and looking round at what the other people are drinking will be surprised by the variety: long, short, a whole scale of colours, some drinks cloudy, others clear or sparkling. Yet the waiter, anxious to give the visitor something he or she will like, usually recommends the familiar favourites: gin, Martini, Dubonnet, porto (the great favourite of the French) or *xérès* (sherry) and now 'le whisky', which the French drink far more generally as an *apéritif* than most British people. It may be some consolation, for the traveller eyeing the exotic-looking concoctions at neighbouring tables, to know that many of these are similar to each other in taste, on the sweet side and not as strong as those coming from a nation of spirit drinkers may expect and like before a meal. But here is a brief guide to those wishing to experiment. In a smart bar, large hotel or café in a big town, the barman will naturally be able to make the classic cocktails and supply drinks from an international range.

The French do not always take an apéritif before a meal at home. Those in the wine trade may be exceptions, and of course in the Champagne area and other regions where the local beverage is an *apéritif*, one may be served as a matter of habit. But otherwise the *apéritif* is usually taken—and very seldom more than one for the average person—in a café, bar or the bar of a restaurant. It is unusual for an *apéritif* to be taken at the table in the dining-room of a restaurant, even if the first course involves a considerable wait. For the French, the food and wines involved in a good meal are one harmony which they will not spoil by prefacing the meal with additional drinks beforehand, which may dull the appetite and palate.

The French tend to prefer a sweet apéritif, unless they want a preprandial digestive of a herby type, such as gentian or *anisette*.

The cost of most apéritifs is less than spirits. Even brandy is not cheap in France, and whisky and gin are in the top price range. But helpings are usually equivalent to doubles in the United Kingdom.

Water, soda and ice Anything drunk before a meal is more refreshing if it is chilled or served with ice. A waiter will usually ask if ice is required, and the ice-bowl will be brought so that you can have as much or as little as required. Most *apéritifs* may be drunk straight, but are very often taken diluted with soda or a fizzy mineral water, according to how long a drink is required. In a cafe you can usually get a free splash of soda from a siphon, in a smart bar you may have to purchase a quarter bottle of Perrier to gasify your drink. Plain water in a jug is also always available if you prefer it. Another ingredient of many *apéritifs* is a slice of lemon, which any café and bar will provide on request. It is up to the individual to decide on the way in which the *apéritif* is most enjoyable.

Wine by the glass This is always available in a café or bar. A smart restaurant may only provide it by the half carafe, although Champagne by the glass may be on sale in such places. (This, like spirits, is not usually very much cheaper than it would be in Britain either.) Wine sold by the glass may be rather ordinary in quality but can be surprisingly good if you are in a wine region or if, in a big town, the patron is keen on wine and buys direct from growers. Half bottles of wine are of course available, and a bottle of wine—which gives eight generous glasses—can make a good *apéritif* for a small party of people.

Vermouth French ingredients are mostly dry. All contain wormwood and many other herbs and ingredients, according to the secret formula of each house. As far as I know, the white vermouth, called *bianco*, is only made in Italy, although it is widely available in France. If your French is of the primitive kind and you order a vermouth, it is advisable to specify 'Sans gin' if you want it neat, as a waiter may assume that you want a cocktail; he will also probably offer you Martini vermouth as he may think that you prefer it, unless you specify otherwise. The most important French vermouth is Noilly Prat, the best-known and classic type being dry. This will always be available, but other vermouths may be tried in the south, especially around Marseille, the vermouth capital. A very good one is from the small house of Déjean. A very dry, delicate and refreshing vermouth comes from Chambéry, in Savoie, and is well worth sampling—it is quite different from, say, Noilly Prat, but it is a difference of character, for it is still vermouth (see pp. 303–304). One of the best-known makers of Chambéry vermouth is Richard—not to be confused with Ricard, which is a house producing 'pastis' (see p. 70)—and others are Dolin and Gaudin, although this type of vermouth is not always easy to come by away from the region and not in a big

69

city. *Vermouth cassis* has a little cassis liqueur added to sweeten the drink.

Absinthe   This drink, based on wormwood (like vermouth) contains aromatic herbs, and the most famous type was invented in the late eighteenth century by a Dr Ordinaire, who lived in Switzerland, and who sold the formula to a M. Pernod, whose establishment at Pontarlier have been producing it ever since. Because of the narcotics contained in the original recipe, absinthe was banned in France in 1915, and it is still forbidden to sell it, either there or in Switzerland or the United States. Pernod today contains aniseed instead and is the most famous drink of this kind, but other well-known houses are Berger and Ricard, and in southern France, especially Marseille, the drink is known as *pastis*. It is always served with iced water, which should be allowed to combine with it slowly, turning it cloudy and yellow in colour. For a 'woman's drink' a lump of sugar is held in a perforated spoon and the water is dripped through this. Pastis is high in alcohol, strong in flavour and never very cheap—the sort of drink to sample first via a sip from someone else's glass.

Dubonnet   This, like the majority of French *apéritifs* and vermouth, is wine based. The best-known kind is a deep pinky-red and slightly sweet, but there is now a Dubonnet Blonde, which is pale gold and slightly dry.

St Raphael   There is a tradition that anyone who drinks a lot of this will never go blind—because, at the beginning of the nineteenth century, a Frenchman called Jupet prayed to the saint to restore his sight. But the original recipe is supposed to date from the time when quinine arrived in France from Peru via Spain, and the Jesuits evolved an aromatic drink using it. Louis XIV, Louis XV and the Emperor Napoleon I all are associated with this type of drink, and during Napoleon's Algerian campaign the troops were issued with quinine to mix with their wine ration as a health measure. Today, there are two types of St Raphael: the red, which is rather full and sweetish, and the white, which is dryer and less fruity.

Amer Picon   A fruity flavour, but bitter-sweet, with a touch of orange invented in Algeria in 1835. Rather like St Raphael rouge.

Byrrh   A syrupy, reddish-brown heavy wine-based drink, slighty bitter, but essentially sweet.

Ambassadeur   A wine-based bright red drink, lighter and dryer than many others, which has a sufficiently fruity flavour to appeal to most people, with the sort of clean, refreshing finish to appeal to the lovers of dry drinks.

Cap Corse   Dark reddish-brown in colour, with a slight smell and taste of vanilla. Medium fruity, medium sweet.

Mandarin   As its name implies, an orange-flavoured orange coloured drink, very light and quite refreshing.

Suze   Bright yellow in colour, gentian based and consequently a type of digestive. It has a herby bitterness, unlike the quinine bitterness of some of the other *apéritifs*, but, like pastis, Suze is something to try by the sip before ordering by the glass, as some people find it disagreeably dry and bitter. Personally it is a drink I myself favour when I have got to eat, for courtesy reasons, a meal that I expect to be heavier and richer than I really want, and I invariably find it a first-rate perker-up of the appetite and stimulator of the digestion. In one of the Maigret books, Simenon refers to Suze as being a drink popular with businessmen and travellers who know that, for commercial reasons, they may have to have several rounds and wish to avoid taking too much alcohol.

Pineau des Charentes   Not to be confused with pinard (French army slang for the wine ration), or *pinot* (a type of grape), this is an *apéritif* of Cognac and grape juice, from the Cognac region. It is, however, often to be had elsewhere, though it may have to be asked for specially. It is both fruity and dry and is unusual among *apéritifs* in having an *Appellation Contrôlée*. There are many brands, but Plessis is the one likely to be known to the British *pineau* drinker.

Banyuls   Strictly, a sweet wine from the place of that name in the south, but generally used as a generic term in France for similar sweet wine *apéritifs* of this type. In this category Bartissol from Languedoc is a well-known name, also the *vins doux naturels* of Rivesaltes and Maury, in the Roussillon, and the Muscat de Frontignan (see p. 252).

Gauloise   This is a drink that gave its name to the cigarette. It is more like a liqueur, and there are three kinds, varying from sweet-ish to fairly aromatic and dry, and in colour from dark to light. It is both herby and slightly sweet. It is seldom met with nowadays but I have included it because of the association with the cigarette.

Vin blanc cassis   This is a Burgundy *apéritif*, made by adding cassis (blackcurrant liqueur) to a glass of dry white wine, but it is often served elsewhere, using the white wine of the region. It is a light, refreshing drink, and the cassis gives the touch of sweetness that appeals to most people. Being lighter in alcohol, it is also usually cheaper than the other *apéritifs* (see p. 198).

Lillet or **Kina Lilet**   Both the same, but the second version of the name is usual in the south. A wine-based *apéritif* from Bordeaux, pale in colour, dry and light—in some ways a little like vermouth, as it contains herbs. It can be drunk by itself, or with soda, or gin.

Soft drinks

Grenadine is possibly the best known. It is pomegranate juice, diluted with water or soda, and is sweetish.

Sirops of various flavours are also usually available: lemon (*citron*), orange (*orange*), blackcurrant (*cassis*—this is rather like Ribena, and the ordinary cassis sirop is non-alcoholic, unlike the *crème de cassis* or *cassis* liqueur used in *vin blanc cassis* or to pour over a sophisticated ice-cream), grapefruit (*pamplemousse*), and pineapple (*ananas*). They are diluted to taste. All are very sweet. Unfermented grape juice (*jus de raisin*) is also sometimes available. But this usually comes out of a bottle nowadays and it is seldom that the newly pressed juice of wine grapes is offered as, for example, it often is at vintage time in southern Spain.

Fruit sodas in various flavours (as above) are sold by the individual bottle. Two of the best known are Vittel Delices and Pschitt, which are rather like Schweppes sodas.

Fresh fruit juice (*orange pressée* or *citron pressé*) is always available in a café. It will be specially pressed for the individual customer, who can add soda or water as liked. But it is worth noting that fresh fruit juices are never very cheap.

Fruit squashes are *jus d'orange* or *de citron*.

Liqueurs

Many French liqueurs will already be familiar to the tourist, but the fact that they are considerably cheaper in France than in Britain is a reasonable excuse for the traveller to enlarge his or her experience of drinking them. It is worth bearing in mind that the helping you get in France will also be more generous than at home.

The two main types of liqueurs are those based on herbs and those based on fruits. In general, the former tend to be less sweet and more 'digestive' in character, some of the latter can be very sweet, although the *alcools blancs*, such as the fine fruit brandies of Alsace, are fruity rather than sweet, as they do not contain added sugar. The purpose of a liqueur is to aid the digestion of a meal,

72

but it is quite usual nowadays for a liqueur to be taken either as an *apéritif* or an in-between times drink, often with plenty of crushed ice or a lump of ice in the glass. The liqueur business is a commercial affair today, and although some of the recipes for the more famous ones did originate in religious houses, where the monks and nuns for centuries had been ministering to visitors with home-made cordials and preparations from their gardens and stillrooms, present-day establishments are completely up-to-date and impressively modern.

Some of the liqueurs have self-explanatory names, such as cherry, apricot, or peach brandy. The *alcools blancs* are simply called after the fruit from which they are made, such as *framboise* (raspberry), *fraise* (strawberry), *mirabelle* (little golden plums), *mandarine* (mandarin) and *poire* (pear, which is also sometimes called Williams, after the type of pear). Certain of the big liqueur houses, such as Cointreau, Cusenier, Marie Brizard et Roger, Regnier and Bardinet, have a range of all the better-known liqueurs under their own label. Some others include:

Bénédictine This is said to have been discovered by Dom Bernardo Vincelli, at Fécamp (see under the section on Normandy, p. 280). It is a herby liqueur, and at one time was used as a preventative and treatment for malaria in the marshy country around the monastery. After the Revolution, the formula came into the hands of Alexandre le Grand, a wine merchant, who revived its production and who also evolved 'B et B', Brandy and Bénédictine, for those who liked to temper the sweetness of the original liqueur with a little brandy.

Chartreuse This was originally made by the monks at their monastery near Grenoble, with such success that a huge distillery was built at Fourvioirie. When in 1903 the Carthusian order was expelled from France and went to Spain, the monks carried on the manufacture of their liqueur from Tarragona until 1931, when they were allowed to return. Only the liqueurs from the monks' distillery at Voiron may today bear the actual name of Chartreuse, although a variety of green and yellow herby liqueurs are produced by the liqueur manufacturers. The green is the stronger.

Verveine du Vélay Another herb liqueur, made in both yellow and green.

Izarra A similar kind of herb liqueur made by the Distillerie de la Côte Basque, at Bayonne, with Pyrenean herbs and flowers and Armagnac in its composition. The name is a Basque word, meaning 'star'. The green type is slightly stronger than the yellow, but some people like to combine the two in a *frappé*.

Trappistine Greenish-yellow, made by the monks of Grace-Dieu, from herbs gathered in the Doubs.

Liqueur des Moines A yellow aromatic liqueur.

Vieille Cure Originally made by the monks of the Abbey of Cénon, near Bordeaux, aromatic and containing both Armagnac and Cognac as well as herbs and plants.

Raspail Yellow and herby, invented in the early part of the nineteenth century by François Raspail, who some people consider as the forerunner of Pasteur. It was devised by him as a true digestive. It is very rarely seen nowadays.

La Tintaine A herby liqueur with aniseed the predominating taste. This is the liqueur that has a sprig of fennel inside the bottle. The name refers to the platform on which a jouster would stand in medieval times. It was the invention of a Languedoc family.

Sapindor, or Liqueur des Pins A green, rather strongly piney-smelling liqueur, put up in bottles like pieces of tree trunk. It is in fact made from herbs in the Jura, and produced at a distillery in Pontarlier.

Sénancole Evolved at the Abbey of Sénanque, who still hold the secret of the formula, although a distillery produces the liqueur commercially. It is herby, bright yellow and with a pungent, refreshing smell.

Aiguebelle or Liqueur du Frère Jean Discovered by a Trappist monk in the archives of his monastery. It is herby and made in both yellow and green.

Crème de Menthe or Peppermint This, of course, is mint in flavour and usually green, although there is a white variety.

Anis or Anisette Sweetened aniseed on a spirit base, this is one of the most popular of French liqueurs. If you like the flavour of aniseed you will like all the varieties—if you do not, choose something else.

Curaçao This type of liqueur first got its name from the Island of Curaçao, where the bitter oranges grow. Nowadays many types of orange are used, though only the peel is utilised for the liqueur. There are several very well-known kinds, the two most popular being **Grand Marnier**, which is made by the firm of Marnier-Lapostolle, and which is a curaçao made on a basis of Cognac (not merely brandy), which is why some people think of it as a type of orange brandy. The other great curaçao is **Cointreau**, made by the establishment of that name in Angers. It was so called because the firm found that many other liqueur establishments were producing a white curaçao called Triple Sec, so, in order to distinguish themselves, they gave the product the family name.

Apry is the name of the apricot liqueur made by Marie Brizard et Roger.

Abricotine is the apricot liqueur produced by the house of Garnier.

Noyau   A pale pink or white liqueur made from almonds.

Maraschino   A white liqueur made from cherry kernels.

Quetsch   A white liqueur made from a type of small plum.

Kirsch   This is in many ways the most frequently encountered liqueur, as it is the one poured over pancakes and often put in fruit salad. The full name is *kirschwasser* and it is a product of Alsace and the Jura, where the cherry trees grow in profusion, for kirsch is made from cherries. The firms of Dolfi and Jacobert are probably the two best-known producers of kirsch, but there is another sweet type, produced by the firm of Peureux, and known as **Kirsch Peureux,** which, because of its sweetness, is rather a different thing.

Crème de Bananes   A sweet banana liqueur, either yellow or white. **Banadry** is Bardinet's brand name for it.

Prunelle   The white liqueur made from sloe kernels; **Prunelle** is the name of the Garnier brand. Cusenier make a **Prunellia.**

Cassis or **Crème de Cassis**   This is the blackcurrant liqueur for which Burgundy is especially famous. It is perhaps worth stressing that it is alcoholic, like all liqueurs, and also that people who at home have been accustomed to drink blackcurrant juice, either by itself or with white wine, will find that a *'vin blanc cassis'* made with the proper liqueur is something very different, and much better.

Cordial Médoc   A dark red, sweet liqueur, made, as would be expected, in the Bordeaux area.

Calvados   Apple brandy, made in the cider country of Normandy and Brittany. It has been found an excellent digestive, especially at some of the enormous meals traditional for celebrations in that part of France and, some say about the eleventh century, the Normans discovered that a quick gulp of calvados in the middle of the meal gave them the appetite to continue without flagging. This habit of drinking—always in one or two quick mouthfuls—in the middle of a meal, became known as the *trou normand*, the idea being that the digestive made a space for the rest of the repast. Calvados is, of course, also used as a digestive at the end of a meal.

Crème de cacao (chocolate), **Crème de Café,** or **Moka** (coffee), are, as one would expect, very sweet, but can be delicious when a single taste of something sweet is wanted at the end of a meal.

Crème de Roses and **Crème de Violettes** are, however, probably too sweet and scented for most people to enjoy drinking these days, but the exotic-sounding **Parfait Amour,** often lilac in colour, is spiced as well as being sweet.

Marc is the pure white spirit which is distilled from the mass of compressed grapes left after the final pressings, and is usually considered the 'perks' of the vigneron. It is usually very strong but, properly made, can attain great character and quality. **Marc de Bourgogne** is the most famous marc, but the liqueur can be made in any wine-producing area. Visitors who may be asked to sample a home-made marc should, however, beware of the strength and, if the spirit has not been long matured, of the extreme fieriness. Like *eau-de-vie de framboise,* the home-made product can be utterly overwhelming to the unwary, especially as the helpings may be double the size of a British allowance of liqueur. Both these have—once—affected me like knock-out drops, and, however good they may be, I limit myself to teaspoonful-sized helpings henceforth.

Fine is a brandy distilled from wine and is usually described according to its origin—e.g. Fine de la Marne. It matures quicker than *Marc* and is often lighter, smoother and more delicate and usually more expensive. *Une fine à l'eau* is brandy (which in a good hotel or restaurant should be Cognac) served with water for the drinker to mix as required.

Arquebuse This is a digestive produced by Cusenier, pure white in colour. It has the enormous advantage of acting on a flagging or recuperating stomach like the more famous Fernet Branca of Italy, yet being easier to drink and not so harsh in flavour.

Mineral waters

There are numerous spas in France, especially in the Pyrenees, Auvergne and the south-east, and fortunately for the French the springs that bubble from their earth are mostly agreeable and suitable for table waters, unlike the majority of British springs. It is usually perfectly all right to drink the tap water in France, but, like much British tap water, it is not always as pleasant as that from a bottle, and the refreshing character of the many French mineral waters accord admirably with rich dishes and clean the palate for the most accurate appreciation of wine. Mineral waters are cheap in France and, if you buy bottles for picnicking, remember that you usually get a small rebate on each returned empty.

The most obviously useful thing to know about mineral waters is whether they are still or fizzy, also if a water has any specially medicinal properties; ignorance of this last can be highly inconvenient. Once in Italy I was unable to understand why I had a continual gastric turmoil, until translation of the small print on the label of the bottles of mineral water that I had been feverishly quaffing revealed that this particular kind was mildly aperient! In the neighbourhood of springs, of course, there are the local waters, which are often suggested as substitutes for the nationally-known brands, and it would be impossible to detail all these. But if you are assured that one is like, say, Évian or Perrier, this is a vague guide. All those listed are widely available. It is worth bearing in mind that fizzy waters can be very bloating to the stomach if drunk when they are only tepid; when they are, as they should always be, chilled, the carbonation tends to disappear into the water.

Evian is the top-selling table water. It is quite still and of a neutral flavour, and is suggested for use in baby foods, as it is both chemically and biologically pure.

Vittel Grande Source is the next still water. It has a very slightly earthy tang to it.

Vittel Hepar   It is unlikely that this will be offered in a restaurant, as it is a medicinal water, but anyone who comes across it should know that it is earthy in flavour and has laxative properties, being especially intended for children.

Vitteloise is what might be called the soda of Vichy Grande Source. It is very fizzy and is advertised as '*l'eau qui chante et qui danse*'.

Vittel Delices   Fizzy fruit drinks.

Perrier   A neutral tasting soda, used to mix with other things, such as brandy or whisky, or to drink by itself, with or without a slice of lemon. Another thing to note about Perrier is that the big bottle is only 7/10 of a litre, whereas the other large-sized mineral waters are 9/10 (32 fluid oz). An interesting thing about Perrier is that its fame today is largely due to an Englishman. The spring, which is naturally fizzy, was discovered by a Dr Perrier near Vergeze, fifteen miles from Nimes, in 1863, though even the Romans had known of the spring; but it was not till the early 1900s that A. W. St John Harmsworth (brother of Lord Northcliffe) visited the region with his tutor during a university vacation. They met Dr Perrier, and Harmsworth was so enthusiastic about the spring that he bought it—with the promise that it should always bear the Doctor's name. Harmsworth became paralysed after a car accident and in order to try to recover the use of his limbs he would perform exercises with Indian clubs—from which he got the idea of designing the Perrier bottle.

Contrexéville is a flat water, with a slightly earthy taste. It is a mild diuretic, which has caused it to become very popular with people trying to slim, and is also said to be advantageous in reducing cholesterol.

Vichy St Yorre, Bassin de Vichy is the well-known table water of Vichy, slightly sparkling with a faintly salty flavour. It does not get exported to Britain, because there are occasional slight variations in the mineral content of the natural spring.

Vichy Célestins has only a faint sparkle to it and is the Vichy known best outside France. However, the pace at which the Célestins spring runs is comparatively slow for the demand, so **Vichy Boussange** has been evolved to augment the supply. It is virtually the same as Vichy Célestins, but very slightly more sparkling. Vichy Célestins is not available in quarter bottles in France.

(*Vichy Grande Grille* and *Vichy Hôpital* are purely medicinal waters.)

Badoit is mildly salty, with a very slight 'prickle'—not quite a sparkle to it. Badoit is usually much liked by people who want something refreshing that isn't really 'gassy'.

Vals St Jean   Neutral and slightly 'prickly'—similar to Badoit.

Charrier according to an authority is the purest water known in its natural state—it is as neutral as distilled water, and is used by people who are on salt-free diets. Some years ago, while Brigitte Bardot was married to Jacques Charrier, the advertising boys promoting Charrier brought out a slogan '*B.B. adore Charrier*', without consulting the star in advance; not only did her lawyers compel the withdrawal of the offending advertising, but she herself almost immediately sponsored a rival piece of publicity which opened with the phrase '*Mais les Charrier préfèrent Vittel*'.

Beer

Most French beer is sold in bottles and is of the lager type. If you do come across so-called draught beer (*sous pression*), it will be drawn from a keg, and in any case it is unlikely that you will find this type of beer served anywhere except a *brasserie* or a café near to or associated with a big brewery.

Beer is invariably chilled, which makes it particularly refreshing, and may be ordered in any type of eating establishment. The big breweries, such as Kronenbourg and Pecheur, in Alsace, distribute supplies throughout the country, and several types of imported beer—now even some British—are also available. Although it is difficult to generalise about such a variable product, it is fair to say that, in strength and style, all kinds resemble lager, and French beer is, indeed, mostly made by the low fermentation method, with a higher proportion of carbonation than the British beer, which is made by top fermentation.

The *'demi'* beloved of Maigret is a measure—5 *décilitres*, which means a generous large glass tankard. *'Un bock'*, which sounds slightly dated as a term nowadays, is not actually a measure, but if you order such a thing, you will probably get a beer in a fat, stemmed goblet, containing about 4 *décilitres*.

Most breweries are glad to receive visitors and show them round, so that if you are in the neighbourhood of any large brewery, this can be an interesting excursion to make.

Hot drinks

There is a greater variety of these widely available than in Britain, so if you cannot like tea in the way the French make it, there are plenty of alternatives.

Tea Nowadays mostly made with a tea-bag and seldom very strong. It comes mostly from Ceylon. You may get both hot milk and cold milk with it, but lemon is always available too, and so is China tea (*thé de Chine, au citron* if you want lemon), which will come in a pot unless you are eating somewhere (such as in Paris) where Russian tea is also served. This is strong tea with lemon and is usually served in a tall glass with a handle or standing in a holder with a handle. It is not unusual for a French man or woman to have a spoonful of rum in tea instead of milk—pleasant on a cold day. Tea is not cheap in France, but can be good.

Coffee is not cheap either and may often be served only by the cup and not by the pot. It varies in quality, but sometimes contains too much chicory for some visitors. Coffee after a meal is always black, so if you want milk or cream, you must ask specially. Coffee at breakfast-time is served with hot milk unless you ask for it black; the coffee and milk will either come in two jugs, for you to mix as you wish, or else the coffee will be already poured into a large cup and the milk in a separate jug. Coffee ordered at any time other than breakfast may be brought already in the cup, in which case it will probably have come out of an urn or a big coffee-pot, or you may be asked if you want *'Un filtre'*; this means that the portion of coffee is put into one of those perforated metal holders with lids that perch on top of the coffee cup and are filled with boiling water, which drips through the coffee into the cup. After all has passed through, you remove the metal lid—it is impossible to do this without risking burning your fingers—stand it upside down by the side of the cup and then put the rest of the filter apparatus on top of the upturned lid, so that any further drips go into this lid. This is what should happen; in practice the coffee either takes so long to filter that it is cold when you can eventually drink it, or else the water refuses to pass through at all, in which case you have either to try and unscrew the metal plate that clamps the coffee down, thus letting the water flow more freely through—taking some of the grounds with it—or else you cup your hand and press it down onto the open top of the filter—heat regardless—thereby making a vacuum that will force the water through. *Café filtre* can be good if the coffee in the filter is of good quality, but the performance involved with it is rarely trouble-free. The espresso coffee machine is now popular in France, so that you may get espresso coffee in a large café or snack bar. But the coffee that a good restaurant or café should serve you —if you ask and, of course, pay for it—is Cona coffee, though usually they only make exactly the number of cups required for one each.

Sugar is always served with coffee, usually in large lumps, and it is not bad manners—though certainly informal and not to be done at a luncheon or dinner party—to dip the corner of a lump of sugar into the coffee and then eat it. To do so is to *'faire le canard'*.

There are also several brands of decaffeinated coffee, and this may always be asked for by people who find strong black coffee in the evening interferes with their sleep. Café H.A.G. is the best-known brand of this *'café décafeiné'*, but there are others. If you order one, the waiter may bring it in a small sachet, which you slit open and pour into the cup, while he adds boiling water, or else a whole tin of decaffeinated coffee may be brought, for you to help yourself (sometimes one can order and get instant coffee in this way too). It must be admitted that personally I have never found any of these otherwise wholesome beverages bear much resemblance to coffee. To my palate all have an odd flavour of vegetable extract.

Milk Travellers who drink a lot of plain milk may encounter problems in France. In the country the milk may come fresh from the cow, which is a taste some people—and among them children, who are notoriously conservative—really do not like. Otherwise the bulk of French milk is pasteurised, but, as the system of daily deliveries is not widespread, a great deal of milk is sterilised, for obvious convenience, and it is this that may result in the flavour of the milk being unappealing to the British taste, especially in tea. There is frankly nothing much to be done about this, except that one can comfort oneself with the fact that milk that is boiled before use is unlikely to be a source of infection. You can recognise the sterilised milk bottles by their crown capsules. When hot milk is served a strainer should ideally accompany the jug, as the skin will invariably be thick.

Milk drinks The milk shake is gaining ground in Paris and large towns, and Caccolac, a type of bottled chocolate milk shake, which may be served hot or cold, is widely available throughout the country.

Chocolate and **cocoa** are widely available and chocolate is an alternative to coffee at breakfast for those who do not care for whatever type of coffee is served.

Grog is hot water with either rum or Cognac, excellent for warming up anyone who has come in out of the wet or cold.

Infusions or **tisanes** The use of herbs, infused in hot water, for healing and soothing purposes, is something that is very common in France, although nowadays in Britain very few people make use of herbs in this way. The herbs to be infused are in a little sachet which is put in the teapot with boiling water just like a tea-bag, and allowed to infuse for a minute or two. Sugar may be taken with the clear drink, but milk is not served with it. I myself find this sort of drink very refreshing and soothing at the end of a day that may have taxed the digestion and taste-buds, but these drinks are 'herby', so all may not care for them. They are a possible alternative to tea, should you not care for this in France, and if you do not like coffee last thing at night. Here are some of the best-known infusions, with their reputed properties:

Camomile (*camomille*)   A sedative for the nerves and digestion
Mint (*menthe*)   Digestive
Vervain (*verveine*)   For feverishness and nervous complaints
Balm (*mélisse*)   For fevers and colds

Orange flowers (*fleur d' oranger*)   A sedative and for the calming of the digestion

Sage (*sauge*)   A tonic in general, and especially for the brain and head

Pansies (*pensées sauvages*)   Soothing and cooling

Elder (*sureau*)   Healing and soothing

Lime (*tilleul*)   For sleeplessness

Tilleul-menthe   For soothing sleep and a good digestion, also to counteract headaches

Wild thyme (*serpolet*)   A stimulant, for the lungs and digestion

Vocabulary and useful phrases

Chacun voudrait payer son addition séparément   Each (of us) would like a separate bill

Bière sous pression   Draught beer

Une grande bouteille   When referring to mineral water, this merely means the full-sized bottle, not a magnum or a similar large size. '*Une demi bouteille*' is either a half bottle or a half litre bottle; '*un quart*' or '*une petite bouteille*' is either a quarter bottle or small size of whatever is being ordered

Café crème and *café au lait*   Both these expressions mean coffee with milk, but '*café crème*' is generally used for white coffee (not with cream), and '*café au lait*' mostly just in connection with breakfast.

Une chope   A type of beer mug

Une chopine   A half-litre measure

Le comptoir   Bar counter

Le consommateur   The customer in a café or restaurant bar

Les consommations   Drinks

Eau fraîche   Cold water

Eau plate   Tap water

Eau de seltz   Soda water

Frappé   Iced

Gazeuse   Fizzy; *légèrement gazeuse*—slightly fizzy; *non-gazeuse*—flat, still

Glaçons   Ice cubes

Mélangé   Mixed

A part   Separately

Un passoir   A strainer

Régler   To settle (bill)

Un seau à glace   An ice bucket

Siphon   Siphon; '*avec du siphon*' signifies 'with a splash'

Sucre en morceaux   Lumps of sugar

Une tournée   A round (of drinks)

Une tranche de citron   A slice of lemon

Un zeste de citron   A twist of lemon peel

Un alcool   A drink of spirits, never wine

Sabler   To gulp or swill down. It is a verb sometimes used in connection with Champagne e.g. *Sabler le Champagne* signifies 'to drink Champagne like water'

To Take and to Bring Back

There are very few things that are quite impossible to buy in the British Isles or France today, although of course some will be cheaper in one country than the other. There are, for a start, those items that the traveller cannot do without, that may be difficult or very expensive in France. Without suggesting that anyone interested in food and drink should stock the boot of their car with tinned produce, here are some things for the lover of picnics to bear in mind when packing:

If you travel with children, then you will be well advised to take any baby foods regarded as essential in their diet. Children, especially tinies, tend to be very conservative, and it is not worth trying to make any child adapt itself to a completely different set of foodstuffs as well as to a different climate and daily routine. Baby foods are of course available in France, although they are a little more expensive than in Britain. For older children, British biscuits are better and cheaper than the average French ones, and breakfast cereals are rare, so take these if the family are wedded to them, or if you give them to the younger ones for supper instead of the full meal that the French serve. Familiar sweets and chocolates are useful, especially barley sugar and boiled sweets to suck on a long drive. The French equivalents tend to be rather dear. French chocolates are excellent, but the hand-made ones, from shops that make their own, contain no preservatives, so that the chocolates must be eaten within a few days and can be adversely affected by the heat.

To take It is almost unnecessary to remind lovers of the British national non-alcoholic beverage that they should take their own tea if they wish to have frequent cuppas. Tea in France is dear and seldom as the British like it, even on the rare occasions when tea-bags are not used. Coffee is expensive in France and may contain too much chicory for individual tastes, so if you have a favourite brand or blend, a personal supply is a good idea when travelling if you have the means of making it, or if you are going to stay somewhere where you can hand your tea and coffee to the manageress for your own use.

Marmalade is something that may be unobtainable where you are staying and as even the most adaptable of us can feel strongly about the rightness of this for breakfast, a pot of the pet kind may be packed, or jam, if there is a favourite variety, as hotel jam is seldom very good. Finally, for the person who loves a fine apple, especially with the last of the wine at the end of a good meal, it is worth noting that comparatively few apples in France equal the crisp succulence and fine flavour of a really good English apple. Apples from warm countries seldom achieve quality, just as trout and shellfish from warm waters are never as good as those from icy seas and streams. As apples keep quite well and as the odd piece of fruit, either for breakfast or a snack can add to the general running expenses, it is a good idea to have a bag of apples, padded with tissue, in the car; an apple can also sometimes be helpful in settling any sort of queasiness that develops during a long hot drive.

What to bring home You are allowed a concession by the customs of a bottle of liqueur and a bottle of wine each duty free, but this must be declared. You are not supposed to bring into Britain raw meat, fish, game, potatoes (other than new or sweet) or plants. Butter, coffee, fresh apples and pears, and sugar, are all subject either to rigid quotas or special licensing arrangements. H.M. Customs and Excise can provide a detailed list of all prohibited goods and the Board of Trade a list of everything that requires an import licence. What other things are good buys and worth the trouble of taking them home?

Drinks Because of the saving in duty, a bottle of a liqueur is a better buy than any wine. Indeed, unless you are fortunate enough to find or be given a very rare and otherwise costly wine, it is never worth while taking table wines home—they either will not travel, if they are the little wines beloved of holiday voyagers and not already on sale in Britain, or else they may be cheaper at home just because British wine merchants do not raise their prices as often or as sharply as most French sources of supply. Of course, if you come across a supply of table wines that you wish to buy and export by the case, you must get the appropriate forms to enable you to do so, whether you are taking the wine back with you or having it sent.

Most proprietary brands of liqueurs and *apéritifs* on sale in France may now be bought in Great Britain, but you may come across some special one, made only on a small scale, that is worth taking back for the interest as well as enjoyment. Duty on *apéritifs* is charged on the rate of strength and if whatever you have in this way is really obscure, it may be a good idea to ascertain the strength when you buy, so that you can tell the customs, as they are entitled, if in doubt, to keep the bottle for analysis.

If you are fond of *sirops*, you may buy a favourite kind in the *épicerie* before returning, especially if you live out of easy reach of Soho or a French provision shop. *Infusions*, which are bought at the *pharmacie*, are not always easy to get in Britain, so if you become fond of these, a packet or selection is a worthwhile buy. **Foodstuffs** Fresh herbs, especially those from Provence, are a good idea for city dwellers, or those who live in the north. They can be kept in plastic bags or plastic containers of the type used in the refrigerator and used days later. The soft cheeses are more difficult to transport if you have a long journey to make, but Cantal and even Roquefort can be kept if wrapped in a moistened cloth over ordinary greaseproof paper.

Tins of *pâté*, tinned truffles and truffle peelings, which are comparatively cheap and as suitable as the whole truffle for most cooking purposes, *foie gras*, which can never be cheap but which will be cheaper than in Britain, and, naturally, any local specialities put up for tourists to take home, such as the mustards of Dijon and Reims, nougat of Montélimar, are worth buying, either for your own use or for presents at home. Local oils and vinegars, too, can be valuable assets in your kitchen at home.

Certain kitchen utensils and equipment can be good buys in France, especially if you live out of very easy reach of London. Heavy enamel on cast-iron casseroles, hachoirs (the curved blade that makes such an excellent chopper), the range of '*Mouli*' utensils, gadgets that catch your fancy or straightforward steel knives that become indispensable make it worthwhile for the amateur cook to spend an hour in the hardware department of a large store, or a *quincaillerie*. Plastic items, too, can be good souvenirs, especially mats, cloths and tablecloths and table and shelf coverings, which can be more attractive and certainly less ordinary than those available in Britain.

Local pottery and china can be worth buying, but attractive things of this kind are rarely cheap; earthenware that is suitable for top of stove use, for example, may be far more expensive than in Britain. Very fine glasses are virtually the same price as in Britain, and their fragility seldom makes it worth while having them packed for transporting home. Tableware for everyday use, such as the chunky *faïence de Béarn*, with dark blue and red criss-cross lines, the Gien pottery, which is rather like majolica, or the blue and white cut-out ware from the Basque region of the Pyrenees are examples of informal tableware that transplant well. Fine china can be very attractive in the more expensive ranges, although if you are matching it up with tableware you already possess, it is worth remembering that the white of continental china is really more skim-milk or off-white and can look strange by the side of some British china.

Table linen is expensive, but local cloths and napkins, although they may cost a fair amount initially, can be very hardwearing. The Basque and Catalonian stuffs, in brilliant colours, are examples of this.

Finally, cookery books, although not as numerous in France as in Britain, are very much cheaper than the same books bought in the British Isles, so that it is certainly worth while buying any big reference work to do with either food or wine, or anything that is rather lavish in presentation and consequently expensive, if you can read French. In the different regions you may find collections of local recipes, which are of great interest, as well as being useful; the various histories of wine and gastronomy, some of them long since out of print and only available secondhand, can be fascinating. Sets of postcards of regional dishes and wines and maps of wine districts or food specialities are usually very well produced and attractive, so that they can be used decoratively as well as for reference; many of these last are given away, either by individual firms or local tourist offices.

Vocabulary and useful phrases

L'ail Garlic ⎫
Basilic Basil ⎬ for names of other herbs, see pp. 48–49
Une brasière A heavy casserole
Une carte vinicole A wine map
Une casserole A saucepan
Cerfeuil Chervil
Ciboulette Chives
Une cocotte A cooking pot with a lid. What we might call a casserole
Les épluchures de truffes Truffle peelings
Estragon Tarragon
Un hachoir The half-moon type of chopper that is expensive in England
Une mandoline A vegetable slicer
Une marmite A stewpot

Oseille Sorrel

Un panier à salade A salad basket, for shaking salad dry (also slang for the police van, or Black Maria)

Un panier touristique A gift basket (usually used of wine put up in gift packs)

Persil Parsley

Une facture A bill (of sale). Remember to get one for presentation to the Customs if you buy anything while you are in France

Vintager carrying four of the Burgundian baskets (*paniers beaunois*) which fit over the shoulder. A hole at each end enables a stave to be passed through so that, if the basket is very heavy when filled with grapes, it can be carried between two people.

French Hospitality and Good Manners for the Visitor

This is not a textbook on etiquette, nor do I suggest that the ordinary civilised person needs to modify his or her behaviour in the slightest when visiting France. But it is always interesting to become acquainted with other ways of life. If you travel with your children, too, it may be necessary to brief them before they visit a French friend's home, as they can find a change in the conventions both strange and upsetting. Anyway, when I began to visit in France, I should have been glad of most of the information I have included in this chapter.

The conventions governing social life vary from country to country and even within different sorts of society within the same country. No traveller need feel that he or she is letting down the reputation of their native land by not knowing all the nuances of the language and the manners of the well-brought-up Frenchman or woman. Being intensely individualistic as a people, the French are usually very tolerant towards those whose ways are completely different from their own, but simply because their ideas about hospitality tend to be lavish the visitor can find a visit to a French household both intimidating and confusing. It may be some comfort to know that, except for those fortunate enough to have been educated in France or to have lived there, studying the ways and whys for some time, most people share in this shyness, even though they may have been travelling in the country for years.

It should be emphasised that Paris is not typical of France in many ways as regards manners and customs; this applies of course to any capital city of importance, but the French provinces, even today, tend to be strongholds of a different way of life, admirable in many ways, irksome in others, rather more so than in the provinces of the British Isles. Those who have stayed mainly in Paris or smart coastal resorts, or who have been to school or for long holidays in French-speaking Switzerland or even in Belgium, will find a considerable change in everyday life and even in the

French language when they get to know the French provincial towns or the country proper.

Speaking French The French are proud of their language in a way that the English seem never to have been. Consequently, although you may have tried to learn idiomatic French, it is risky to make use of slang words and phrases; at best, it implies that you were taught by an ill-educated person, at worst, you may inadvertently say something definitely not fit for polite company. Better to talk in a stilted fashion that is at least correct, until you are really fluent. The subtleties of the language are great and phrase books are not always to be relied on. Once I learnt what appeared to be a gay, informal phrase of greeting, signifying, more or less, 'How are things with you, chum?' only to find that, whereas it would be permissible for it to be uttered by a man to another man, with whom he had been a lifelong friend, it was not at all the sort of thing a woman would ever say!

The sort of slang and jargon current among young people, and the use of English and American expressions in French sentences are also frowned on by serious-minded French people, although of course they may be an accepted way of talking among the young and gay in the resorts or in Paris. It is wise to be cautious about copying the way radio announcers speak, or using turns of phrase acquired in popular newspapers or detective stories. And great bewilderment can be caused by the employment of words and expressions that are actually French but which, in Britain, have a completely different significance from their meaning in France. The most obvious of these are: '*faux pas*', which means a definite and deplorable going astray (the French term for *faux pas* is '*gaffe*'); '*cul de sac*', which in France is an '*impasse*'; '*aider*', which is to help in the sense of helping someone down steps or into a bus, as opposed to '*assister*' which means to give monetary or material aid; '*demander*' which is a perfectly polite word meaning to ask, not demand; and '*sensible*' which means sensitive. There are many of these unlike pairs and it is interesting to see how the meaning changes. The use of regional and special words for things in the worlds of wine and food, however, is helpful—providing that the visitor gets them right.

Similarly, do not use what little French you may have to ask a question requiring a detailed answer unless you can be pretty sure of following the reply. If one can generalise at all about any people, it may be said that the French are intellectual and exacting and for anyone who is like this there is nothing more exasperating than to understand, by a vague or inadequate answer, that the person to whom they have delivered a short speech has failed to grasp the significance of what has been rather carefully said.

French conversation is one of the great social arts and it can be amusing, stimulating and highly intelligent all at the same time, in a way that seldom seems to be possible elsewhere. But once a company of people get going and rattle away in this fashion, they tend to forget about the visitor who can only follow the general trend of the talk, the nuances of which cannot be exactly translated anyway. This is not very kind and it can be both tiring and boring for the person left out. The only thing to do, should this happen to you, is to listen as amiably as possible. Sometimes after a concentrated dose of French talk, one suddenly gets the sound of the language and can understand a great deal better. Do not demand explanations, which will only slow up the whole thing, to the possible exasperation of those playing leading parts. In France everyone talks, about general rather than personal matters in company. But if you cannot join in with moderate ability, keep quiet.

Meeting French Friends   The rules for introductions are the same as for ourselves—men are presented to women, unless a high official, religious personage or elderly eminent man is concerned, and young people are presented to older ones. Hands are always shaken, both when meeting and when saying goodbye, and this applies to everyone—host, hostess with whom you stay, and business colleagues each time you meet or leave them. French men kiss the hand (or rather incline over it) of a married woman, but usually only actually kiss it when they have met her before and are on friendly terms. Little boys bow rather deeply and make the gesture of raising a lady's hand to their lips, and little girls curtsy, both offering their hands—and not, unless you are a great family friend, expecting you to kiss them. A man says either '*Mes hommages, madame*' or simply '*Madame*', or '*Mes respects, mademoiselle*', or just '*Mademoiselle*'. A woman inclines her head, smiles slightly and merely says '*Madame*' or '*Monsieur*', at the moment of being introduced. You may also say '*Bonjour*', or, in the evening '*Bonsoir*', which is correct as an opening phrase at any time from 6 p.m. onwards. '*Bonne nuit*' is only for when you are going to bed. '*Au revoir*' or '*A bientôt*' are correct when saying goodbye, even if you are never likely to see the people again at all.

There is a great deal of uncertainty about the use of the word '*Enchanté*' when being introduced. Some manuals of etiquette and some very well brought up people advocate it, others shudder in horror. My researches have resulted in the following: a woman certainly *never* says '*Enchantée*' just by itself (it has the sort of significance of 'Pleased to meetcher'), although if the friend who makes the introduction is a close one and she really is delighted to meet the other person, she may well, either early on in the conversation or at the end, say, '*Enchantée de faire votre connaissance*'. A man being introduced by a close friend to someone who is a good friend of the person performing the introduction may, except on very formal occasions, say '*Enchanté*', as the phrase has some validity—rather as we might say 'Delighted to meet you', on an informal occasion. But in this post-Mitford era the French have become almost as self-conscious about it as we have in saying 'Cheers', so you may hear the word even in very polite company.

If you have to edge past someone or for any reason want to say 'Excuse me', the phrase is either '*Excusez-moi*', or simply '*Pardon*', to which the properly brought up and automatic reply is '*Je vous en prie*'.

Asking after someone's health, the phrase is '*Comment-allez-vous?*' to which the response is '*Très bien, merci—et vous?*' Should you wish to send a greeting to a friend via someone else, the phrase is '*Dites lui bonjour de ma part*', or, slightly more formal, '*Donnez mon meilleur souvenir à Madame Dupont*', signifying 'Give Madame Dupont my best wishes'. And should you meet French friends any time before noon, they will invariably inquire '*Vous avez bien dormi?*' to which the polite reply is '*Très bien, merci, et vous?*' even if you've just passed the worst night of your life. If you wish to be particularly deferential when saying goodbye to anyone you have met for the first time, you can say '*Très heureux d'avoir fait votre connaissance*', or with a really important person, suppose you are wishing to defer a little to them, you can say '*Très honoré (or privilégié) d'avoir fait votre connaissance*'.

As far as what may be called the 'social kiss' is concerned, French women (apart from those in the international smart set) use it only with very close friends indeed. Leave it to them to take the initiative. A Frenchwoman only rarely kisses a man, even a friend of long standing and although kisses may be exchanged when you all meet in someone's home, greetings may be a little more formal if you are in a restaurant or hotel foyer.

The use of the first name, too, is something of a privilege and it is always for the older man or woman to suggest that anyone younger may make use of it. Although the use of the second person singular has become fairly common among friends in the international set in Paris and also is merely a mark of friendship in Switzerland, this is not so in provincial France. There are even still families who, while saying '*tu*' to their children, expect a formal '*vous*' in reply, and although older people do use '*tu*' to those much younger, it is a familiarity for anyone else to make use of the second person without being invited to do so, rather like Edwardian clubmen using first names instead of surnames. Even the first declaration of love may well be '*Je vous aime*', rather than '*Je t'aime*', so the visitor is advised to stick to the security of '*vous*' until absolutely sure of the nuances in the language. You may find, in old-fashioned manuals of conversation, the instruction to address servants in the second person, but this is *not* the way to get good service nowadays.

When having a drink, it is not invariably the custom to say anything, but if you are among old friends the conventional exchange of greetings is '*Santé*', or '*À la vôtre!*' If the host wishes to make a slightly special point of an initial toast, he may '*trinquer*' or clink glasses with everyone, or else all clink glasses lightly together.

Children on the social occasions are definitely seen and not heard, even when they are almost grown-up. It is unusual for a French child or teen-ager to address a visitor without first being spoken to, unless offering refreshments, and young people never raise their voices in company. Any bad behaviour is dealt with by the offender being immediately taken away from the company—there is never any question of ticking off a child or slapping it in public. If you are not sure whether your children will be able to maintain an equal standard of rather rigid good manners, then it is probably a good idea to arrange for them to go out to play after a short time.

Do not expect, when you meet friends for a drink, or for any sort of light refreshments in between meals, that the occasion will be prolonged or involve a lot of drinking. It is always perfectly in order for you to have a mineral water or even a cup of coffee at any time, if you wish.

Being entertained in a restaurant If you have been invited to a meal, it is possible that you will, when you arrive, be expected to go straight in to the restaurant and not have a drink in the bar. If you do have an *apéritif* first, then you may only be offered a single one. It is important to be on time for a meal which may have been ordered and most carefully planned in advance.

When entering a restaurant, or going downstairs in the company of the host, it is he who goes in front, to see that all is as it

should be and, if necessary, to support a woman should she trip.
Invited to tea 'Le five o'clock' can be a formal as well as an
informal occasion in France. Whatever time mentioned when you
are invited, it goes by a name that the French imagine is tea-time,
but with a mid-day meal of a size usual in that country, tea
generally is later than it would be in Britain. Bread and butter is
seldom served and the cakes, biscuits and little sweet things all
tend to be small and easily manageable, although you may sometimes be offered a slice of a large cake or tart. If so, you will
certainly get a fork with which to eat it.

The tea itself may be offered with hot or cold milk or cream (an
American influence) or lemon. Sometimes tea is served with rum
—the light Martinique rum, so different from the heavy rums
more usual in Britain. Or for those who prefer a drink, *'porto'*
or sometimes another *apéritif* or sweet wine will be available.

Breakfast in a French household The breakfast tray will
usually be brought to your bedroom, but in a country house, or
one by the sea, especially where there are a number of young
people, breakfast may be served downstairs *en famille*. The coffee
may be served in a large, bowl-like cup without a handle, which
it is perfectly polite to raise to your mouth with both hands. This
is called a *bol*, it is slightly old-fashioned and definitely informal.
Plates are not always set, though of course the hostess will always
provide one if asked, and the spoon with which you will be
provided in addition to a knife will be quite large, almost like a
small dessert spoon. This is because it is usual and perfectly polite
to dip your roll or croissant or even bits of bread into your
coffee, and then fish it out with the spoon, if you are unable to
keep hold of part of it with your fingers. Very few British grown-
ups can sincerely enjoy doing this, but children often do. However, it is not rude to refrain. Butter may be the only accompaniment to bread, rolls or rusks, but jam or honey are quite often
served.

Invited to a French house for lunch or dinner The remarks
about punctuality apply likewise. You may be offered an *apéritif*
which, unless you are in a region where there is a local speciality
of this kind, will probably be *'Un porto'* (which can occasionally
turn out to be sherry), or whisky, out of compliment to you, or
simply because whisky is nowadays a smart drink in France. Do
not be surprised if neither the hostess nor the other women have
an *apéritif*, or indeed if you merely sit round for a short time
talking, without any drink at all.

If the guest wants to visit the bathroom or should a woman wish to repair face or hair, he or she must ask to do so. It is likely that you may be offered the chance of going upstairs or to a cloakroom should you be in the country and have come some way, but in a town your coat will be taken in the hall and you will be shown straight to the salon.

If you are the chief guests, you will sit on the right of the host and hostess, as in Britain. They will give the signal to sit down. Your napkin may conceal a roll or piece of bread, so be careful to put it on your side plate—if there is one—or on the cloth if not, instead of sending it flying as you shake out the napkin. It is strictly correct only to unfold part of this and to lay it across your lap. French good manners require the hands always to rest on the table and not in the lap—a reversal of ours—and the wrists are usually propped either side of the plate.

Dishes are nearly always handed twice in France, so avoid taking too large a helping on the first round since you will be expected to have a second one. And you will be expected to finish everything on your plate. It is not rude—rather the reverse—to comment on the food.

Glasses are set above your plate and cutlery on either side, forks with tines downwards, but it is unusual to have all the cutlery needed for the meal on the table at the beginning. It is supplied with the courses. However, for anything less than a very formal meal, you will have a knife rest set to the right of your plate; the knife and fork are rested against this either when you are going to help yourself to another portion, or when the same implements are going to be used for another course. A French manual of etiquette is firm that you should never put knife and fork on the 'porte-couteau' when the plates and cutlery are both going to be changed, but leave them on the plate. However, this is one of the things that you learn by instinct and not by rule. The fact that you have been eating fish does not invariably mean that the cutlery will be changed before the next course, but it may be. The wisest course is to keep an eye on what the hostess does and follow her example. But even if you forget, whoever is waiting at table will either put your cutlery back on the knife rest, or transfer it to the plate without anyone being inconvenienced. I never get the use of the knife rest right myself; perhaps one has to be born in France to do so.

Soup is eaten from the point of the spoon in France, and the use of the fork for eating, rather in the American style, is fairly general, but as the tableware is the same as in Britain, there is no reason why you should not use it exactly as you do at home. Snail tongs and picks for shellfish are not difficult to manipulate, and if necessary you can, except on the most formal occasions, use your fingers. In the same way, it is quite usual to pick up the oyster or mussel shells and drink the liquid from them, and also to pick up and put in your mouth the joints of small game birds, which are difficult to strip of meat with a knife and fork. Finger bowls usually arrive after such dishes and generally accompany the service of fruit at the end of the meal.

If, at any meal given by members of the wine trade, the conversation relates largely to the wines, it is always wise to keep a little of each in the glasses set before you and not to empty any one. The wines can then be sampled again and then compared according to any discussion. To quaff down a rare old vintage early on in the meal not only implies a casual attitude to a prized commodity but can deprive you of the opportunity of trying it again during any subsequent relevant comments. If you have emptied your glass there may be none left to replenish it—and it might be the host's (even the world's) last bottle.

Depending on the circumstances, the coffee (always black) may be served at the table, or else everyone will move back into the salon at the end of the meal. Sometimes the hostess will offer the women guests a chance to go to the bathroom and tidy themselves before a glass, but she may not always do so. If you ask 'to wash your hands', the chances are you will be shown a tap, with soap and a towel. The euphemism to mutter at need is—'*Voulez-vous m'indiquer le petit coin?*' (But it is possible that the foreigner will be the only one to require it. French ladies seem to be trained not to.)

It is not only bad manners but indicates a positive contempt for food and drink to smoke at table at any time, and certainly before the end of the meal. Quite possibly cigarettes and cigars may not be offered in the dining-room at all, and it would be an affront to the host to bring out your own, with the possible exception of households in the Basque country and Rouissillon, which may have been influenced by their Spanish neighbours.

It is likewise 'not done' for a woman to make any repairs to her face or hair in public, especially not at the table. The only times you see anyone touching up in this way, she invariably turns out to be a foreigner. Nor will a Frenchwoman ever walk about with a cigarette in her mouth.

Coffee after a meal in France is always black and surprise is shown if you refuse sugar. Rarely is more than a single cup served. Liqueurs are usually offered and as they may be served in far larger quantities than in Britain, it is prudent to ask for a very little—'*Une goutte*', or '*Très peu*'. There is no separation of the sexes and although, especially before the meal, it is quite usual for women friends to get together and catch up with news for a few moments, the company mix throughout and conversation continues to be general. Luncheons may go on until late in the afternoon, but remember, if you are invited out to dinner, in the country people tend to go to bed well before midnight. It is therefore considerate to take your leave—if you are the guests of honour, no one will leave before you—about eleven o'clock, unless, of course, your host is elderly, when you may think it polite to leave a little earlier.

Gifts for friends Anyone feeling hesitant about taking food or drink to France should be reassured; there are certain national delicacies that will be very welcome:

Drinks Whisky is always acceptable, although recently the price has dropped so that it is not quite as costly in France as previously. Visitors can bring in half a bottle of spirits each and naturally it is a good idea to buy this in the duty-free shop at the airport or on the boat. If you want something rather special, then a straight malt whisky is a true rarity and prized by the recipient, or if a smaller gift is wanted a quarter flask of Drambuie, the whisky liqueur with the romantic Bonnie Prince Charlie history—sure to appeal—or one of the other liqueurs with a whisky base, such as Glayva, or maybe Atholl Brose. A small flask of mead, too, and even English wine would interest the historically minded, even if only academically.

Foodstuffs Most Frenchwomen love English tea, but it should always be the strong Indian type if you are in doubt. Earl Grey or a similar blend are also liked by many, especially those who have lived outside France a lot; it is possible to get selections of attractive canisters of different kinds of tea from most big grocers or stores and these make first-rate presents. Coffee is so dear in France that, especially if you are going to stay with friends, it will be appreciated if you take some beans, and preferably fairly high roast.

Stilton cheese, especially when put up in a gift container, makes a good gift, but as few French people know of the existence of any other British cheese, it could be an inspiration to take a pound of Double Gloucester, Lancashire, Dunlop, or a whole baby Cheddar, or a Blue Cheshire (it will all, anyway, be referred to as 'le Chester'—no one seems to know why) if you are going to reach their destination within a fairly short time. Food of this

97

kind should be declared when entering the country, although it is possible that the experience of a friend may be repeated: he declared a large chunk of Leicester cheese, to which the customs official replied that monsieur must obviously be in transit and marked the luggage through without a moment's further questioning.

Biscuits, especially in decorative tins, delight children, and shortbread is very popular indeed. Bath Olivers are appreciated by lovers of cheese. Fruit cakes or iced cakes of the Christmas variety are liked, and if you are visiting a friend recently married, or having moved to a new home, or having had a new baby, it might be an idea to have a cake of this kind made and specially iced. The wedding or birthday cake, as we know it, is not usual in France (it is served as a dessert cake on festive occasions) so that this would be an unusual present. One of my friends took a complete wedding cake out to a family celebration; although carefully packed and padded, it arrived a little damaged, but the local patissier was delighted to repair it and it was the centrepiece of the family party. Dundee cake, gingerbread, or any good cake in a tin would be a suitable present for one's hostess.

Marmalade, especially the vintage kind, makes a good present, and the small pots of assorted British honeys and marmalades likewise. Tinned puddings, which are not known outside the British Isles, are also much liked, particularly Christmas pudding, and also mincemeat, although the recipients should be briefed about the preparation and service of both. Gentleman's relish and really good mint chocolates are other presents recommended and appreciated by French friends.

One of the most acceptable presents of all, if you are going to see the recipient within a day or two of arriving in France, is smoked salmon. There is nothing as good as first quality Scotch, cut sliver thin, and *saumon fumé*, well packed in greaseproof paper, can be put into a hotel refrigerator overnight, or even for a couple of nights, so as to be a very appreciated and truly status symbol present. Smoked fish are not, curiously enough, a speciality of France, and although I have not taken smoked herring or trout to France as gifts, I think that either would be appreciated, and smoked cod's roe makes a good small gift.

Tableware   Although the French are so particular about tableware as to make anyone hesitant about offering anything of the kind, they do appreciate pieces of fine china and glass and silver, providing that these are typically English. Crown Derby, Worcester, Spode, Wedgwood or English cut crystal are all good presents, either as little gifts in the form of ashtrays or trinket boxes or butter dishes and knives, or sets of dessert cutlery, or plates; sets of little ashtrays, or bon-bon dishes are appreciated in France, where a *service de table* is more important as a status symbol than it might be here, and English or Irish cut-crystal dishes or goblets, salad dishes or bowls, or finger bowls will be prized.

If you are choosing sterling silver, sets of small pieces or even one piece are liked and antique silver is always a good choice: silver coasters, decanter labels, grape scissors, ice-cream or dessert knives and forks or spoons, coffee or tea spoons, cake or pastry servers, salts and peppers, sugar bowls and tongs or sifters, or small salvers, dishes, cake stands and cream jugs. For a rather important sort of present, a tray is something that is fairly easy to pack, but if you have the gift, whatever it is, packed for you at a shop, remember to get them to give you a bill for the customs, which should also state whether or not the present is an antique.

Antique and modern pewter ware is another idea for a present to a gourmet friend, or fine linen. As a rule, the French do not use table mats for formal occasions, so as far as table linen is concerned the present should be a cloth and napkins, (for a tea table this need not be very large or expensive) or the sort of small cloth or large mat or runner that can be used for a tray or side table, or put on top of the tablecloth. A small-scale present, but one that is usually very much liked, is linen drying cloths; in France these are generally cotton and more expensive even than linen cloths in Britain. Sets of small napkins, such as are suitable for buffet parties, are another good idea. Remember when choosing linen that even in a small household the table, centre of so many important activities, will be on the large side, also that the Frenchwoman has access to much fine lace and embroidery work within her own country.

Saying thank you   Apart from thanking host and hostess when you leave, a note of thanks sent afterwards is a polite expression of gratitude. Flowers or chocolates or sweets, or fine fruit are of course appreciated by the hostess, but they should never be brought by guests, only sent beforehand or afterwards. It is worth pointing out that it is not the custom in France to send bunches of mixed flowers. They should be all of one kind although they can be of mixed colours. If, for a birthday, flowers are sent to a young girl, they must only be white ones. Red roses, in provincial France anyway, imply intimate affection. Also sweets and chocolates, presented with the delightful packing and decorations in which the French *confisiers* excel, can be very expensive—the box alone can be a costly item. But to send a gift, accompanied by a card that briefly expresses your thanks for the kindness of host and hostess, has one enormous advantage for the visitor: it does away with the complex and time-consuming task of writing a letter when this has to be done in French. Should the hosts speak or read English, even only moderately, it is far wiser to write in your own language. If they do not, there is the really difficult business of composing a thank you that will be both adequate and correct—and with the correct ending. One friend of mine, very experienced in living in France, is so appalled at the prospect of this that she invariably sends telegrams. The delicate shades of respect, gratitude, affection and propriety implied by the numerous variations of 'Yours sincerely' in the *'How to write letters'* books are really intimidating. The most important thing, after all, is to make sure that you have said thank you in a way that will really show your appreciation and that will not cause you too much trouble, heart-searching and waste the time that, on holiday, should be spent enjoying the country.

What to wear when visiting   Visitors on holiday in a warm and sunny part of France sometimes forget that a town is still a town and not invariably a seaside resort. When you visit friends in the country, informal clothes are naturally in order, although, when invited to a meal, even in an easy-going household, men should wear trousers, not shorts, and unless you know the hosts well and are sure it is a casual party, a tie should be worn, even though it may be hot enough for the very young to wear just a short sleeved shirt without a jacket. Frenchwomen on their home ground tend to wear darker clothes even in the country as soon as they cease to be able to call themselves 'girls', and it may be a source of surprise to find that, even when visitors are still in light cottons and silks in early autumn, the Frenchwomen will be in woollen suits and dresses. One rather curious thing is that Frenchwomen tend not to wear green as much as the British do. The convention of wearing mourning is still far more widely and strictly observed in France than in Britain. A Frenchwoman of thirty or more is unlikely to receive guests without putting on stockings, unless actually at the seaside or in the country. Trousers and shorts for women are naturally not worn when visiting, and very low-necked or sleeveless dresses are seldom seen round the table—except on the rare occasions when cocktail or semi-evening dress is worn, when you will almost certainly be advised in advance. As, even in very hot weather, French country houses can be cool if they are stone, it is practical to be moderately covered up. Gloves are seldom worn, except by the older women or for really formal parties, and are removed when one comes indoors, and hats are seldom worn at lunch, though possibly for *'un cocktail'*, or *'un lunch'* (which is a buffet party) if you know that hosts and guests are habitually rather smart. Strange as it may seem to the visitor, who may have been stumbling over cobbles and gravel drives and in gardens, most Frenchwomen do not wear 'sensible' shoes when visiting. Even if you can't cope with high heels on these occasions, informal sandals are too informal. But the sort of fashions that are shown in magazines as suitable for the international resorts are highly inappropriate for a French provincial town where women usually dress more quietly though not necessarily more inexpensively, than in the English provinces. The visiting British man on holiday can go anywhere in the daytime in a light jacket or blazer with flannels or light trousers, shirt and tie or cravat, but if dining out it is of course polite to wear a suit.

Vocabulary and useful phrases

Bon retour! Safe return

Chez This expression means 'at home', e.g. 'Chez Mme Dupont' —'At Madame Dupont's'

Ça m'est égal means 'Either (of two alternatives, or even more) is all right for me', a phrase useful when you are asked whether you would like to do various things, such as making excursions. But not to be used if you are offered a choice of food— indifference, even of the politest kind, to food or drink implies that you don't consider it worth bothering about

C'est pour offrir? This phrase is very frequently used by the shop assistant from whom you may be buying flowers, sweets or anything that could be a present. Or you can use the phrase as a statement to imply that you are buying a present. The significance is that therefore the purchase should be gift wrapped, which will be done without extra charge, but which may very well take considerable time

Ce n'est qu'un petit rien means 'It's really nothing'—the sort of useful phrase to use if you have brought a small gift or given something to a friend's children and are being thanked elaborately

Je ne suis pas un matinale   I am not an early riser. A most useful phrase for the business visitor or for anyone being shown around the region, because in general the French both start work and make appointments much earlier than the British, and 8 a.m. or 8.30 a.m. is not considered an unusual time for a meeting. Remember, too, that the French do not generally have any break or 'elevenses' mid-morning

Je soigne ma ligne   I'm watching my figure

Je suis au régime   I am on a diet (diets of all kinds are of great interest to the French and it is not at all incorrect to mention that you are dieting, although if you do—out of politeness to avoid getting stunned with hospitality—be prepared for everyone to recommend their diets to you as well)

La lettre du château   Bread-and-butter letter, written after a stay

Meilleurs vœux   Best wishes

Mille remerciements   Thank you very much indeed

Merci   Thank you, but also signifying 'No thank you' to anyone offering you food or drink, when you do not want anything

Soignez-vous bien   Look after yourself

Oui, s'il vous plaît or *Volontiers*   If you are accepting a helping, or anything offered, i.e. 'Yes, please'

Le colis, le paquet   The package or parcel

Un coup de téléphone or colloquially, *un coup de fil*   A telephone call

Un convive, un invité   A guest

Une fourchette à huîtres   Oyster fork

Goûter   As a verb, this means to taste or sample—but for food, not wine. As a noun it stands for something that might best be translated as 'elevenses in the afternoon'—an afternoon or even picnic snack, and also the light refreshments children have when coming home. It is *not* 'le five o'clock'

Un grog   A hot rum and water, perhaps with lemon, or any hot slightly alcoholic drink, which a thoughtful hostess may offer you if you have got wet or cold

La maîtresse de maison   The mistress of the house. Used in the sense of signifying the hostess, as '*hôtesse*' is not employed in this context

Les pinces, fourchettes et pointes à crustacés   Tongs, forks and picks for shellfish. The fork may be a very thin one, rather like an elongated and pronged hatpin

Pendre la crémaillère   To have a housewarming

Une serviette   A table napkin

Prendre un verre   To have a drink

Trinquer   To clink glasses (as at a first meeting of friends)

Une maison particulière   A private house (not, as I used to think, a dubious establishment, for which the phrase is *Une maison tolérée*—if you really want to know)

Voulez-vous prendre quelque chose?   Literally 'Do you wish to take anything?' phrase frequently used signifying 'Will you have a drink?'

Le Pique-Nique

The French take picnics seriously. Food is important and they will pack up chairs, tables, an umbrella for shade, linen, tableware and glasses, plus a portable cookstove, to make meals by the wayside enjoyable and attractive. They are also great campers, so that should you be able to afford the time as well as the money to buy picnic and camping equipment in France, you will probably be very satisfied with your purchases; even quite small provincial towns have a '*maison du campeur*' where every sort of accessory is sold. But there are good guide books in English and manuals of advice for the serious camper and person who picnics regularly. As it must be admitted that I am not among the number of those who enjoy picnics and camping (France, for me, is somewhere to eat as a treat) this chapter is chiefly concerned with the impromptu sort of meal that is a time and money-saver and which any traveller may have to cope with at some time or another.

Buying food   The arrival of the supermarket makes shopping easy for even the non-French speaking visitor. Usually you will find everything you require in such a place and you certainly also will in the grocer's (*épicerie*) or '*alimentation générale*' (with the exception of bread), plus even probably a string bag in which to carry the shopping. The French are practical about checking whether or not you have a tin opener with any cans of *pâté* or soup you buy, and they will also usually give you a bottle opener for the mineral water unless it merely has a foil cap. Mineral water bottles can be returned and a small sum refunded, and you can generally do this at any shop that sells them, not necessarily the one where you bought them (see vocabulary).

Remember that most shops are closed on Mondays, although some food stores may open in the afternoon or briefly during the morning. But do not rely on this. On Sunday mornings food shops will usually be open until mid-day but stores will be closed. In very small villages without shops you will see a sign '*Dépôt du pain*' indicating that this is where a baker's roundsman leaves his delivery. Otherwise, any village that has a shop will also have its own baker. Do not leave buying bread until late in the day, though, as not only may all supplies of the most enjoyable loaves have gone but French bread goes stale quickly. The names of some of the many different kinds are given at the end of the chapter, but there are such a variety that it is worth while asking the baker to tell you his particular name for any kind you especially like—often loaves have local names.

Butter   Although farm butter, especially in a region such as Normandy, may tempt you, remember that it does not usually contain preservative and can therefore go off quickly in hot weather unless put in a refrigerator. Small packs of butter are practical for picnics.

Pâté and cold meat   If you buy this loose, it is worth bearing in mind that the temptation to try a variety of different kinds can result in your getting more than can be eaten at one session, for a price that would have paid for a light meal in a restaurant. Cold food is bought from a *charcuterie*.

For general purposes, a *pâté* is the same thing as a *terrine* (which is the vessel in which it has been made), but a *pâté en croûte* has a pastry crust around it. A *ballotine* signifies something boned and rolled, so that, for example, you can have a *ballotine de caneton*. A *pâté maison* should have been made in the establishment and can be composed of an assortment of meats, a *pâté de campagne* will be a rather rough-cut *pâté*. *Hure* is a type of brawn made out of pig's head or boar's head—it looks like little tongues in jelly. A *pâté* or *ballotine 'aux pistaches'* has the bright green pistachio nuts in it. *Lièvre* (hare), *caneton* (duck), *gibier* (game), *volaille* (chicken), *porc* (pork), *foies de volaille* (chicken livers), or just *pâté de foie* (liver) are some of the most usual types of *pâté* found in the average charcuterie.

Anything *truffé* (with truffles) tends to be more expensive and *pâtés* in which there are slices or large pieces of truffle will be dearer than those merely speckled with bits of truffle. *Pâté de foie d'oie* is goose liver *pâté*, but with the addition of the word *truffé* it will be in the luxury class, although *mousse de foie gras*, which is to the *foie gras* world rather what pressed caviare is to the Beluga and Sevruga category, will be less expensive than *foie gras*.

Although *pâtés* and similar concoctions are delicious, they do not, especially in hot weather, provide an altogether satisfactory main course for anyone not accustomed to rich food. The fat content is high and therefore some plain cold meat, which is also available at the *charcuterie*, is sometimes a better choice. Small *quiches* (egg and bacon tartlets), variations of pizza (especially in the south), and other savoury pies and flans are also available and make welcome variations from too much bread. *Tripes à la mode de Caen*, in jelly, and *tête de veau vinaigrette* can also be bought in individual portions and many kinds of sausage and salami. If you are buying sausages to cook, check whether they should be fried, grilled, or plain boiled.

Fish At the sea it is usually possible to buy quantities of shellfish with which to picnic. Be sure that you have the wherewithal to open them if you are going to take them off into the country. And in order not to smell of fish for the rest of the day, see that you have either a sponge or flannel in a plastic bag, or the appropriate damp cleansing tissues with which to clean up afterwards. The attractive made-up fish dishes, such as you may see in the cooked meat shops and delicatessens, are not very good ideas for the traveller who may have some distance to go in hot weather.

Vegetables Various salads are also on sale at the *charcuterie*, but once again, for transport in the heat, those that are fairly plain are probably going to be the most appetising after a journey. *Céleri-rave* (celeriac) is always refreshing, and of course tomatoes in a dressing, tiny green beans (*flageolets*), and a macédoine of vegetables, sold in small cartons, can provide the vegetable course. Radishes, lettuce, tomatoes, green peppers and many other vegetables that are good eaten raw may usually be found in a market, but it is a good idea to make sure that you have the opportunity to wash these before the meal.

Cakes and sweets Brioches, croissants and pastries are bought at the pâtisserie, and many other delicious sweet things as well. Small fruit tarts are probably a more satisfactory choice than anything with a lot of chocolate and cream, should you be travelling in hot weather, and *palmiers* (the curled sweetened flaky pastry), *madeleines* (small sponge cakes), and *frangipane* (tarts with soft almond paste) are suitable for children as well as grown-ups. Indeed, a fresh *brioche* or croissant, perhaps with a dab of jam, is both cheaper and simpler than anything very rich or elaborate, and sometimes one can buy croissants with a chocolate filling. French fruit preserves are quite expensive but very good; the currant preserve, *Bar-le-Duc*, is a luxury, but there are plenty of small pots and tins—including the Swiss Hero jams—at more moderate prices. Individual foil containers of *crème caramel* and other custards and creams, including the small '*pots de crème*' flavoured with chocolate, coffee or vanilla, are also good buys while you are en route (but remember you will require spoons

with which to eat them). The same applies to the excellent yog-
hourts in a variety of flavours, and the light, fluffy cream cheeses,
such as Chambourcy.

Sweets and chocolates tend to be more expensive than those in
Britain, and candied fruits, although delicious, are always dear.
Ice-creams, however, are very varied and usually of fair quality.
Toffee and sweets to be sucked long-term while driving are seldom
as satisfactory as British ones, but the ubiquitous chewing-gum
is available in all varieties.

Biscuits These can be bought loose or in packets, as at home,
but one of the most useful presentations for the traveller is the
kind—of which there are many varieties—that come in individual
sealed packets, joined together so that you need only open one at
a time. Often these biscuits are of the plain Marie type, sometimes
with chocolate filling, or various fruit fillings, all good, and there
is also a variety of delicious wafers.

Drinks The mineral waters have been described on pp. 76–78,
but small bottles or tins of fruit juices, either for mixing with
mineral water or drinking straight, can be bought in general food
stores. For picnics, the vins ordinaires are the best buys as regards
wine, unless you are in a wine region, where the good local
product may be bought cheaply.

Although some of the firms responsible for vins de consum-
mation courante distribute all over France, there tends to be a
regional supply, rather as with breweries in Britain, of certain
types. You will always be able to get a red, white and *rosé*. Very
often these wines will have the strength marked on them, and
usually visitors prefer those of a higher strength, even though
this may merely be a matter of 12.5° against 11°. Do not forget
that the bottles in which ordinaires are sold are often of litre
size, about a bottle and a third. Wines of this kind sometimes have
corks in them, so remember to get a corkscrew if you don't carry
one, but nowadays most either have a top like a soft drink bottle,
for which you need an opener, or a plastic stopper under a metal
capsule, which is the simplest of all as it can be replaced. Wines
suitable for picnic purposes are also now being put up in cans
rather like beer. Wine bottles with three stars in the glass are
always returnable to any shop.

There is no sense in being highly critical of a branded wine
bought for casual drinking but after shopping around you will
probably settle on one type that you like best. It is sense to chill
the white and *rosé* wines if you can, either in the picturesque way
by trailing them in a stream or by packing them in an insulated

bag if you have one. At worst, you can cool a bottle moderately well by packing it in wet newspaper and letting it stand in the draught of a car window while you are driving. As it may be cool when you buy it, the thing is not to let it get hot in the first place, so wrap it up immediately. The same applies to beer, if you want it cool. If you plan to stop near a village, of course, you can buy your drinks ready chilled immediately beforehand.

Since thirst is not quenched by wine—though a mixture of claret and water is most refreshing—one of the most useful things the traveller can take is a vacuum flask that can be filled up with cold water. It is surprising how much money can be spent by stopping on the way just to get a cool drink. Your hotel or restaurant will gladly put drinking water into a flask for you, but take care not to put ice into a vacuum flask with a narrow neck, as it may break the flask when you try to get it out.

Snack foods The French have become aware of the need for what they often refer to as 'le quick snack', but in the provinces most people work near where they live, so that, except in large towns, you do not always find a snack bar of the sort now established widely in Paris. A café will give you a 'sandwich', which usually consists of several inches of crusty loaf halved, buttered and filled with whatever they have to offer—invariably ham, but sometimes you can get *pâté* or cheese. You may also be able to get bacon and eggs, or *'une assiette anglaise'*, which is a plate of assorted cold meats or at the sea, a dish of shellfish, with drinks or coffee, at such places if you want something quick.

Bringing your own food Outside many cafés by the roadside or at the coast, you may see the sign *'Ici on peut apporter son manger'*, or *On reçoit avec provisions*, which means that you can bring your own food and eat it in simple comfort at a table, being charged only for your drinks, or anything extra to eat that you order. This is often a pleasant and economical way of dealing with the picnic problem when you travel with young children who need special food anyway.

Eating in hotel bedrooms The British have become rather notorious for doing this and naturally enough hoteliers do not like it. Personally, I deplore the practice, which seems to complicate a holiday quite unnecessarily, for if one cannot afford to eat either in the hotel or at some nearby café or snack bar, then why not stay somewhere that is altogether cheaper? There are however, several ways in which legitimate economies may be made without putting any strain on goodwill.

Those who find the usual continental breakfast inadequate may easily augment it with cold meat bought the evening previously, or, should the butter supply, when you are en pension, prove meagre, extra butter may likewise be brought in. As even French friends admit to the poor quality of the jam in the majority of hotels, I do not regard it as a slight to suggest that those who really care for a special jam or for marmalade in the morning should always take their own. If any of these items have to be ordered through the hotel they will cost considerably more.

If you are a great fruit eater, then it may also be a good idea to bring in whatever you may want to consume and the same naturally applies to biscuits or small plain cakes, such as children often like before going to bed. And if you are a lover of a generous alcoholic drink round about six in the evening or last thing at night, then it is a great saving if you buy or bring your own bottle of Cognac (or whisky or gin) and merely order a mineral water of the requisite still or fizzy sort to be brought to your room. For even moderate spirit drinkers this will effect a real economy.

Quantities The decimal system, although is is essentially simple, can be bewildering to anyone accustomed to the British system of weights and measures. The mathematically minded can work the conversion tables, but as I have never been able to do anything of the kind, here are some simple approximations:

1 kilogramme equals just over 2 lb, so a half kilo is a generous 1 lb.
100 grammes equal about $3\frac{3}{4}$ oz, or a 'short quarter' of a lb.
1 litre equals 1.759 of a quart (a very generous $1\frac{1}{2}$ pints)

You can, of course, always point to indicate how much you want, or say '*Une tranche*' when it is a matter of cutting a slice of something, and with fruit and vegetables you can pick them out individually or give an approximate number and see how much it weighs. If, however, you are trying to order food 'enough for three people', remember that the French appetites, especially in the country, will probably be in excess of your capacity.

Vocabulary and useful phrases

En boîte In a tin
Boucher To stop up, to cork (a flask or bottle)
Une bouteille consignée A returnable bottle. '00 *centimes pour la consigne*' means the amount repayable when the bottle is returned
Un casse-croûte A snack, or a snack bar

Cake   Always fruit cake and, in a café, packed in separate slices in cellophane

Chocolat à croquer   Eating chocolate

Une fermeture à vis   A screw stopper

Un filet   A string bag

Un ouvre-boîte   A tin opener

Un ouvre-bouteille   A bottle opener

Une pochette   A bag, paper-bag

Une poche   An envelope

Pour emporter   To take away. If you say this when buying a sandwich, you will get it wrapped up

Tartiner   To spread

Une tartine   A slice of bread and butter or bread and jam

Un tir bouchon   A corkscrew

Different kinds of bread

Un pain   A loaf, usually a large one

Un pain de campagne   The thick, long crusty loaf that may also be the '*pain de deux livres*' or '*gros pain*' that accompanies the working class meal. A *pain deux livres* is actually slightly smaller than the really huge *gros pain*. '*Un bâtard*' is a small version of a *pain de deux livres*, quite a useful size for a family loaf for a picnic

Une ficelle   The very thinnest long loaf, with maximum crust

'*Bien cuit*' is the description to use if you want a well-done loaf

Une baguette   A long loaf, but slightly fatter and thicker than a *ficelle*

Un pain polka   A loaf that can be round or long, slashed across on the top, and slightly less crusty than the *baguette* or *ficelle*

Un joko   A long, slashed loaf, moderately crusty, rather like a Vienna loaf

Une tresse   A long plaited loaf, slightly sweet dough mixture

Une couronne   A round twist of bread

Un pain provençal   A very light, crusty loaf, round in shape with a twirly crown on the top

Un pain boulot   A fattish, slightly crusty long loaf

Pain de mie   The nearest the French have to a tin loaf, with only a light crust; this is the kind of loaf from which you can make breadcrumbs, and sometimes the dough is slightly sweet

Pain de seigle   Rye bread, but the term is more loosely used of a bread dough that is merely pale brown in colour

Pain russe   Black bread

Pain bis, Pain de son Brown bread. But although this may be served with appropriate dishes in a good restaurant, it is seldom found in a bakery

Pain brioché Slightly sweet, spongy bread, suitable for bread and jam, or good toasted, especially for those who find the ordinary bread too hard toasted

Pain d'épice The definition of this is often given as gingerbread, but I have never found it as gingery as this description leads one to expect and would personally give the nearest equivalent as 'honeycake'

Un petit pain A roll, either long or round, with a fairly hard crust

Un petit pain au lait Roll made with milk

Une galette A round roll

Un pain sandwich A light roll, long, with a soft crust, rather like a bap

Un pistolet What we might call a dinner roll—small, round with hardish crust

Un petit pain opéra or *grand opéra* Different sizes of long roll, slashed across, fairly hard crust

Un croissant A crescent-shaped roll, which should have a flaky, rich crust. Unfortunately croissants are only really good when absolutely fresh and when they are made with butter. Nowadays the majority are made with margarine and have been hours out of the oven by the time they are put on a plate. But it is possible in Paris, and occasionally elsewhere, to get a straightened-out croissant, which is made with butter. It is more expensive but correspondingly better in quality

Une brioche A semi-sweet dough roll, very light, sometimes a better choice for breakfast than an indifferent croissant, and good with butter or butter and jam at picnic teas

Cloakrooms and First Aid

It is only foreigners who insist on retaining their coats, dispatch cases and paraphernalia other than a woman's handbag with them in a restaurant or the restaurant section of a café. The French either go to the *vestiaire* and deposit their property or hand it to the waiter to take away for them. It will be perfectly safe and the small tip need never be more than, say, one franc in a very smart establishment, or even 25–50 centimes in more modest eating places. If you wish to keep a large handbag or a camera or guide books with you, the waiter in a good eating place should put a chair at the side of yours on which they may be placed. Things that may trail over the backs of chairs, dangle onto the floor or risk tripping passing customers, staff or the dogs of other customers should, out of consideration, be put out of harm's way.

The vestiaire is where coats, umbrellas and hand luggage are left, masculine and feminine property together. Frenchwomen do not automatically wish to touch up their hair or make-up when they enter a restaurant and no Frenchwoman would ever attend to repairing her appearance in public, and least of all at table. So there may not be a looking-glass alongside the *vestiaire*.

In many small establishments there may be only one cloakroom for both sexes and the washbasin and looking glass may also be communal, sometimes even in a corridor outside. No need to feel shy about tidying hair or face, however.

In public lavatories where there is an attendant, a very small tip is given, but there is seldom any charge for soap and towel, unless you want the use of a private washroom on a station.

Any eating establishment of reasonable size or pretensions will, of course, have lavatories for both men and women, but sometimes the very small, humbler cafés only have them for men. A *salon de thé*, however, will have a ladies' cloakroom. The public lavatories, especially the modern ones, are in many instances far superior to those in Britain, although of course there are the black spots. The type in which there is a hole in the floor, with two stands for the feet, presents some hazards for women, especially those who may, in addition to a handbag, be carrying a coat, a camera and perhaps books or other things; as there may not be a hook or shelf on which to put these, and as the flush in such places may be of a vigour that sends one leaping to the door and dry land, it is a good idea to get a friend to hold one's belongings outside, or, if this is not possible, either to have a bag you hold over your arm, or even tuck it in a pocket for the time being. I have, on occasions, held mine between my teeth, so as to be able to control the folds of a full skirt and bulky travelling coat.

Should you be unable to see a sign 'Toilettes' in a café or restaurant, it is, of course, possible to ask where the cloakrooms are. But whereas *'toilette'* implies a lavatory with, possibly, a washbasin either in it or near at hand, if you merely ask to *'laver les mains'*, the washplace is all you will be shown. This may be some distance from the toilette, and even unable to be found without a further query.

If this section seems mundane and elementary to many, I would like to remind them of Miss Freda White's sensible reply to the reviewer who said, of her including drains and lavatories in a book, that they were non-U. Miss White retorted, 'I have yet to be introduced to the traveller whose digestion is more U than that of common mortals; and believe me, you will not enjoy either a Roman arena or a Romanesque abbey if you are desperately in need of a lavatory.' Nor will anyone who feels sick, faint, in pain or merely embarrassed and needing help to deal with their problem be capable of enjoying the finest foods and rarest wines. But the French are, in my experience, both helpful and unobtrusively kindly towards anyone who becomes unwell and it would be very unusual, even in a restaurant apparently staffed entirely by men, to be unable to find a woman—*la patronne*, or even *une dame* to help another woman (*aider*, NOT *assister*, which word implies you are in need of money).

Here, however, are a few cloakroom phrases that are a relief to have in the back of one's mind in case they should be required.

Vocabulary and useful phrases

I feel faint (or generally unwell) *Je ne me sens pas bien*
I feel sick *J'ai mal au cœur*
I have become unwell (euphemistic way of saying you have started a monthly period) *Je suis indisposée*
I am pregnant *J'attends un bébé*
I have broken down *Je suis en panne*

I need   *J'ai besoin de*
The lavatory does not work   *Le lavabo est bouché*
The water does not run   *L'eau ne coule pas*
The water does not run away   *L'eau ne passe pas*

Adhesive dressing   *Pansement adhésif*
A bandage   *Une bande*
A crêpe bandage   *Une bande Velpeau*
Cotton-wool   *Le coton*
Disinfectant   *Un désinfectant*
A dressing   *Un pensement*
Lavatory paper   *Papier hygiénique* or *papier de toilette*
Sticking plaster   *Sparadraps*
A towel   *Une serviette*
A nappy   *Une couche* (*disposable* for the disposable kind)
A sanitary belt   *Une ceinture périodique*
A sanitary towel   *Une serviette hygiénique*; Plural *garnitures périodi-
   dique*; *soluble* if you want the disposable kind. If the internal
   sort are required, the adjective is *interne*, though it is usually
   easier to ask for 'Un Tampax'; these may not always be as
   easy to obtain as the other sort
Smelling salts   *Les sels volatiles*

A brassière   *Un soutien gorge*
A corselet   *Un combiné*
A girdle   *Une gaine*; a panty girdle   *Une gaine culotte*
A pair of knickers (briefs)   *Un slip*; Knickers   *Une culotte* (But
   '*Quel culot!*' means 'what a cheek!')
A slip or petticoat   *Une combinaison*; a half-slip *un jupon*
A pullover or sweater   *Un pull*
A jacket or cardigan   *Une veste*
A jacket of a man's suit   *Un veston*
A woman's coat and skirt   *Un tailleur* or   *Un deux pièces*
A topcoat or greatcoat (for man and woman)   *Un pardessus*
A tie   *Une cravate*
A raincoat   *Un imperméable* (often shortened to *Un imper*)
A waistcoat   *Un gilet*
A shirt   *Une chemise* (for man or woman); a stiff shirt   *Une
   impesée*
A nightdress   *Une chemise de nuit*
A man's vest   *Un maillot de corps*
A pair of men's under pants   *Un caleçon*
A coat hanger   *Un cintre*

A housewife (hussif—mending kit)   *Une trousse*
To mend a garment   *Raccommoder*
To mend invisibly   *Stopper*
Lining   *Une doublure*
A needle   *Une aiguille*
A needlecase   *Un sachet d'aiguilles*
A press stud   *Un bouton pression*
A safety pin   *Une épingle de nourrice*
A thimble   *Un dé*
A thread   *Un fil*
A zip fastener   *Une fermeture éclaire*
A button   *Un bouton*
A hook and eye   *Une agrafe et une porte*
To bleach   *Décolorer*
Dry cleaning   *Nettoyage à sec*
To launder   *Blanchir*
A laundry   *Une blanchisserie*
To remove (a stain)   *Détacher*
To soak   *Tremper*
Clothes pegs   *Les pinces linge*
To steam (a garment)   *Vaporiser*
A stain   *Une tâche*
A stain remover   *Un détachant*
A sponge   *Une éponge*
To iron   *Repasser*
An iron   *Un fer à repasser*
Warm water   *Eau tiède*
The tap   *Le robinet*
To scorch   *Roussir*; A scorch   *Un roussissement*

A shoe-horn   *Un chausse pied*
A shoe lace   *Un lacet*
A shoe repairer   *Un cordonnier*
Heel   *Le talon*
Sole   *La semelle*
A strap   *Une courroie*
A shoulder strap   *Une bretelle*   (also means laces in the plural)
A suspender   *Une jarretelle*
A suspender-belt   *Un porte jarretelles*
Elastic   *L'élastique*
A plastic bag   *Un sac plastique*
A nail brush   *Une brosse à ongles*
A nail file   *Une lime à ongles*

Nail scissors   *Des ciseaux à ongles*
Tweezers   *Une pince à épiler*

N.B. *Le lavabo* means washbasin, lavatory basin and washroom (either or all of them and can be merely the place where you wash), but the polite word for the comprehensive cloakroom is '*toilette*'.

Keeping Well While Being Greedy

Even before I married a doctor, I was always the one to take quantities of medicines on holiday and invariably they were required by other people, for I have only once been even uncomfortably ill in France. Any form of illness is not only a waste of a trip, but awkward for friends and family and possibly very expensive. So this section must be taken as my own personal recommendations and suggestions, evolved for the sort of malaises I risk incurring; my remedies have, up to now, worked for me, but doctors' wives are notorious for having theories and illnesses that are never quite according to the textbook. Also, whereas during my husband's lifetime I might have described myself as up-to-date about everyday medical preparations, in many years much has changed, and though two doctor friends have vetted the chapter (one was very critical, the other very enthusiastic), I must, in accepting the ultimate responsiblity for it, also urge readers to check, if in the slightest doubt, with their own doctor as to what may be suitable for their particular needs. Finally, it may be said that although there are certain situations when the right thing to do, as far as a doctor is concerned, is to go to bed, keep still, fast or be sensible in other ways, we all know the occasions when none of this is possible and yet life has to go on; one may *have* to get on a plane, go to a dinner, make a speech or simply stand on one's feet looking intelligent, when it seems impossible to do so. Lay recommendations, such as I can occasionally make, may help out without undue risk. But if there should be any real doubt, play safe and get the medical opinion.

Looking on the gloomiest side Check with your insurance agent that any policy covering you and your family for any accidents or illnesses incurred in France (where there is no reciprocal agreement with the National Health Service) also includes medical expenses, such as the cost of transport home, the attention of a doctor or nurse, or just hotel accommodation while you are unfit to travel.

With your passport and any other documents (car papers, etc.) have a card giving:

Blood group (if known)
Inoculations (especially tetanus)
Drug allergies (e.g. penicillin)
Recent relevant illnesses (e.g. heart disease)
Whether contact lenses are worn
Relevant disabilities and current treatment (e.g. diabetes, epilepsy)

Anyone who has to fill in details in the latter category might consider joining the international organisation Medicalert, which issues a wristlet with coded information about the wearer (i.e. whether he or she is a haemophiliac, diabetic, or has a rare blood group). The British Diabetic Association has most useful pamphlets about foreign travel for the diabetic, and anyone with diabetes is certainly advised—if they are on insulin—to take away a few plastic disposable syringes in case of breakage or loss of their own. Remember that, in France, it is an offence not to carry your identification papers (e.g. passport) on you at all times. It is easy to put a card with the other data in with this.

A first-aid kit should be part of your luggage anyway, but it is *essential* if you are travelling by car. Get your doctor to check that any kit bought ready-stocked really has all you may need, and also that it includes things for the kind of holiday you have in mind, e.g. travel sickness tablets if you are en famille or in a party and are in doubt as to anyone's stamina, sun oil or cream, and calamine lotion if you are going south, eyebrow tweezers (can be invaluable for far more first-aid operations than just plucking eyebrows), scissors, smelling salts (it is astonishing how difficult it is to get these if you need them in a hurry for faintness or nausea) and any special remedies for incidental illnesses to which you may be prone—when you need them it is time-wasting to have to try to explain. Take a fahrenheit thermometer unless you are capable of reading a centigrade one, and remember that the French take a temperature as they usually administer a sleeping draught—in the rectum.

Taking children abroad This is a special subject and not really for this book. Ask the doctor who knows them. Some readily adapt themselves to different climates and diets, others find this very difficult, and some, especially the very young, can be bothered by unusually hot weather.

Travel sickness This also can be a subject on its own. But certain proprietory preparations can completely remove any risk, if—this is the important thing—they are taken in time, and not when the sickness is making itself evident. I am a terrible sailor, but I can vouch for this being true. And reasonable amounts of food and drink should also be taken, once the preventative has started to work.

Heat It is hardly likely that tropical treatment for the traveller to France is required but, apart from avoiding the risk of sunburn (and, as far as women are concerned, the ageing effects of too much tan), if anyone is likely to sweat a great deal the salt loss should be made up, either by taking salt tablets or just having more salt with your meals.

Hazards for the gastronomic traveller These are usually self-invited. If you eat about twice your normal quantity of food, most of it unexpectedly rich, washing it down with spirits and wines, some of which may be very young and very acid, expose yourself to the sun regardless, and go on travelling when you are tired and full of food and drink, you may well expect your digestion to protest. Many travellers, too, are tired from last-minute chores when they arrive and need a day or two to relax and adapt themselves to a holiday tempo and different diet. Discriminating indulgence is commonsense at the beginning of a holiday.

The French rarely eat between meals. So if you eat as they do—copiously at lunch and dinner—and add a big breakfast, mid-morning coffee or ices and pastries or drinks, afternoon tea with more sweet things, and strong drinks bfore the main meals, you are combining the diet of both countries and this will not go well into the average stomach or the ordinary waistline. If you cannot, after a day or two of deliberately light diet, adapt yourself to French eating habits, but simply must eat little and often, then make sure that your menus are short and nourishing, and beware of quantities of cream and lots of sweet things.

Drinking water As far as hotels and restaurants are concerned, this is as safe for the traveller as it is in Great Britain—if there should be anything about it that has been known to upset visitors, a reputable establishment will certainly inform you. On camping sites, or when getting water from public taps, it is of course sensible to take more precautions (though many French camping sites are far more hygienic than many British public cloakrooms). But as worry or doubt can upset you more than almost anything, *don't* take a risk. Either boil the water for your picnic or use a few 'Aquaclene' or chloramine tablets, which will make it safe—or simply buy a bottle of mineral water.

Large quantities of fruit This is responsible for vast numbers of tummy upsets, in Britain as well as abroad. Anything bought in an open market should of course be washed, and the bowl of water that comes with dessert fruit is intended to wash it, not merely your fingers. But over-indulgence in fruit, however, delicious, may bring on a bout of indigestion and loosen the bowels. Fruit that may be fermenting or otherwise decomposing can cause an upset that will feel more serious. It is difficult to tell if fruit is 'on the turn', but anything kept in the sun, in a plastic bag, in the car boot or a knapsack for some time may be risky. If in doubt, don't eat it. If you can detect the slightest 'beery' flavour, or notice a 'prickle' as you bite into it, throw it away.

If you are allergic to shellfish State firmly '*Je suis allergique à . . .*'. If anything else, such as garlic, oil, fried foods and so on, doesn't agree with you, be definite—'*Il m'est défendu de manger . . .*' (I have been forbidden to eat . . .). The French will always respect such a limitation, though if, for example, you can't eat garlic, you will have to restrict visits to the south of France to large hotels where you can get non-regional food.

Young wine or wine tasted from the cask This can upset you, if you swallow it in quantity, either because it is still fermenting (it will taste 'prickly' and have a 'beery' smell), or because of the nature of the acids in it. This is why it is correct to spit on such occasions. Anyway if wines are fermenting they reveal nothing of themselves by either smell or taste.

Large quantities of wine This will naturally upset you unless you are accustomed to drinking copiously. Just because a wine is cheap does not imply that it can be quaffed lavishly without ill effects. The strength of the wine, which cannot be detected by tasting, though sometimes it may be stated on the label, may have nothing to do with the way it can upset your stomach. Bad wine, too, does exist and this will probably upset you even more. Just because you can't drink the litre per day of '*gros rouge*' like the boys in the café, don't think that you're slipping as a connoisseur.

Garlic and oil and quantities of vegetables cooked in butter These can have a loosening effect on the bowels, even if you're accustomed to them at home. But unless you feel really ill, the fact that you may have to empty your bowels more often than usual is nothing to worry about. Don't over-load your stomach directly afterwards, and see below if you think that something more serious is amiss. A little abstention—starvation even—will calm the over-active colon. But drink plenty of plain water.

If you become constipated Any major change of diet and routine can cause constipation which, in mild forms, really does not matter. Take plenty of liquid, both because you may be sweating and because dehydration in a mild form can cause many of the minor ailments from which the British tourist seems to suffer. (In case this sounds overstressed, may I hint that maybe the fact that I am so seldom ill when travelling could be due to the fact that I invariably drink 8–9 pints of *water*—in addition to any other liquids—every day of my life?) The British sometimes seem to be as obsessed with their bowels as the French are with their livers. An occasional glass of health salts and a balanced diet should keep the ordinarily healthy person functioning perfectly well. But if in doubt, ask the doctor.

Sickness and diarrhoea If this is a slight bout it will probably cease as soon as what has been causing the irritation in stomach or bowel has been expelled. If you are being sick, drink plenty of mineral water and one *mild* solution of health salts until the attack passes—you may immediately be sick once more, but this will be the end. (This applies, too, to travel sickness.) Afterwards continue to take plenty of still water—not iced water, and *never* take fruit juices, fruit, salads, tomato juice while you are still within thinking distance of a tummy upset—it will make matters worse. What you need is plenty of water, mineral water (not too fizzy), and, when you do feel like food, a little *consommé* and a dry biscuit or rusk. You will be dehydrated, so the liquid intake is really important. Stay in bed if you have both sickness and diarrhoea. A period of semi-starvation is always a good idea for a slight attack, and, until you are better and eating normally avoid anything very hot or very cold, or anything highly seasoned. The same rules apply to an attack of 'the trots'—and remember, hot tea or coffee can start the whole thing off again. If you want a warm drink, have consommé or a suitable infusion (see pp. 81–82).

Diarrhoea without sickness If you don't feel sick, keep up the liquid intake and don't eat until you really feel better. This is when such preparations as Enterovioform, Ivax, Mist kaolin et morph, or Mist cret et opii, or Sulphasuxidine can soothe and help you—but do, before you go away, get detailed instructions from your doctor or chemist on exactly how to administer them, and *write* the instructions down plainly. (In an emergency you may be quite unable to remember them.) Your doctor may even make you a special prescription to calm things down and enable you, for example, to travel confortably when you may feel it will be necessary to do so actually in the lavatory.

Severe tummy upsets If in any doubt at all, get medical advice. Today it is wonderful how what feels like a serious illness can be quickly cleared up with the right drugs—but you must do *exactly* as instructed with these, and not play around with doses, times of administration or, most tempting of all, stop taking them just when you feel better but before the doctor has said you may cease. Do not, however, worry too much if you get an apparently inexplicable upset; one can develop a sudden adverse reaction to a food that has previously suited one perfectly well. Do not assume that a particular food or dish was bad or infected.

Never take an aperient should any upset be accompanied by the slightest pain. If you have a grumbling appendix or incipient ulcer it can be risky. The 'good dose' that many parents still inflict on their children should likewise be avoided except on medical instructions.

Guarding against infection Certain kinds of tummy upset can be infectious, especially for children, so anyone looking after even a slightly ill person should wash their hands before having contact with anyone else, and use a disinfectant, such as T.C.P., for tooth glasses, any personal washing, the bedroom telephone. Of course towels and personal toilet articles should be kept strictly apart.

Anal irritation or a slight split This can develop after a lot of diarrhoea and is so uncomfortable that if you even think you risk incurring it, get your doctor to recommend a soothing, healing ointment.

Hangovers As we all know, prevention is better than cure, but they do occur even with the most carefully-disposed people. Remember to take plenty of water, both with any alcohol you drink, and lots more before you go to bed. A couple of aspirins —of the kind such as Bufferin, which does not upset the stomach —can help with any headache. But never take large quantities of aspirin unless directed to do so by a doctor, and on no account ever take aspirin without at least a glassful of water with it—it can even cause vomiting blood. Lots of water before you sleep and when you wake, breakfast, and a brisk walk after a cool shower will work wonders with any *gueule de bois* (hangover). You won't, if suffering, feel like doing any of these things, but they work. Should you still be unable to face whatever the day has in store for you after you have done all this, order yourself an Arquebuse (see p. 76) or the Italian Fernet Branca.

Coming home Just as it takes a day or two to get used to French food, so it requires a little while to adjust to home fare when you return. Moderation, even in favourite things, is the best policy on these occasions.

Vocabulary and useful phrases

Fatigué Signifies that you have some slight malaise, as well as being actually tired

Souffrant Implies that you are really in pain

To be *malade* is to be definitely ill with a known complaint

Un calmant A sedative

Une pharmacie A chemist's shop, dispensary

Un pharmacien A chemist

Une bouillotte A hotwater bottle

La tête me tourne I feel giddy

Un bleu A bruise

Une morsure An insect bite

Une ampoule A blister

Un coup de soleil Sunburn

Un mal à l'éstomac Stomach ache

Une piqûre An injection

Un somnifère A sleeping draught

Un radio An X-ray

Une pillule A pill (not to be confused with *Une pellicule* which is either a roll of film, skin (on milk or grape), a film of ice, or, in the plural, dandruff)

Une crise de foie A liver attack. The liver (*le foie*) is, understandably, a very important thing in the life of any gourmet. But do not in a moment of stress, confuse *foie* with *foi* (faith), as *mauvaise foi* means dishonesty or insincerity

Une guenle de bois A hangover

Avoir trop bu To have taken too much to drink. There are, of course, gradations of this. To be *grisé* signifies being mildly tipsy (the verb is *se griser*), to be *ivre* (*s'enivrer*) is to be really intoxicated, and to be *soûl* (*se soûler*) is to be virtually blind drunk. (You can of course be drunk with pleasure, success, love or the beauty of the landscape)

Words such as aspirin, toxic, allergy, penicillin are virtually the same in French.

Great Names in French Gastronomy

A guide book is not the place for a history of French gastronomy, and those seriously interested will find plenty of books on the subject especially if they can read French. But there are certain names that crop up in any conversation or account of the evolution of French food as it is known today, so I have put together some notes on the most important of these for the gastronomic tourist to use as a handy experience.

France seems to have been receptive to culinary influences from different countries from the time of the Crusades, when spices were introduced from the East and formed an essential part of the stores of the kitchen, both to season the dull, often salted meat that was all that was available in the winter, and often as disinfectants and remedies. Much use was made of soup, even in early times, and up to a dozen would be served at a banquet. Joan of Arc is said to have mixed several soups together with a little wine.

The first renowned French cook was a little fat man named Taillevent, in the fourteenth century; he was chef to Philip VI of Valois, Charles V and Charles VI, and wrote the first French cookery book, *Le Viandier*. Shortly after the appearance of this at the end of the fourteenth century another and even more famous one was produced by an unknown writer. This was called *Le Ménagier de Paris*, and is a guide to young people setting up house. From this time interest in food (though not yet in drink), becomes important in the various great households; Agnes Sorel took care to engage good cooks, and with the arrival of the young Italian, Catherine de Medici, to marry the King of France, a gastronomic revolution took place. Catherine had always liked food. The Comte Cesare de Frangipani invented a sweetmeat to which he gave his own name as a parting present from Italy to her, and she abolished the custom of the women feeding apart from the men at state banquets.

Herbs, including parsley, and all kinds of culinary refinements were introduced by her and even today many Italians boast that French cooking derives from Renaissance Italian. Food was very varied, poultry was much liked and a lot of whalemeat was eaten, though the rich people would only eat the tongue. Henry III made the use of forks fashionable and everyone took quantities of garlic, even before the reign of Henry IV, who, as a Gascon, was said to have had his tongue rubbed with it at birth and at the same time as having his lips moistened with the wine of Jurançon. Under Henry, who certainly loved wine, wine was drunk increasingly, though hippocras and other drinks were served too.

It was about this time that vegetables became popular and Montaigne writes about the predominance of salad everywhere. But it was Olivier de Serres (1539–1619), a great botanist as well as a lover of food, who gave impetus to the careful cultivation of all kinds of vegetables in France. Ironically, de Serres actually was the first Frenchman to advocate the large-scale planting of potatoes, but the idea did not appeal and the plants were cultivated only for their attractive flowers in France, while more prosaic neighbours, such as the Low Countries and England, began to adopt the plant from the New World as a valuable cheap foodstuff.

Louis XIII is the first French monarch who liked to cook for himself, and although none of his recipes have survived, he has the reputation for making good jams and preserves and for cooking eggs in more than a hundred different ways. In the seventeenth century two more important books appeared about food: *Le Cuisenier François*, in 1651, by François La Varenne, who was among other things the first chef to describe pastry and its making in detail, and *Les Délices de la Campagne* in 1665, by Nicolas de Bonnefons, a book which deals in particular with vegetables and fruit. It was at this time that Denis Papin, born at Blois in 1647, invented the first pressure cooker, known as the 'digester'. As a Huguenot, he had to leave France at the Revocation of the Edict of Nantes and it was in England and in Germany that his writings on the subject were published first.

Food became socially important under Louis XIV. The dining-room was a great meeting place, and in 1660 a Sicilian, Procopio, started the first café in Paris. During this time tea (from China), coffee and chocolate were also introduced to France, with, as might have been expected, some people saying they were as bad for the health as others that they were good. It was one of the golden ages of culinary discoveries: about the middle of the century Dom Pérignon at Hautvillers found how to harness the sparkle of the secondary fermentation in Champagne and to blend the wines. At the siege of Budapest (some authorities say it was Vienna) the victorious garrison made the first 'croissants' to celebrate the defeat of the Turks; Louis de Béchamel, the financier, evolved his sauce, and poor Vatel committed suicide because, according to Madame de Sévigné, he thought that the fish had not arrived in time to be served at a royal banquet, though after all it had. It is therefore quite consistent with all this to read that Louis XIV had a stomach three times the size of a normal one, and, rather horribly, that when his body was examined after his death, this royal corporation sheltered a worm of unusual size. It was Louis XIV whose taste for sweet things gave us the regular service of a sweet course. Previously sweets were known (as they still are) as *entremets* because they were served in the middle of the meat courses of special banquets. The King enjoyed them so much that he had them served at every meal, but as few others could equal his capacity, it gradually became customary to end the meal after the sweet.

In the Regency and under Louis XV gastronomy became more refined and intimate; it was, says one history, the age of the little supper, and both the king and many of his courtiers and mistresses really enjoyed cooking and serving their own meals, without the attendance of servants. Food became simpler: in 1739 *Les Dons de Comus* appeared anonymously, although it was later attributed to Marin, *maître d'hôtel* to the Maréchal de Soubise (of sauce fame), stressing the importance of the pleasing presentation of food, and in 1747 *La Cuisinière Bourgeoise*, by Menon advocated quality in comparatively everyday dishes. Gastronomy was the smart thing in society. The satyr-like Duc de Richelieu, Governor of Bordeaux, was influential in persuading the traditional Burgundy drinkers at the Court to make a change to claret, and served Sauce Mahonnaise to commemorate the taking of Port Mahon, and the Maréchal de Luxembourg's chef evolved the first *chaud-froid de volaille*. In 1782 *pâté de foie gras* was invented by Jean-Joseph Close at Strasbourg and in the same year Beauvillier opened the first restaurant in Paris. The first, that is, that served complete meals, for in 1765 a man appropriately enough named Boulanger, who sold soup, had opened a shop in which to distribute this in the Rue Bailleul. The actor Desessarts fought a duel with a friend who had played a practical joke on him, but the friend, taking out a crayon and outlining his opponent's huge stomach, informed the seconds that any hit outside that area would not count and the whole affair ended amicably around another dinner table.

Two great men carried on their work at the end of the eighteenth and beginning of the nineteenth centuries, one being Parmentier who, during his time as a prisoner of war in Germany, recognised the value of the potato as a basic food and tried to popularise it on his return to France. King Louis XVI praised his work and Queen Marie Antoinette wore potato flowers in her hair. Parmentier assured his sovereign that famine could never again occur in France. But the Revolution came too soon for his potato plantations to be of use and it was in fact the potato cultivated in England, established against much opposition and suspicion in the earlier part of the century, that enabled the English to feed themselves and resist Napoleon's attempted blockade.

Another French discovery taken full advantage of by the English was that of canning foods; François Appert, known as *le roi des conserves*, was born in 1750 and the secrets of his researches, aimed at nourishing Napoleon's troops, were stolen by the English and developed for their own purposes. 'Bully beef' got its name because one of the first things satisfactorily preserved in canned form was boiled beef (*bœuf bouilli*) from which the English took the name.

Napoleon was, according to even the most patriotic French sources, the antithesis of a gastronome and seems to have been really not interested in food at all. He ate pasta, not bread, and although he did drink Chambertin, he tended to add water to it. However, he had the intelligence to see the influence that could be exerted by entertaining people and often appointed his Lord Chancellor, Cambacérès, to give magnificent dinners, and Talleyrand, that tortuous diplomat, of whom it was said that the only friend he never betrayed was Brie cheese, had the great Carême as his chef at the Congress of Vienna.

This was the age of some extraordinary as well as various great chefs and gastronomes; Grimod de la Reynière (1758–1839), whose name constantly crops up in accounts of exaggeratedly strange meals, wore gloves all his life, whether because, as some made out, he had webbed hands or whether, as he said, his fingers were bitten off by a sow when he was only a few days old, there is now no means of telling. Curiously enough, all his life he loved pork and all products of the pig. He was obsessional, not only about food and drink, on which he wrote numerous pieces of advice, but about parties in general: once he invited every one of his supposed friends to his own funeral—and appeared out of his coffin; following this, he gave another dinner for those invited to the first who had not turned up, at which coffins were provided for each of them. Appropriately enough, he died at the end of a dinner-party. Grimod was absolutely detested both by Talleyrand and Carême, and the latter wrote savage attacks on his meals. Carême was not only a great chef in general, but a superb pastry-cook; he started his career with a caterer and aimed at becoming supreme in all branches of cookery. He came to London as chef to the Prince Regent, but the sly Talleyrand, asked hopefully by the Tsar if he thought there was a chance of persuading Carême to go to Russia, was right in averring that Carême would only be able to stand the English climate for a short while, and off Carême went to St Petersbourg, after which he was for a time chef to the Emperor of Austria, then to Prince Bagration, Lord Stewart and finally Baron de Rothschild.

It was also during the latter part of the eighteenth and beginning of the nineteenth centuries that Brillat-Savarin was giving his wonderful small dinners to friends and writing *La Physiologie du Goût*, which appeared in 1825, after his death, and when Benjamin Delessert, 'Le roi du sucre', was establishing his great refineries. Gastronomy at the highest levels had become international; Prince Kourakine (1752–1818), a great gourmet, started the fashion of serving each person separately at a dinner-table, whereas previously only the very important had been served, the others having to help themselves from the food placed all at the same time on the table. Kourakine's so-called democratic method, which is that still observed in restaurants and private houses with staff to this day, was known as *service à la russe*.

Louis XVIII was another king fond of cooking and he despised those who were not interested in food, saying nastily about his brother, the dreary and unfortunate Louis XVI, 'My brother goes to the table with as much enthusiasm as to his wife's bed'. But he was the last French sovereign to be much concerned with *haute cuisine*; Charles X revived the habit of royalty dining formally in public, which not only prevented the creation of any intimate and friendly atmosphere, but cut out the sort of delicate dishes that spoil if kept waiting.

In the Second Empire and to the end of the nineteenth century, however, there was a great deal of gastronomic writing and many dinners and lunches that are now historic occasions. Gas cooking was invented, so was Sauce Béarnaise by Chateaubriand's cook, Montmirail. Alexandre Dumas the elder published his *Dictionnaire de la Cuisine* in 1869; in spite of his enormous success as a novelist he was an impassioned cook, always experimenting and cooking for his friends, and he hoped that it was by his Dictionary that his fame would survive. All sorts of people were really critical gastronomes, writers, artists, singers and dancers; Dr Véron, famous for a patent elixir, which made him so much money he was able to keep and launch the great tragedian Rachel, was equally renowned for his cook-housekeeper, Sophie, whose skill was so great that Véron's friends were always trying to entice her from him. The Baron Louis Brisse (1803–1873) was one of the first gastronomic journalists, and Charles Monselet (1825–1888), who wrote the *Almanach des Gourmets*, actually composed a sonnet to soup. Thomas Genin, called 'the Gambetta of the kitchen', organised the first Concours Culinaire in 1889; he was concerned with maintaining the reputation of French cooking and protecting its traditions against abuses by indifferent cooks. He was no mean cook himself, as well as being a first-class administrator; he wrote in detail about the cooking of various kinds of animals—rats (said to be good), donkey (also good), dogs, and billy goat, of which he said that absolutely no cooking process could make it palatable. This sort of exotic cooking was given a fillip in the Siege of Paris in 1870, when 300 animals at the zoo were killed and sold for food and a famous banquet was given featuring the elephant as the chief course.

Margarine was invented in 1869 by a man called Mège-Mouriès. He had great trouble with the producers of butter and, in spite of the Emperor's encouragement, it was only with difficulty that the new substance went into production. About the same time the word tournedos came into use, due to the Italian gourmet and composer Rossini (who so loved his food that he married his cook). Rossini was dining at the Café Anglais and announced his boredom with the usual cuts of meat. He suggested an alternative method of cutting and preparing the steak, to which the horrified and conservative *maître d'hôtel* announced that he could not, would not present a dish that was—well, unpresentable. 'Very well,' said Rossini, 'then don't let us see you do it—I'll turn my back' (*tourne le dos*). And the name caught on. Tournedos Rossini, however, was evolved at the Restaurant Magny, in the Rue Contrescarpe Dauphine. Here, on 22 November, 1862, a series of monthly dinners were started by Dr Veyne Robin (the anatomist, whose last words were 'Apoplexy? Curious . . .'). Gavarin, the illustrator (at that time very depressed), the critic Sainte-Beuve and the brothers Goncourt. These dinners continued until 1872 and were attended by Gautier, Flaubert, Georges Sand, Renan and Turgenev as well. Magny always insisted that his *Châteaubriand* was named for M. de Chabrillan and not the writer.

He called his *bécasse à la Charles* after his head waiter Charles Labrau. *Purée Magny* was potato baked in its jacket in the oven then sieved and served with fresh butter. Magny was also famous for his *petites marmites* and for *écrevisses à la Bordelaise*.

Coming nearer to the present time, there are too many names to mention, but C. Reculet's *Cuisinier Pratique*, and *Le Gastrophil* of Paput-Lebeau are books worth keeping an eye open for if you look through secondhand bookshops. One great cook of the later nineteenth century was Jules Gouffé, who had worked under Carême in Austria, and who became chef to Napoleon III and then was at the ultra-smart Jockey Club. Léon Daudet was responsible for arranging the monthly discussion lunches of the Academy Goncourt which some members criticised; however, at one time at the Grand Hotel it was Auguste Escoffier who cooked for them, and their later reunions made the reputation of the Restaurant Drouant. Prosper Montagné, born at Carcassonne, was one of the great cookery writers, a caterer of renown and a cook of individual genius, whose works are still most valuable. And there was the great Maurice-Edmond Sailland (1872–1956), better known as Curnonsky, a name he invented from the words *Cur non?* (Why not?), who founded the Académie des Gastronomes, and whose writings and influence have probably done more than anyone in this century to establish the high reputation of French provincial and the simpler restaurant cooking, as well as haute cuisine. Cur, as he was known to friends, only had one meal a day (lunch), and lived very simply, refusing to allow the exploitation of his name for the slightest publicity. Finally, there was the great Fernand Point, of the Restaurant de la Pyramide, at Vienne, who also died in 1956. Even those who had the opportunity of comparing him with every other great restaurateur in the world admitted that he was incomparable as a restaurateur, a chef (he was proud of the fact that his staff called him 'Chef'— as a practical tribute—rather than 'Patron') and a judge of wine. Fortunately his window, Madame Point, on whose judgment, especially with regard to wine, he relied a great deal, continues his restaurant in the same tradition of fine French food, where the most simple, everyday thing is perfection and the great classics of cookery make the visitor realise why so much has been talked and written about gastronomy.

The Regions of France for the Lover of Wine and Food

No single human being could know all France in detail, and it will be plain that I have been able to give fuller documentation to the regions that I know best. Because I have, when in doubt, relied only on my own personal experience and knowledge of a place, there will be many omissions of well-known places reported enthusiastically to me, but without sufficient corroborative evidence to warrant their inclusion.

Apart from the special foods and wines in the various regions, there are many things of interest for the gastronomic traveller, such as reconstructions of kitchens and dining-rooms of former times, or even the real thing, still preserved; collections of objects connected with wine and food, which are frequently found in folk museums; and wine museums, as well as places and catering establishments famous for various reasons. I have listed those that I know, but it is worth pointing out that the folk museum, which has a slightly dreary sound, can be a really enjoyable place to visit, even when members of the party are not, on holiday, museum-minded; everyday things have often a more direct appeal than works of art, and the curators of such places are usually both informed and enthusiastic. There are few historic buildings and small museums in which the visitor is allowed to wander unaccompanied; this can be a bore, but there is nothing much to be done about it unless, should a member of the party be fairly fluent in French, the guide can be persuaded to cut the trip short and only indicate the most interesting things. Museums and many of the historic houses on view are often shut on Tuesdays.

There are many things that will not be listed in detail in the different sections, simply because they are numerous. For example, in Burgundy the signs indicating *Vieux pressoir* occur every five miles on some roads, and the wine premises open to the public and the regional tasting rooms increase every year. It has also not been possible to list and differentiate all these tasting rooms that are the property of commercial establishments intent on direct sales from those that are either the joint property of the wine growers of a particular district or else belong to a commercial house which is not, at this point, concerned with selling. The words *salon de dégustation* can imply several things from an ordinary bar to a serious tasting room but the phrase *dégustation gratuite* often signifies that the rest of the proceedings will not be free at all and that the visitor will be expected to buy something. This does not apply to the enormous establishments that, after showing you round, will certainly offer you a free glass of wine, and in which you can often buy more if you wish, but where you are not necessarily expected to do so. Nor would it be possible to list the paintings, sculpture and carvings to do with food and drink in detail, although where certain examples have seemed to me of special delight I have indicated them. If it seems disproportionate, that, for example, Chartres Cathedral is included under 'things to see and do' because of the windows showing vignerons, coopers and wine merchants, and the Abbey of St Benoît-sur-Loire because one of the capitals shows a monk cooking, I would suggest that, especially in France and up to this century anyway, artists and craftsmen have very often acknowledged their indebtedness to food and drink. The vine appears in religious art before Christian times and the most sacred moment in Christian history took place at a meal. No traveller would wish to concentrate solely on food and drink, of course—but there are many other guide books dealing with art, archaeology and history; this one does not attempt to cover any subject except gastronomy —where it is good there are usually other good things as well.

Part II   Visiting in the Wine Regions

There are many excellent books on wine available, some of which are listed in the recommendations for further reading at the end of this guide. But a brief outline of the way in which French wine law works may make it easier to understand certain terms and attitudes of mind that the visitor may encounter. It must not be assumed that because the French are inhabitants of a wine country they are all knowledgeable about wine; the traveller may find himself better informed than all but the wine-lover or specialist; he will almost certainly enjoy a wider experience of wine drinking than the Frenchman who, because he has lived all his life in, say, Burgundy, hardly ever troubles to try anything from Bordeaux. Because wine is an everyday commodity, too, there is seldom very much reverence displayed towards it, except in the top-flight hotels and restaurants of the principal wine regions; food may get far more of an introductory flourish and detailed discussion among French people than the contents of the bottle on the table.

Nor, with very few exceptions, will the traveller find very old wines on the restaurant list, or the shelves of a wine merchant in France. Especially since the war, the French have had to turn their stocks over rapidly and in very many instances methods of vinification have been changed or modified so that wines are ready to drink far earlier than they used to be. A preference for older vintages is often referred to as an English taste. Although one may be fortunate and find old wines at reasonable prices they are not usually as low in price as the same wines would be in Britain —the moral of this being to drink the local wines while you are away, and save the comparatively expensive rarities for enjoying at home. In the principal wine growing areas, of course, this ruling does not always apply, though even so the wine lists of the provinces do not show the catholicity of certain restaurants and many wine merchants in Britain; you might, for example, find hundreds of clarets on a list in a good restaurant in Bordeaux, but there would probably only be half a dozen Burgundies, and only a few German wines.

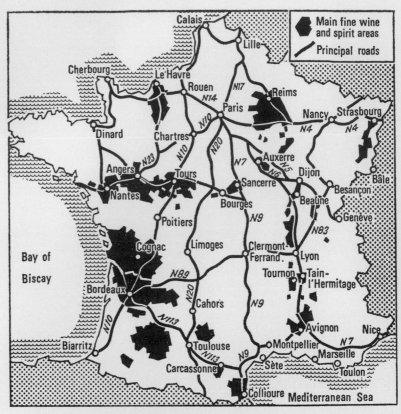

Main fine wine and spirit areas with principal *routes nationales*

Wine is made and spirits distilled in many parts of France in addition
to the areas indicated here, which are the regions devoted to the production of the best-known classics, the majority being in the A.O.C.
category. New methods of cultivation and production, to cope with
growing demand, have resulted in regions such as the Hérault, in the

The wines of the chief wine growing areas are dealt with in the
sections of the guide devoted to those regions. Here is a general
outline of the wine world in France with advice for the visitor
who hopes to learn while in France so as to enjoy increased
appreciation when home again.

Wine is one of France's most important resources and although,
up to the time of writing, Italy has been the largest wine producing

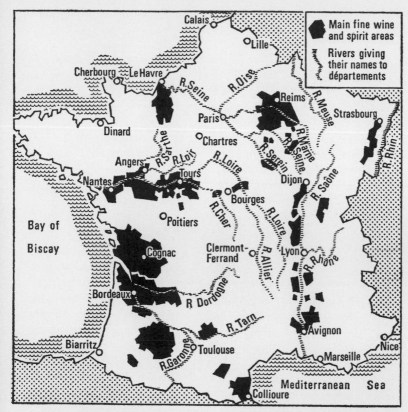

Principal wine and food centres and some of the rivers giving
their names to *départements*

---

hinterland west of Marseilles, becoming increasingly important. This
in fact is the biggest and most copious in yield of all the wine regions,
but until recently the wine was seldon exported, being used mainly for
blending and for vermouth making.

---

country in Europe, it looks as though France will surpass her
any year now. Certainly the greatest quantities of fine wines in
the world come from France. More than three million Frenchmen
are engaged in the wine industry and there are about a million
and a half wine growers, plus approximately 500,000 wholesale
and retail wine merchants. (There are, however, very few specialist
wine merchants in France comparable with those in Great

Britain, where families may have been in the business for generations, or who may be part of huge combines, with vast capital
resources at their disposal.)

About 2·6 million acres of France are under vines, yielding in
the region of 190 million gallons annually of wines of Appellation
Contrôlée d'Origine, 87·99 million gallons of Vins Délimités de
Qualité Supérieure, and 989 million gallons of wines of current
consumption. What do these terms signify?

Appellation Contrôlée Early in the twentieth century a series
of laws concerned with what we should now call consumer protection were brought in, affecting wine as well as other produce.
In 1935 a decree law, often called the Capus Law after the senator
who drew it up, resulted in the establishment of the Institut
National des Appellations d'Origine des Vins et Eaux-de-Vie,
popularly known by its initials—I.N.A.O. This is a government-
appointed body, supported solely by a small levy exacted on
every hectolitre of wine vintaged in France; it keeps a strict
control over all wines and spirits distilled from wine grapes to
which an *appellation d'origine* either has been or may be granted.
By exerting this disciplinary control, protecting the finest French
wines coming from areas and vineyards with reputations sufficiently high and stable as to tempt the unscrupulous to make use
of them unfairly, I.N.A.O. enables these fine wines to maintain
and improve their quality. An *'appellation d'origine contrôlée'* is
rather the same sort of thing as a pedigree that has been investi-
gated and officially approved; it does not only say what the wine
is, but what it should be in relation to its ancestors, its upbringing
and capabilities. An A.C. or A.O.C. is a prized and important
acquisition. As the phrase will come into conversation in all the
major wine regions, here is a brief description of the way the
system is applied.

An A.C. is granted by I.N.A.O. subject to application. Each
granting of the award is individual to the area which it concerns
and takes into consideration the demands of the local syndicates
of wine growers. In brief, the rules governing the award
define:

The exact area.
The type of grapes planted.
The amount planted per hectare (a hectare = 2·471,05 acres).
The minimum amount of sugar in the 'must' (the unfermented
    grape juice).
The minimum degree of alcohol in the finished wine.

The maximum production of wine per hectare in hectolitres (a hectolitre = 22·4 gallons approximately).
The method of pruning and training the vines.

The A.C. is also subject to the granting of the 'label', a word which means something rather more than just 'label'; this is awarded each year as the result of the tastings of wines organised by the local committees.

How the A.C. works All the fine wines of France are now A.C. wines. The wines of Alsace were included as recently as 1962. By French law every A.C. wine must have the words '*Appellation Contrôlée*' printed clearly on its label, either above or below the name of the wine. The sole exception to this is Champagne, which is permitted by I.N.A.O. to use merely the traditional phrase '*vin de Champagne*'. It will be appreciated that the A.C. is of tremendous prestige value, but the phrase is not always used on the labels of even the finer French wines offered for sale in Britain, because, to date, we have not installed a system of controls to maintain the French regulations. The wine trade in Great Britain consider that the British wine drinker is protected both by the laws of the country and the reputation for knowledge and fair trading of British wine merchants and shippers. The matter is much under discussion in the UK and the Common Market.

The A.C. regulations can apply, first, to an area: Bordeaux, Rhône, Beaujolais, or to a smaller area within a large one: Médoc, Graves, Côtes du Rhône, St Émilion, with the type of wine—rouge, blanc, rosé—often appended. Then there are the names of parishes within those areas, such as Pauillac, St Julien, within Médoc, Meursault, Fixin or Beaune within Bourgogne, Moulin-à-Vent, Fleurie within Beaujolais, Châteauneuf-du-Pape and Gigondas within Rhône. In some areas, such as Bordeaux, the individual properties within a parish are each owned by individual proprietors, so that further detailing is not necessary; a wine that bears on its label the words '*Château Palmer, Appellation Margaux contrôlée*', gives an exact statement of the contents of the bottle in terms of the estate and the parish—and, by implication, of the area comprising the parish from which it comes, though some older wines may be found bearing only the general district name. There have been some problems, involving estates where boundaries do not quite coincide with the parish boundaries, and consequently the wine vintaged from that portion of the vineyard is not, strictly, entitled to the A.C., but most of these anomalies have been smoothed out.

In Burgundy, where a single estate such as Clos de Vougeot may have many proprietors, there may be what the great authority Morton Shand calls an *'inner appellation contrôlée'*, such as Clos de Vougeot, Corton, Montrachet, because products of the different sections of the vineyards are all different and there the vineyard name has the same sort of significance as that of the parish. Usually one A.C. fits inside another and the system reaches its limit with the tiny vineyard of Château Grillet in the Rhône, which produces a mere eight casks a year; it lies within the parish of Saint Michel, which has the A.C. Condrieu for its wines, but Château Grillet has the unique distinction of being the sole vineyard in France to have an A.C. all to itself.

It should be stressed that the A.C. regulations only control the wines to the extent of where they come from and how they are made; as regards quality the responsibility rests solely with the proprietor. There are all sorts of problems which the traveller may hear discussed: suppose a vineyard yields more than regulations permit, because the year is favourable and the owner's methods very up-to-date. The wine he makes in excess of what the A.C. regulations have laid down cannot bear the A.C. and must merely take the name of the area—which means that it will not be sold at as high a price as that bearing the higher ranking A.C. within France or the countries within which the rules apply—one reason why the British wine trade often enjoy the advantage of being able to buy a good wine at a lower price and why the trade are not all anxious to see the A.C. regulations enforced in Britain. Then there is the problem of wines such as the dry Sauternes now being made at Châteaux Yquem, Filhot, Lafaurie-Peyraguay; although originally the wines of Sauternes were dry, the A.C. regulations were made when they had all become sweet, and so today these dry wines from top ranking estates are only able to bear the A.C. 'Bordeaux Supérieur'.

Other wines Below the A.C. wines come those marked V.D.Q.S.—*vins délimités de qualité supérieure*, some of which have lately been sent to Britain. In France each must bear a label giving its description as V.D.Q.S., either in the form of a stick-on label or with the equivalent phrase incorporated in the bottle label. Below these come the *vins de consommation courante*, or the *ordinaires*. Of these last, some are referred to as *vins de marque*, which sounds rather important but which merely means wines having a brand name such as those put out by many of the great wine houses for everyday drinking and of which the quality is maintained at a constant standard.

Fortified wines, known as *'vins vinés'*—port, sherry, Madeira—are not made in France, but the sweet *vins doux naturels,* such as the Muscats of Frontignan and the wines of Maury and Rivesaltes are slightly higher in alcoholic strength than the table wines, and so are the vermouths.

Strength   As far as the traveller is concerned, there is no point in bothering about alcoholic strength if you drink for enjoyment. It is, in any case, impossible to tell this merely by tasting. A wine with a flowery bouquet and glorious flavour may be a degree or so less in alcohol than a thin little carafe beverage. Within the groups of different kinds of wines the difference of strength can only be a matter of a degree or two. Here is an approximate idea of the strength of French wines and spirits expressed in percentage of alcohol by volume (this system is known as Gay Lussac, after the man who made it famous), which is easier for most people to understand than 'proof':

	Average
All tables wines, red and white	$8-12°$
The great Sauternes	$12-14°$
Champagne and other sparkling wines	$12-13°$
Vins doux naturels	$15-20°$
Vermouth and many *apéritifs*	$16-20°$
Brandy, including Cognac, Armagnac and marc	$45-55°$
Liqueurs and fruit cordials	$30-60°$

Where to go   Although it sounds picturesque to say that you are spending a holiday visiting vineyards, these are, after all, part of an agricultural economy and sometimes more attractive by their associations and implications than the beauty of their countryside or charm of their towns and villages. There is, of course, beauty and charm for the wine lover in every vineyard, but the family may soon get bored with endless rows of vines and equally so with lines of bottles and casks in dusty cellars.

France is well organised, however, as far as the wine regions are concerned, for the tourist who wishes to see a lot in a short visit. It is usually indicated, when you are driving in one of the main wine districts, how to follow a *route du vin,* or *route des grands crus;* large diagrammatic maps show how you can make détours off the main road and see a number of vineyards and properties without even getting out of the car. Quite often the local wine growers, or various individual restaurateurs, make tasting rooms or *salons de dégustation* at some point on this wine road, so that you can sample typical wines from the region and see more maps and pictures of the vineyards in pleasant surroundings. You can usually also buy postcards, souvenirs and gift packs of the wines. A small sum may be charged per glass sampled, or occasionally visitors are merely asked to pay what they think fit.

If you have not visited vineyards previously, it is above all worth while trying to start by seeing something of one of the more important wine regions—Burgundy, Bordeaux, Alsace, Champagne, or the Loire or Rhône—and getting an impression of the way a classic wine is made. It is not only more impressive and enlightening to see the processes by which a great wine comes into being, but you stand a greater chance of being able to drink such a wine again, at home, than something obscure that is mostly consumed locally. Also, for anyone beginning to learn about wine, it is really important to start with the first-rate—whether you can afford to drink it often or not—so that some sort of standard may be formed and an idea gained of what the best is like for future reference.

To arrange a visit to a vineyard or a cellar, the best way of all is to get an introduction from your wine merchant to someone on the spot who will show you round. It goes without saying that any specific appointment made for the traveller should be punctiliously kept—just because you are on holiday, it does not mean that some-one can wait in an office all day for your possible telephone call—but, so as not to circumscribe your timetable, it is a good idea to ask whoever is arranging the introduction merely to say that you will be in such-and-such a place on or about such-and-such a date, and suggest that you will telephone when you arrive to fix a definite meeting. Remember the sacred lunch-hour is from mid-day until two o'clock and that offices will be closed during that time.

If you are not able to make any arrangement of this kind, then the hotel where you stay or any restaurant where you are able to ask the advice of the management will probably be able to put you in touch with one of their suppliers. Failing this, the local tourist offices usually can help, although naturally enough they are seldom able to give more specific information than details of conducted visits and hours when places are open for visitors. But the French in the wine areas are easy-going and happy to show visitors round if at all possible, so it is never difficult to get to view the details of wine growing and production, especially if you see a notice beginning with the word '*Visitez*' or '*Visite*', which is an open invitation to inspect cellars, tasting rooms and installations.

Although only the large establishments have multi-lingual guides, anyone who understands the basic procedure of wine making will not be bewildered, even if the French at his or her command is slight. A list of some of the words that may occur in wine talk is given in the vocabularies, plus some local words that may not be in dictionaries and for which you may need explanations. A little goodwill, however, can go far in overcoming any language problems. One thing that British visitors, with their fairly catholic experience of wine, do not always realise is that the inhabitants of a particular wine district do not, on the whole, either know or care very much about the produce of other regions, and certainly not about that of other countries. It may not be very interesting to them to have the visitor make a comparison, say, between Muscadet and Chablis when in the Nantes region, and it might be tactless to refer constantly to hocks and Moselles when tasting Alsatian wines.

Another circumstance that can bewilder the visitor (especially if he or she is as mathematically moronic as I am) is the quoting of vineyard sizes in hectares, the agrarian measure (ha.) and the yield of a vineyard or size of a vat in hectolitres (hl.) If one is able to calculate at all it may be of use to recall that one hectare equals 2·471 acres, and 1 hectolitre equals 21·997 gallons.

When seeing round any establishment that has organised trips arranged for visitors, it is, of course, polite to thank the guide at the end of the tour, but it is not invariable to tip, unless it is made delicately obvious that something is expected. Usually you can judge this as being so should the guide take off his hat and thank each visitor. If he, or she, merely hopes that you have enjoyed your visit and that you will return, and especially if any move is made to shake hands, then on no account offer anything except thanks and a smile. The guide may be a director or high personage in the firm, or, in the country, the *maître de chai* or cellarmaster, or even the owner of the property or a member of his family; the fact that he wears blue overalls and espadrilles and has not shaved for a day or so is not necessarily any indication of lowliness, especially at vintage time. Nor should it ever be assumed that the people who show you round cannot speak or understand English. As far as many of the big wine dynasties are concerned, they may have had English nannies or governesses, or been educated in Great Britain.

When to go There are two main pivots of the annual cycle of wine—the flowering of the vine in the spring and the vintage in the autumn. The dates when these take place naturally vary according to the weather and where the vineyards are, those in the south being slightly more advanced than those further north,

141

but there are usually official dates, rather like the Queen's official birthday, for these occasions, near enough to when the actual flowering or vintage takes place. There are then usually some celebrations, processions and ceremonies, according to the regions.

It is worth stressing, however, that the vintage is a time of great activity for anyone connected with wine, as not only does the actual picking and wine making go on from early morning as long as light lasts, but directors and senior members of firms are additionally pre-occupied with the visits of business people, wishing to taste the young wines of the previous vintage before they are bottled, as well as to see the current vintage being made. In the spring, too, all these people are concerned with tasting the young wines of the previous year in the same way, although they may not be quite as hectically taken up with business visitors as in the autumn, when many of their customers combine a trip to the vineyards with a holiday. All this means that during the vintage the casual visitor may not get a lot of time from even the most hospitable members of the wine trade he has come to see, and, more important, that hotels and eating places in all the wine towns will be crowded out. Except for Bordeaux and Reims, the wine towns are not large and the major wine firms in all of them reserve rooms and accommodation for clients from year to year, so that it is not wise to count on finding anywhere to stay at the last moment.

The vintage is not as picturesque as many people imagine. It is an agricultural affair and though there is plenty of good humour throughout and there may be dances and celebrations on the last evening, the most important thing is to get the grapes picked and the wine made, not to put on a show. This may sound discouraging, but those who have imagined a vintage as one long carnival tend to be disappointed. It is better, especially if you are travelling with your family, to visit a well-organised property, see the process thoroughly once, and only if you are endlessly enthusiastic to try and repeat the experience.

French holidays are taken in August, so that owners and directors of firms tend to be away from their headquarters then, but June and July, or early September before the vintage starts are good times for seeing vineyards and cellars. At vintage time it can be far too hot for many people to stand about in the sun listening to explanations. Beforehand the vineyards look beautiful and opulent in a good year and after the vintage, when they turn crimson and gold, they are spectacular.

Cellars, tasting rooms and tasting The individual character-
istics of these in the chief wine regions are dealt with in the
sections on the different districts, but a few general pieces of
advice are useful. It is sensible to wear flat, comfortable shoes
for any visiting and anyone seeing round cellars in cool weather
will be glad of boots or heavy shoes, as it may be wet underfoot.
Anyone going round a cellar will need a jacket or, should the
cellars be in the rock, a coat, as the temperature may be very
much lower than outside. There may also be steep stairs or
wooden or iron ladders that women find difficult to manage in
tight skirts and high heels. Many cellars are dusty, so fragile
fabrics in pale colours risk getting soiled and in the red wine
areas light coloured clothes and shoes may get splashed.

When tasting in a salon de dégustation, where a host in the wine trade
may take a visitor, the wine will be ready to drink and offered in
glasses to each person. If you do not want to finish each helping
you are given, it is quite in order to leave it, especially if you are
going to drive.

When tasting in a cellar the wines drawn from the cask will be young
ones, because, with only a few exceptions, all the table wines of
France go into bottle when they are between a year and three
years old. As far as the fine wines are concerned, they will not be
at all pleasant to drink while still young and may even be fermenting, which will upset the stomach of anyone who drinks them; it is
because of these factors, as much as because of the sheer impos-
sibility of continuing to sip endless mouthfuls, that the visitor
should spit the wine out. There may be a box of sawdust or an
elaborate spittoon, but if not, one spits onto the floor or, if the
cellar is small, it is usually possible to go outside and spit on the
ground. Visitors tend to be self-conscious about spitting, but it
is the sensible thing to do. It is only necessary to take a small
quantity of wine into your mouth anyway, and if you then direct
your aim away from your own feet and those of anyone else, it
is quite easy to get rid of the wine tidily.

The procedure of tasting is the same anywhere, whether at a dinner-
table or in a cellar. Swing the wine round in the glass so as to
release the bouquet, look at its colour, and take a little of it into
your mouth; it seems to clarify the sense of taste if a small
amount of air is drawn in at the same time, but it is not necessary
to make gargling noises or grimaces, however seriously you are
tasting. The visitor may find him or herself running out of suit-
ably appreciative or interested comments after some time at
this, and the vocabulary gives some expressions which can be

143

both polite and useful for such occasions. Those experienced in tasting generally hold their glasses by the stem or the foot, instead of the bowl, as this gives the wrist greater play in moving the glass so that the wine swings round easily without spilling. The professional will often hold the foot of the glass, with fingers underneath and thumb on top of the foot—this looks awkward, but once you can hold a glass this way it is surprising how easy it is, and it is also easy to change the hold from the stem to the foot without using more than one hand or putting the glass down. *In a tasting room or office* the wines offered to you may be young ones, or those that have been in bottle some while but are not yet really ready to drink, or of course they may be the finished product, ready for you to enjoy. If the latter, naturally you do not spit the wine out, but otherwise make use of the spittoon or sink as your host will suggest.

If you are invited to a tasting room to look at wines with any sort of seriousness, or if other people who may be professionally concerned are likely to be there, it is polite not to arrive smelling strongly of anything—hair lotion, after-shave, anti-mosquito ointment, or scent. Nor is it considerate to light a cigarette in the tasting room, even after the tasting, unless your host suggests doing so—though he will probably take you into another room before he does—and a woman should not repair her make-up, as all of this will impinge on the atmosphere of the room. As the annual turnover of large concerns often depends on the reactions of the nose and palate of one or two men, it is only right that you should not risk distracting their attention. Many of the wine trade do smoke, however, and in any case will offer cigarettes when the tasting is finished, while women who fear damage to their make-up, and anyone whose fingers are sticky—inevitable when tasting—can always remedy this in the cloakroom.

A small point that sometimes causes surprise is the way in which, as far as the professionals are concerned anyway, there may be one glass standing in front of each wine to be tasted and everyone will use that glass. Visitors are sometimes given glasses to themselves, but in the country, when tasting in a cellar, you may be handed a glass which you will be expected to share with other members of your family. But unless you have a cold, a mouth infection or, as a woman, use the kind of lipstick that comes off on the glass anyway, do not hesitate unduly—wine is a great disinfectant.

Work in vineyards This is something definitely not to be undertaken unless you are in good health and are prepared to work and live hard. In most of the wine regions the vines only grow about three feet high, so that picking the grapes is back-breaking, and it is work that has to be carried on under a usually very hot sun, though sometimes also in vineyards drenched after showers, every day while the vintage lasts and from early morning to evening. Unless you work for a friend, a work permit is required and although the work is paid and meals are usually provided, vintageing is not the easiest way to earn a lot of money. Vintagers may sometimes be offered accommodation at the property, but this may merely consist of dormitories. Profes-sional vintagers can be tough characters too, who do not always welcome amateurs. It is also difficult to be definite about when the vintage will start and how long it may last, so that cut and dried holiday plans may be upset. If you can get yourself invited by friends who have a vineyard, this is the comfortable way of vintageing, but otherwise those interested can make arrangements as to where to go and how to see about work permits through: *Concordia Ltd*, 188 *Brompton Road, London SW3*.

Wine orders In medieval times most of the French wine regions had their orders in much the same way that the towns had their guilds. These orders were in many ways the governing bodies of the particular region; for example, the Jurade of Bordeaux was virtually the town council. The *'Ban des Vendanges'*, or proclama-tion as to when the vintage might start, prevented any vigneron from having the advantage over his fellows by beginning the harvest and wine earlier—and therefore selling his wine first when the buyers arrived. Nowadays the wine orders do not enjoy this sort of power, although their chief officers are usually pro-prietors and shippers of standing and importance in the district. They may be active in forming and administering the laws applying to wine, they arrange local ceremonies and, in their picturesque robes, attract the tourist trade and by admitting people of importance and influence as honorary members, they stimulate interest in their region and its wines.

The oldest surviving order of all is possibly the Jurade of St Émilion, whose *'jurats'* were also magistrates, tax collectors, military leaders and administrators. They controlled the quality of the wine, destroying any that they judged to be inferior. With the unification of France the wine orders fell into decline, but in 1904 the wine growers of Anjou founded the first of what are termed *'bacchic associations'*, the Chevaliers du Sacavin. In the time of great depression between the wars, the Confrérie des Chevaliers du Tastevin was started at Nuits St Georges to stimulate interest in wine, and this proved so successful that 'chapters' of the order were started in many other countries and eminent persons from all over the world were invited to the ceremonies of the order. In 1944 the Chevaliers du Tastevin bought the Château du Clos de Vougeot, where the grand banquets and installations of new members have been held ever since. The example of the wine growers has been followed by the great cheese makers, who have also formed themselves into fraternities, with picturesque robes and ceremonies that are gay in spirit even if only superficially serious. The guild of goose roasters, oldest gastronomic fraternity in the world (1248) was revived in 1950 as the Chaîux des Rôtisseurs. Any of the ceremonies in which these orders take part are worth while watching.

Wine and spirit fraternities

Confrérie de St Étienne d'Alsace
Connétablie de Guyenne
Commanderie du Bontemps du Médoc et des Graves
Jurade de St Émilion
Les Compagnons du Beaujolais
Confrérie des Chevaliers du Tastevin (Côte d'Or)
Confrérie Saint Vincent des Vignerons de Mâcon
Les Piliers Chablisiens
Commanderie de Champagne
Ordre Illustre des Chevaliers de Méduse (Côtes de Provence)
Les Mestres Tastaires du Languedoc
Ordre des Chevaliers du Cep (Montpellier)
Ordre de la Dive Bouteille et Confrérie Albigeoise de Rabelais (Gaillac)
Viguerie Royale du Jurançon
Confrérie des Chevaliers de la Chantepleure (Vouvray)
Confrérie des Chevaliers du Sacavin (Angers)
Ordre des Chevaliers Bretvins (Nantes)
Confrérie Vinuese des Tire-Douzil (Vienne)
Confrérie des Baillis de Pouilly (Pouilly sur Loire)
Sabotée Sancerroise et Comité de Propagande des Vins A.O.C. de Sancerre
Confrérie Saint Vincent des Vignerons de Tannay (Nièvre)
Confrérie des Chevaliers de la Canette (Deux Sèvres)
Confrérie des Chevaliers des Cuers de Baril (Loches)
Ordre des Fins Palais de Saint Pourçain en Bourbonnais

Paierie des Grands Vins de France (Arbois)
Compagnie du Sarto (Savoie)
Compagnie des Mousquetaires d'Armagnac
Principauté de Franc Pineau (Cognac)
Commanderie de l'Ile de France des Anysetiers du Roy (Paris)
N.B. The names in brackets indicate the town or region of wine with which the various organisations are chiefly concerned, should this not be clear in their names.

General wine vocabulary

People

Être dans le vin   To be in the wine trade

Un courtier   A broker

Un fermier   A peasant farmer—not to be used instead of 'propriétaire'

Le maître de chai   The cellarmaster, in charge of the care of the vineyard and making of the wine, hence a very important person

Un marchand de vin   A wine merchant, usually in France a small-scale distributor

Un négociant éleveur   A shipper

Un propriétaire   A vineyard owner, large or small

Un vigneron   A worker in a vineyard

Un régisseur   A bailiff, estate manager

Places

Un château   The house—large or small—to which a vineyard belongs, but also used to signify the vineyard or property in general. It is chiefly used with reference to the big properties in the Bordeaux region, but can be used anywhere

Un clos   An enclosed property. Used in wine regions to signify a vineyard, especially in Burgundy, where several owners may have different portions of one vineyard and the 'clos' marks out the different sections

Une propriété   A property

Le terroir   The type of soil, i.e. clay (*argile*), chalk (*craie*), sand (*sable*), gravel (*gravier*), stones (*pierres*). *Un goût de terroir* is the taste given by the vineyard to the wine but it can also be used in a pejorative sense, to signify a wine that tastes badly of earth

Un vignoble   A vineyard

147

Vines

Un pépin   A pip (used of any fruit)
La pellicule   The (grape) skin
La tige   The stalk
La sève   The sap
Le cépage   The type of vine
La fleuraison   The flowering of the vine
La grappe   The whole bunch of grapes
La greffe   The graft
Une pépinière   A nursery garden, used in connection with vines
Un porte-greffe   The vine stock that carries the grafted vine shoot
Le raisin   The grape
La souche   The vine root. To buy wine '*sur souche*' is to buy on
   spec, before the vintage, on the reputation of the vineyard and
   its owner and the expectation of the type of wine that may be
   made
La taille   Method of pruning and training
Tailler   To prune

Vintage and vineyard work

La charrette   The cart used to take grapes to the presshouse
La douille   The small wooden tub used in vineyard work
La hotte   The tall bucket-like basket carried on the back
Un panier   A basket (for gathering grapes)
La serpette   The knife used for cutting grapes, or pruning knife
Les vendanges   The vintage
Trier   To select (sometimes grapes are sorted out before being
   used for wine making)

Making wine and in the cellar

Un alembic   A still
Bande de côté   When the bungs are round to the side of the casks
La bande   The bung
Le linge de bande   The bung cloth
Bande dessus   Bung up. When the casks have been filled and
   bungs are uppermost. *Bande dessons*, when bungs are at the side
La cave   The cellar
Le chai   An above ground wine store, a term used chiefly in the
   Bordeaux region, where the particular locality makes it
   difficult to excavate cellars below ground
Le châpeau   The mass of grapeskins and pips that rise to the top
   of the vat

Chaptaliser   The process of adding sugar to the must to increase the alcoholic content. Strictly controlled, but practised in northern vineyards such as Burgundy, and elsewhere in years when the weather prevents the alcoholic strength being naturally attained. Named after its inventor M. Chaptal

Coller   To fine, the process of clarifying wine in cask

Coupage   Blend

Couper   To blend

La cuve   The vat

La cuvée   The contents of the vat, sometimes used to signify a blend

La cuverie   The vat house

Cuves closes   The sealed vats in which some sparkling wines are made, also termed Méthode Charmat, after its inventor

Dégorger   The process whereby the first cork of a sparkling wine is taken out and any dosage put in and the final cork inserted

Dosage   The sweetening added to sparkling wines before the second corking

L'égrappoir   The mechanical device that strips grapes off the stalks

Un entonnoir   A funnel

Entreiller   To bin

Fermenter   To ferment

Filtrer   To filter

Gazéifier   The method of making a wine sparkling by pumping gas into it

Méthode Champenoise   The method employed to make Champagne and that followed where the finest sparkling wines are made elsewhere (which is always stated on the label)

La mise en bouteilles   Bottling. Sometimes shortened to *la mise*

Le moût   The grape juice before it ferments, or 'must'

La pipette or *la sonde*   The velenche, a large metal or glass pipette, used for drawing wine out of the cask or vat

La pompe   The pump

Le pressoir   The wine press

La récolte   The crop

Soutirer   To draw off (wine), rack off from the lees

Viner   To add alcohol to wine. *Un vin viné* is a fortified wine

Vinifier   The process whereby grape juice is turned into wine

Un vin de garde   A wine worth keeping

Un vin de presse   Wine made after the first pressings have been drawn off and usually one less good, that may be reserved for local consumption

Casks

Une barrique A cask, of variable but not greatly differing size, according to local usage. In Bordeaux, a barrique holds 47–49 gallons, and the term is generally used for a cask in that region. In Burgundy, a barrique holds about 48–51 gallons. The most adequate English translation is hogshead

Une barrique de transport A cask strengthened so as to be suitable for despatching wine, usually with metal rims at each end

Un demi-muid A very large cask holding varying quantities, according to the area

Une feuillette A cask of smallish size, varying according to local usage from about 25–35 gallons. The term is chiefly used in Chablis

Un foudre A cask, usually generally applied to any large one

Un fût A cask, of any kind, sometimes used of any empty cask

Expédier en fût is the term used when wine is despatched in wood

Une pièce A Burgundy cask

Une pipe A large cask holding about 116–121 gallons, according to the area. Chiefly used for spirits

Le porte-fût The scantling, or wooden trestles that support the casks

Une tonne A very large cask, not used nowadays

Un tonneau A cask holding about 4 hogsheads, term generally used to signify a measure rather than an actual cask and chiefly in the south-west

Un tonnelier A cooper

Bottles, tasting

Une jolie robe Expression used to describe wine with a beautiful colour

Un grand cru A great growth. Used to apply to fine wine from an individual vineyard

Un vin fin Signifies something rather more than a fine wine—a wine of quality

Une véronique A type of flûte bottle, used for some rosé wines. It must have four ridges or rings on its neck to differentiate it from the *boûteille de Rhin*, used for German wines (and which is the shape used for many roses and some local wines). Not to be confused with the *flute d'Alsace*, the longer bottle used for Alsatian wines and some others

Il se laisse boire Literally 'It lets itself be drunk'—a phrase of understatement, implying that a wine is in fact highly drinkable and 'moreish'

Avaler To swallow down, gulp, as compared with *boire*—drink. *Avaler le bon Dieu en culottes de velours* (to swallow the Good Lord in velvet breeches) is a fairly common phrase in wine regions, supposedly describing what it is like to drink a great red wine

Charnu Fleshy. Sometimes used to describe a wine that is so full bodied that it seems almost possible to chew it (*mâcher*)

Charpenté Literally 'built' or 'framed'. Sometimes used to describe a wine that is well constructed or constituted—*bien charpenté*

Bien equilibré Well balanced

Vider To empty. *Vider d'un coup*, or *d'un trait*, is to empty (a glass) in a single gulp or draught

Une gorgée A mouthful

Un crachoir A spittoon

Une bonbonne Large container (looking rather like an acid bottle) for wine or spirits in insufficient quantity to go in a cask, usually employed for despatching, and generally with a cover of wicker or straw, i.e. carboy or demijohn

Le bouchon The cork

Bouchonné 'Corked' in taste

Bouqueté Fragrant

Une bouteille fantaisie An unusually shaped bottle, such as may be put up for the tourist trade, or a special market

La capsule The metal cap covering the cork

Corsé Full-bodied

Cracher To spit

Décanter To decant

Déguster To taste

L'emballage Packing

L'étiquette The bottle label

Le goulot The neck of the bottle

Humer To smell

Un millésime A vintage date. The term is usually applied only to a fine wine of a good vintage—i.e. *un grand millésime*. *Un vin millésimé*. A vintage wine

Un tastevin A tasting cup, nowadays used only in the Burgundy region

Un tire-bouchon A corkscrew

Velouté Velvety

La contre étiquette The back label (often gives information about the wine)

L'étiquette de collier The neck label

L'étiquette de millésisme The label giving the vintage (if this is not on the main label)

Le passe partout The strip label (which means the thin strip of label which gives the name of the shipper or supplier when it is not on the main label)

Tastevins: The three top sketches show a Burgundian tastevin, with irregularly patterned indentations and a thumb-rest, with a loop underneath by which the tastevin may be hung round the neck. Sometimes there is no flat rest for the thumb. The bottom sketch shows the Bordeaux tastevin, which is no longer in use, and which is a plain saucer, without thumb-rest and with a raised centre.

Alsace and Lorraine

A variety of outside influences have produced many distinctive dishes in the north east of France. Belgium, Luxembourg and Germany are on the external boundaries, yet the cooking of Alsace and Lorraine has changed and transformed many of their recipes and culinary traditions, so that the food only bears a distant resemblance to the national dishes of these countries.

In addition, the area received a tremendous gastronomic boost during the eighteenth century in a rather curious way. Stanislas Leczinski, the exiled King of Poland, was the father of Louis XV's wife, Maria, and when the Duke of Lorraine, François III, decided to exchange his duchy for that of Tuscany, the King of France made his father-in-law governor in 1738. Stanislas settled at Nancy and Lunéville, surrounded by many people who were both charming and able. For an account of the kind of life they led, see Nancy Mitford's *Voltaire in Love*. Delicious foods streamed from the royal kitchen and were often sent to Paris and Versailles, as when *bouchées à la reine* (cheese puffs) went to Queen Maria, and it was Stanislas' cook, Madeleine, who evolved the little orange-flavoured cakes to which her name was given, and which became fashionable at all tea-tables. King Stanislas himself is supposed to have had the idea of soaking the traditional *kugelhopf* (a light yeast cake, usually with a hole in the centre), in rum, and so the *rhum baba* was created.

During the eighteenth century there was a boy, Claude Gelée, apprenticed to a pastry-cook in Toul; he grew up to become the famous painter, Claude Lorrain, and to invent *pâte feuilletée* or puff pastry. At least, this is the story and it is possible that he did introduce it to France, as he worked in Italy for a time and the Italians claim to have made puff pastry first. At the same time, the Maréchal de Contades became military governor of Alsace in 1762 and settled in Strasbourg with his personal chef, Jean-Joseph Close, who is claimed by some authorities to be a Norman and by others as a native of Lorraine. This man evolved a special way of serving goose liver (praised by Horace, Pliny, Martial, Rabelais and Montaigne), prepared with truffles and cooked in a

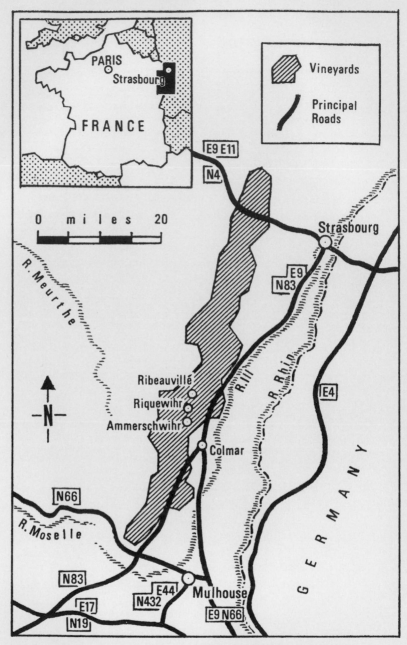

Alsace: showing the extent of the vineyards of the area.

The vineyards of Alsace are on the lower slopes of the range of the Vosge mountains which cut the region off from Lorraine. The *villages fleuris* along the Route du Vin make the region extremely attractive.

pastry case. The Maréchal and his friends liked this *Pâté de Con-tades* so much that some was sent to the French court and the King was so pleased that the Maréchal was given an estate in Picardy and Close a purse of money. Close later left the Maréchal's service to marry the widow of a Strasbourg pastry-cook, and set up in his own business, making *pâté de foie gras*, for which, it is interesting to note, he only ever used truffles from Périgord. The fame of this culinary creation spread rapidly and it is reported that Maréchal Rapp, when only a lieutenant, achieved promotion to the staff of General Desaix (and the first step to becoming a marshal of France) by presenting his general with a Strasbourg *pâté*. Today *foie gras* and the *pâtés* (there are said to be 42 different kinds) are an important Strasbourg industry, though it is only comparatively recently that Alsatian truffles have been considered superior by outside authorities. During the nineteenth century the Alsatians were prohibited by the Germans occupying the country to use pigs to hunt the truffle, and therefore dogs had to be trained for the purpose, spaniels, pomeranians and poodles being sup-posed to have the keenest sense of smell.

Food in this part of France is very copious, many French writers describing Alsatians as *'forts mangeurs'*; the tourist will usually find that a single portion will satisfy at least two visitors, and although there is a wide range of plain dishes, there is also a lot of cream and many sweet things to tempt the traveller. Something that I have never seen mentioned in any guide book, and that has often affected me, is the very sharp rise of the Vosges mountains and their foothills, which divides the two provinces, and towers above the vineyards. If you have been travelling and staying in the comparatively flat plain on either side of the Vosges and then go up into the higher regions, it is possible to feel a vague malaise, neither sickness, giddiness nor indigestion, which, in conjunction with creamy food and a lot of rather acid young white wine, can make you feel definitely uncomfortable, though not really ill. I have found in my own experience that it is merely a modified form of height sickness, which soon passes and is relieved with a little brandy and a lot of fizzy mineral water, but travellers who whisk up and down into the mountains several times daily in fast cars may certainly find that the abrupt change in altitude upsets them.

Food in general

Lorraine is a great source of salt, something reflected in many place names, such as Salival, Château Salins, Salins les Bains; Alsace is dominated by the pig and the goose, hence there is a huge variety of sausages, salted meats, and things involving the use of pork fat or goose fat whereas in Lorraine the cooking medium is usually butter.

Carp (*carpe*), pike (*brochet*) and a variety of freshwater fish such as the grayling (*ombre*) are found in the rivers and lakes, and crayfish and *sandre* (defined as a cross between pickerel and perch) in Lorraine. The description *à la juive* in both meat and fish recipes is thought by some authorities to result from the fact that there has always been a strong Jewish community here, especially at Metz, which may also have affected the widespread use of spices and certain herbs in the cooking. But the fish the traveller will perhaps appreciate most is the trout, for this is always best when it comes from a mountain stream or cold lake.

The great vegetable is the cabbage, and much of the cabbage crop becomes *choucroute* (sauerkraut or pickled cabbage), for which a special type, known as *chou quintal*, is used, with juniper berries. Red cabbage and potatoes are also popular mountain fare and appear in many soups and the asparagus of Metz is famous. Sometimes hop sprouts (*jets de houblon*) are served.

Sweet things and confectionery abound: the *vacherin glacé*, which is a meringue and cream concoction, *kaffeekrantz* (coffee cake), *krapfen* (rather like little light doughnuts), *nonnepferzlas* (a type of fritter-cum-cream puff), *bireweka*, a very rich, fruit and spice cake, *eïerkuchas* (pancakes with raspberry jelly), *tarte alsacienne*, which is a large open tart with custard and fruit, always beautifully arranged, *quiche aux chanottes*, a poppyseed and onion tart, *talmouses* (puff pastry and almonds) and *tarte au Mengin*, a tart of eggs, cream, sugar and fresh white cheese. *Bretzels* or *pretzels* (salted biscuits) are often served with beer and *apéritifs; pastilles au kirsch*, made with kirsch liqueur are sweets. Chocolates of various kinds are made in and around Strasbourg.

Specialities and dishes

Although there are many things special to either Lorraine or Alsace, for the purposes of simplification I have treated the two provinces as a single region, indicating where appropriate anything that is the product of one place.

Choucroute Pickled cabbage, plus all kinds of other things according to the local tradition where it is made and the inclination of the cook—pork or goose fat and so on. It is served with ham, sausages and sometimes a pork chop or piece of goose or game— so a *choucroute garnie* is a formidable dish! Sometimes potatoes cooked in their jackets and a *purée* of yellow peas accompany this dish also. *Choucroute royale*, a version of the dish popular in smart restaurants nowadays, has a bottle of Champagne (or Dopff & Irion's sparkling wine) put in the middle of the choucroute, which is then opened and the wine poured over the whole at the table. It looks luxurious, but many people dismiss it as a gimmick—dry white wine, they assert should already have been added during the cooking; what can it do as a drench at the last stage?

Sausages *Cervelat* is a smoked pork sausage, *mettwurst* a sausage that is mainly beef, *saucisse de Strasbourg* or *schniederspettel* is mixed pork and beef, lightly smoked, and contains caraway seeds. Then there is the *boudin à la langue* which is blood sausage containing tongue, *kalerei*, 'head cheese', and *boudin blanc*, a white sausage.

Schifela is shoulder of pork with turnips, *porcelet farci à la peau de goret* stuffed baby sucking pig, *civet de porc* a pork stew.

La potée is a vegetable soup, varying according to where it is made—for example, *la potée Lorraine* has bacon in it.

Beckenoffe A stew of mutton, pork and potatoes.

Pikefleisch or **bœuf salé** A Strasbourg speciality, this is smoked brisket.

Derentifleisch Lorraine smoked beef rib.

Grenouilles à la Boulay Frogs' legs are not found so frequently on menus as they used to be and one reason why the storks are scarcer in Alsace (they bring luck to the house on which they nest) is because there are not enough of the frogs on which they feed (pesticides are responsible, I suppose). But this dish dates from 16 November 1821, when a reservoir of frogs next to the fish market in Metz was inadvertently opened and the housewives doing their shopping had to devise a means of coping with the sudden glut. The recipe involves rolling the legs in crumbs and shallots and parsley and then frying.

Knepfl Like little dumplings, served on toast with gravy or grated cheese.

Grillade à la Champagneules This has been described as the French version of Welsh rabbit. It is a Lorraine speciality, and is fried ham on toast, covered with a sauce made from cheese and beer.

Le zewelwai or **tourte aux oignons**   Onion tart.

Pflütten   A type of potato pie or gratin.

Waffelpasteta   A very rich truffled goose liver and mushroom dish.

Tourte Lorraine   A flaky pastry tart, filled with strips of pork and veal, onions, spices and topped with beaten eggs and cream.

Quiche Lorraine   The most famous dish of the region, a bacon tart topped with eggs and cream. Sometimes it is a large tart, but individual tarts are also made, and variations include the addition of onions or cheese. A local name for the *quiche* is *féouse*.

In general, the term *à l'alsacienne* implies the dish is served or cooked with cabbage or *choucroute*, and possibly sausages and/or potatoes. *À la vosgienne* implies the use of onions and possibly mirabelles.

Fish or chicken cooked in wine are often described by the name of the wine—*coq au Riesling*, or, in Lorraine, *coq au vin gris*. *Poisson à la gelée du vin* is usually carp or pike cooked and allowed to cool in red wine, which gives it the appearance of pink aspic.

Bar-le-duc   This is the name given to the red and white currant preserves of the town. They are expensive, because each currant is separately pierced so that it shall fill out correctly when cooked. A spoonful of this preserve is sometimes served with a fluffy fresh white cream cheese.

Bergamottes de Nancy   Sweets flavoured with bergamot.

Mirabelles de Metz au sirop   The mirabelle plums of Metz in syrup—very luscious and rich. Metz has always been famous for fruits and fruit tarts, and Grimod de la Reynière used to have a regular supply of *silvanges*, a type of specially fragrant pear, sent to him from there.

Chanoinesses   A type of honey cake from Remiremont.

Macarons des sœurs   These are a speciality of Nancy, where records have existed as to their being made since the twelfth century. The '*des sœurs*' suffix dates from the time when the religious houses were dispersed at the Revolution and some nuns found refuge with a family whom they tried to help by cooking. Their macaroons were so popular that they put their name to them and the macaroons have been produced ever since.

Meringues   A speciality of Langres.

Cheeses

Munster This is the great cheese of the region, made throughout the Vosges as well as in the Munster Valley. It is made from
cows' milk and is round, between 1½ and 2 inches thick and has an
orangish crust. It is not a hard cheese but is extremely strong—a
good ripe Munster makes the strongest Camembert seem positively delicate and fragrant. Originally it was made in the various
religious establishments of the region. Nowadays some of the
cheeses are made by *marcaires*, who are cheese makers who take
their cattle up to the high pastures on St Urbain's day (25 May)
and bring them down at St Michael's day (29 September), accompanied by their cheese-making equipment. The summer installations are known as *marcaireries*, and are rather like little chalets.
The cheese produced in them is not quite the same as that produced in ordinary farms, because the milk is heated up slightly in
huge cauldrons, whereas the milk for farmhouse cheeses is not
heated.
Gérome The name of this cheese is a corruption of the name of
Gérardmer in the Vosges, and it is like a Munster in outward
appearance, shape and strength of flavour, but is much larger in
size. It takes about four months to ripen and is at its best from
October to May. Some of these cheeses are flavoured with either
aniseed, fennel or cummin. Occasionally Gérardmer is encountered under its own name.
Lorraine A large Munster.
Saint Rémy is a very fat (in terms of richness) version of Munster.
Some lighter cheese of the region are *Fromgi*, *Thionville*, and *Noyer
en Barrois*. Fresh white cheeses, like cottage cheese, are also made
throughout the region and are sometimes served plus the addition
of a piece of strong Munster as a *canapé*.
Carré de l'Est (See p. 280)

Drinks

Beer Hops are grown on the flat lands throughout the region
and the Alsatians are great drinkers and connoisseurs of beer. The
great breweries, such as Kronenbourg at Strasbourg, Le Pêcheur
at Schiltigheim, La Meuse at Champigneulles, and others at Metz
and Thionville are well organised to receive visitors all the year
round. The patron of brewers is Saint Arnoult, twenty-ninth
Bishop of Metz, who lived in the seventh century. A verse in a

stained-glass window dating from the sixteenth century, asks the saint to allow his followers to drink his beer and promises that as long as it is drunk, they will serve him all the days of their lives.

Wines

The vineyards of Lorraine have been considerably reduced in size and the wines today enjoy only local reputations. The *vin gris*, which is really a pale pink and rather like a light *rosé*, is the best known, and that made around Toul, Metz and Vic-sur-Seille is supposed to be the best.

The Alsatian vineyards, on the contrary, are expanding and, because of the carefulness of the producers, the wines are increasing in popularity. During the German occupation of Alsace the local wines were prevented from developing as quality wines and vast quantities of them were exported to Germany for blending or making into sparkling wine. Consequently, anyone tasting Alsatian wines was usually disappointed by them. In recent years, however, they have become both good in quality and highly competitive in the medium price ranges of French wines; some extremely fine ones can be found as well.

The majority of Alsace wines are named after the grape from which they are made; there are six varieties of what are called *cépages nobles*: Riesling, Traminer, Gewürztraminer, Muscat, Pinot Blanc, Pinot Gris (also called Tokay d'Alsace) and the Sylvaner, which is considered by some authorities as being noble, although others merely class it as belonging to the *cépages courants*. If a wine is made from a blend of the noble grapes it is called Edelzwicker, if any of the *cépages courants* are involved in a blend, it can only be called Zwicker. *Grand Cru* implies superior quality. The producers put their names on their labels so that it is possible to compare, for example, the Riesling of Hugel or Kuehn with that of Preiss Zimmer or Dopff & Irion, or many others. In a few instances there are certain site names given to wines, of which the best known are Kaefferkopf from Ammerschwihr, Sporen from Riquewihr, Mamburg from Sigolsheim, Zahnacker from Ribeauvillé (in which the vines are not only very old but are replanted one by one as they decline, which makes it impossible to describe this wine as from a single grape), Rangen from Thann, Kanzlerberg from Bergheim, Wannen from Guebwiller and Brand from Turckheim.

The Alsace bottle is known as the *flûte d'Alsace* and is tall, tapering and a true dark green colour, like most Moselle bottles. It is strictly very slightly (2 centilitres in capacity) larger than the brown bottle used for Rhine wines, but this difference, like the very slight difference between the Alsace flûte and some of the tall tapering bottles widely used throughout France for some *rosés* or white wines, is not perceptible to the lay eye.

Generally, Alsatian wines are drunk young when their freshness and crisp quality is especially enjoyable. Occasionally a grower may make a wine of great quality, similar to the auslese and even beerenauslese wines of Germany and this can be kept for some time, but such wines are rarely found. Although it is very difficult to describe wine, the approximate styles of the Alsatian wines are as follows:

Riesling The great wine, dry, subtle, with a beautiful fragrance that many people find 'grapey'.

Traminer Slightly spicy and sometimes definitely full in flavour. The Gewurztraminer is, as it were, even more so, and this is now the name most often seen on labels. The fragrance and fruitiness of these wines appeals very much to people who may not care for anything wholly dry, and they are good with certain dishes whose flavour might be overwhelming to the Riesling.

Muscat Somewhat similar to Traminer in being full and fragrant, but the fragrance is fruitier and of special appeal. Either you like it very much or hardly at all.

Sylvaner Light, dry and refreshing.

Tokay or **Pinot gris** Light, dry, but without the definite crispness of the Riesling and fairly full-bodied. Can live to a considerable age.

There are a very few red wines made in Alsace, but they are not quality wines and only produced in small quantity.

Fruit brandies

The quantities of fruits, both soft fruits and berries, grown in this part of France has resulted in huge quantities of brandy being distilled locally, both on a commercial and personal scale. Many hoteliers make a large range of these *alcools blancs* every winter. They are called 'white alcohols' because they are quite colourless, due to having been made in glass and not wood, hence gaining no colour during the process of maturation. They are also not usually sweetened, so that the flavour of the fruit is strong. The way they are served is for a medium-sized glass to be filled with

161

lumps of ice, which are swirled round so as to cool it thoroughly, then for the ice to be emptied out and the fruit brandy poured in. The cold helps release the bouquet in exactly the opposite way to the service of Cognac or Armagnac. A fruit brandy is not a liqueur except in the most general sense, but it has the advantage of some liqueurs in being an excellent digestive, and especially after a huge Alsatian meal, which has probably ended with something creamy, nothing more quickly restores the diner to feeling comfortable and alert than a little helping of an alcool blanc.

Kirsch (cherry) and *framboise* (raspberry) are possibly the two most famous of all fruit brandies, but others are made from *fraise* (strawberry), *myrtille* (bilberry), *sorbe alisier* (a type of rowan-berry), *prunelle sauvage* (sloe), *mûre* (blackberry), *mirabelle* (a type of small golden plum), and *quetsch* (another type of plum). A brandy called *tutti-frutti* is a mixture of fruits.

Things to see and do

Nancy In the Ancien Palais Ducal et Musée Historique de Lorrain, there are important collections of china and pottery, handicrafts and furnishings, a pharmacy museum, and, in the Galerie des Cerfs, a series of tapestries of La Condamnation du Banquet. These show the shocking consequences of over-indulgence at table.

Strasbourg At 23 Quai St Nicolas, there is the Musée Alsacien, containing reconstructions of Alsatian rooms and domestic utensils. There is a section devoted to wine and fine reconstruction of a kitchen and a pharmacy. The Musée de l'Œuvre Notre Dame, by the Cathedral, contains magnificent still-lifes of food by the Strasbourg painter, Stoskopf, reconstructions of rooms of different periods, and a seventeenth-century dolls' house, showing excellent detail of a kitchen of the time.

In the Musée des Arts Décoratifs in the Château des Rohan there is a fine collection of the different types of china of the region.

The Maison Kammerzell, now a restaurant, dates from 1467.

Riquewihr The whole town, the pearl of Alsace, has been most carefully preserved to show an Alsatian wine town as it has been for centuries. There are numerous beautiful old houses which have belonged for generations of wine growers, many of them belonging to houses still active in the business today, and the visitor will see signs indicating those that are open to view in which old presses, huge decorated casks and all the paraphernalia of wine can be seen. Riquewihr, because it is so compact and comparatively small, makes an ideal stop for a visit if time is limited.

Thann The Rangen is the local vineyard, the wine from which has been famous for centuries, although its reputation for making people drunk very quickly led to the local curse—'I hope the Rangen will harm you.' By the vineyard there is the guardhouse, built in 1483 for those who kept watch over the vines, and in which there are records of the vintages from 1483–1832. There is a Fontaine des Vignerons in Thann and a small museum containing exhibits relating to folklore and local history.

Wintzenheim The Château de Hohlandsbourg belonged in the fifteenth century to Lazare de Schwendi, who introduced the Tokay grape from Hungary to Alsace.

Verdun The establishment of Dragées Braquier, 'sugared almonds', is open to visitors.

Wangen The justices of Wangen used to be paid in an annual levy of wine, but although at the Revolution this was changed into an ordinary tax, and then abolished, an attempt was made in the nineteenth century to revive it, and the inhabitants had to go to law to protect themselves. To commemorate winning their case, the people built a fountain, which yearly flows with wine to celebrate the event, on the Sunday after 3 July.

Colmar There is the Fontaine du Vigneron, erected in honour of the wines of Alsace, and the Fontaine Schwendi, in memory of Lazare de Schwendi, who holds up a bunch of Tokay grapes, because he brought this type of wine to Alsace from Hungary.

The Musée d'Unterlinden, formerly a Dominican monastery, houses among other treasures a reconstructed Alsatian wine cellar and museum of wine. The wrought-iron inn-signs and elaborately decorated casks, as well as a collection of all the equipment used in wine making, are very fine; there are also collections of kitchen utensils, water irons, moulds for anis bread, butter, and so on.

The Maison des Têtes is a handsome house, dated 1609, in which a restaurant, with the tables divided from each other by pew-like partitions, is exactly as an Alsatian eating-house might have been a century or more ago.

Sainte Ménehould was the birthplace, in 1639, of Dom Pérignon (see p. 212).

Lunéville The museum in the château has an interesting collection of glass and china.

Château du Haut-Koenigsbourg The reconstructed medieval castle, burnt in 1633 and rebuilt for Kaiser Wilhelm II, is open to visitors who can see the cellar, kitchen and dining-room.

The Route du Vin runs from Marlenheim, near Strasbourg, to Thann. Tourist offices or the Astra Company, Place de la Gare, Strasbourg, can provide full details of this circuit, but perhaps the visiting of Ribeauvillé, Hunawihr, Riquewihr, Mittelheim, Sigolsheim, Kaysersberg, Ammerschwihr, Kientzheim and Turckheim, with possible excursions to Haut Koenigsbourg and Trois Épis, makes the most picturesque shortened version, possible in a single long day for anyone staying in or near Colmar.

Langres Musée du Breuil de St Germain, has collections of china, a room devoted to Diderot, born here, son of a cutler, and another room with an exhibition of cutlery.

Baccarat Glasses which are at the same time beautiful and perfect for fine wine come from the crystal works in this town, but unfortunately the factory is not open to the public.

Mulhouse The Musée Historique in the sixteenth-century Hôtel de Ville has reconstructions of rooms of different periods and a good exhibit of the equipment and tools of a vigneron and a cooper.

Other things to note

The Pfiffertag The expression means 'day of fifes', and is the name given to a very ancient celebration that takes place in Ribeauvillé on the first Sunday in September. Among other events, there is a big free wine tasting and a procession that generally includes a giant *kugelhopf*.

The Foire Régionale des Vins d'Alsace This takes place annually in Colmar during August. The Weinmarket at Ribeauvillé is held in May and other towns hold spring and autumn wine festivals, at which one can taste wines on payment of a small sum.

Funerals of the Dukes of Lorraine were formerly regarded, with the coronations of the kings of France at Reims and that of the emperors at Frankfurt, as one of the great spectacles of Europe. The Dukes of Lorraine always celebrated important events, such as baptisms and weddings, with enormous feasts; for the funeral of Duke Charles III in 1608 the usual custom was observed of presenting a series of dishes to an empty chair, while the body lay in state in company with everyone who had come to the funeral. All the dishes offered to the duke were afterwards distributed to the poor, and for Charles III these curious 'suppers' lasted from 9–13 July.

Auvergne and the Massif Central

Although very beautiful, this is not a region famous for its wines and dishes. It is poor agriculturally, except for the flocks from whose milk the regional cheeses are made, and the poverty and hardness of the mountain life do not encourage the making of delicate foods. However, much good simple fare is available.

Food in general

The two great vegetables are potatoes and cabbage, and there are also vast quantities of mushrooms. Le Puy is famous for green lentils and in the Liagne, north-east of Clermont-Ferrand, there is a great deal of fruit, especially apples. Trout, salmon and eels are found in the mountain streams. Pork, mutton and veal are the main meats and there is some small game, especially the thrushes of Brioude, and *coq au vin* is another favourite local dish.

There are many sweet dishes, especially a variety of cherry tarts, called *milliards* and *clafoutis*, although these are also a speciality of the Limousin. *Fouasse* is a type of *brioche* of the Cantal region, *picoussel* of Mur-de-Barrez a type of wholemeal fruit loaf. There are many candied fruits and jams, and Royat specialises in chocolate. Coffee may be served in a vessel like a small flower vase, or elongated eggcup, known as a *mazagran*.

Specialities and dishes

Soupe aux choux The substantial soup of the region (another variety of it is the *potée*, which is cooked in a covered dish), which can contain meat as well as vegetables.
Tripaux Stuffed sheep's feet.
Fricandeau A type of pork *pâté* in a casing.
Tourte à la viande Pork and veal in pastry.
Friands de Saint-Flour Sausage meat wrapped in leaves.
Œufs à l'Auvergnate Poached eggs with cabbage and potatoes.

Truffado This is a potato dish, rather like a potato pie which may contain cheese, or garlic or other things according to where it is made. *Aligot* or *alicot* is a similar potato dish, in which the potatoes may be cooked and mashed first, and sometimes cabbage is included with them. *Pommes de terre au lard* contains diced bacon and onions as well, and possibly herbs.

Bourrioles d'Aurillac Sweet pancakes made with buckwheat flour.

Cornets de Murat Cream horns.

Tarte à la crème A cream tart, speciality of Vic-sur-Cère.

Jambon d'Auvergue and other sausage specialties.

Cheeses

The high pastures make several fine cheeses, often in the *burons*, the small stone houses in which the shepherds live in the uplands during the summer, the cattle being kept overnight in small stockades known as *fumades*. It is in the buron that the cheese is made in a *fourme* or mould, the word that derives from the Latin *formas casei*, from which we get *fromage*.

Cantal This is the great cheese of the region and one of the few French cheeses to resemble a matured British cheese, such as a Lancashire cheese. Cantal was mentioned by Pliny the Elder two thousand years ago. It is made from cows' milk, from single herds, during the summer, put into the *fourmes* shaped like stocky cylinders (the size of a large Cheddar) and then left to mature in the cellar of the *buron* for several months. This is *Cantal fermier*; *Cantal laitier* is a creamery-made product. It is sometimes referred to as *Fourme de Cantal*. *Cantalon* is a small cheese of the same type. *Laguiole* is a type of Cantal from the town of the same name. *Fourme d'Ambert*, and *Fourme de Montbrison* are types of Cantal that are blue-veined. Rochefort is another similar cheese.

Chevrotin d'Ambert A smallish, rectangular cheese, sometimes all goat, sometimes goat and cow milk, rather strong in smell and flavour. *Chevrotin de Moulins* is a pyramid-shaped goat cheese, *Picotin de Saint Agrève* similar to the Chevrotin d'Ambert, round, and a little like a Camembert.

La Rigotte A thin round cheese of cow and goat milk, which, when it appears in a square shape, is known as *La Brique*, or *Chevrotin Cabion* (this appears in the Rhône Valley as well).

La Tomme de Brach A Corrèze cheese, made from ewe milk.

Saint-Nectaire Made in the Mont Dore region, from superior cows, called Salers and Ferrandaises. It is semi-hard, and is matured on mats of rye straw, often in cellars underneath Clermont-Ferrand, during which process it often develops a yellowish-red crust. *Murol* is a type of this cheese, which has a hole in the centre, *Vachard* another type.

Bleu d'Auvergne This blue cheese has been made for the past century according to the same procedure followed with Roquefort, which is inoculated with *penicillium glaucum*, but it is made from cows' milk. It is both farm and creamery made, from May to October, and is sold the year following that in which it is made, in its silver paper marked with its name. *Bleu de Laqueuille* is thought to have been the first type of this blue cheese made, by a man called Antoine Roussel, to whom there is a statue at Laqueuille. There are several other *bleus*, such as *Bleu du Vélay* and *Bleu de Thiesac*.

Gaperon A spherical, very hard, strong cheese.

Drinks

Gaspo or buttermilk is quite a favourite drink in this region of pastures, but there are also a number of 'little' wines, in the V.D.Q.S. category. Most are white, and not even the most chauvinistic would claim that any are more than pleasant light drinks. The best known is probably the white Saint Pourçain, from the Allier, although a red and a *rosé* are also made, and there is a light red wine from near Clermont-Ferrand, called Chanturgue, also red wines called Chateaugay and Corent may be found. Local liqueurs are naturally made, but the availability of these rather depends on the type of hotel in which you stay or where you eat. *Arvèze* is the brand name of a local gentian bitter *apéritif*, slightly resembling Suze (See p. 238)

Verreine du Vélay is a local liqueur (See p. 73).

Things to see and do

Aurillac In the Musée J. B. Rames there is a room devoted to folklore.

Chateaugay In the donjon of the château there is a Musée de la Vieille Auvergne.

Clermont-Ferrand In the Musée du Ranquet, in the former

Hôtel Fontfreyde, there are costumes and furniture, souvenirs of Pasteur, and local art.

Thiers The Société Générale de Coutellerie et d'Orfévrerie (Thiers is an important cutlery centre) will arrange to show visitors who apply to 45 de l'Avenue Pierre-Guéron how cutlery is made.

The Musée de la Coutellerie et d'Art Locale is at 8 Rue de Barante, and includes local folklore and industries.

Château de Tournoël Visitors see the pressroom and old press and the huge stone container for 13,000 litres of wine, also the kitchen with its large fireplace.

Vichy The Maison du Baillage has a folklore and local history museum. The establishment of the mineral waters of Vichy-État are open to visitors.

Moulins The Grand Café has remained exactly as it was in 1900, ornate and gilded. The shop of Sérady in the square is a chocolatier of the same period, all blue, gold, with medallions and completely '*belle époque*'. Their chocolates (the speciality is a type of caramel-truffle called '*palet d'or*') are good too.

Bordeaux and the Landes

Bordeaux is not at all typical of France. Standing, as the city does, on an intersection point of rivers and roads and with the harbour, sheltered by the long Gironde estuary, affording easy access to the sea, it has received all kinds of foreign influences for centuries. The Romans, the northern pirates, the pilgrims en route for Compostella, the English (to whom the whole region belonged for three hundred years), scholars coming to the university, those suffering from religious restrictions in Spain, Portugal, the Low Countries and Germany—all have settled in Bordeaux and left their traces. It is a wine city, as contrasted with the wine towns elsewhere, and the majority of people there are at least interested in wine, if not actively concerned with it. It has been called '*la cuisine de la France*', and the cooking seems to have made the best of all worlds, the homely and the fine, which makes it very acceptable to Anglo-Saxon visitors, as, while comprising many succulent touches that make holiday fare of many dishes, it is invariably balanced and never overwhelmingly rich, however copious.

The Landes, the great stretches of pine forest south of Bordeaux, were a desert waste, in danger of being literally blown away by the end of the eighteenth century, when the engineer Nicolas Brémoutier started the pine plantations which now yield both wood and resin. The pastures are poor, but the woods are the resort of a lot of game, and there is plenty of fish in both the streams and ponds and, of course, in the Bassin d'Arcachon and the Gironde estuary itself.

Food in general

One of the surprises of the region is the *caviar* of the Gironde, where the sturgeon comes—and loses its roe. M. Émile Prunier was largely influential in developing the local caviare business, when, in 1917, he was unable to get supplies from Russia, and thought of his native Gironde. The *lamproie* (lamprey) is another curious eel-like creature found in the estuary and of course there are the usual freshwater and sea fish. At Arcachon the oyster beds are extensive; the local type or oyster is known as a *gravette*, and there is the curious custom of serving oysters in this region accompanied by either little hot sausages, usually garlic flavoured, or slices of cold sausage or salami. The regular types of oysters, *Portugaises* and *plates*, are also cultivated in the oyster parks, and there are mussels and shrimps, eels and snails, though these last are usually not the fat Burgundian type. Bordelais cooking makes use of garlic, but sparingly, and shallots come into many dishes. Butter is the cooking medium.

The *agneau de Pauillac* is famous, because of the pastures by the river and sea. Game includes *palombes* (wild dove) and *becfigues* (p. 283) from the Landes, and *ortolans* (the same, or else wheat-ears), tiny birds which used to be a feature at medieval English feasts; they are served grilled or roast, and it is customary to eat every bit, even the head, though I can never bring myself to do this. Special dishes for ortolans, like plates for oysters, but decorated with ears of wheat, may occasionally be found in the British Isles. A great deal of beef is eaten, perhaps because grills and roasts are excellent partners to the great clarets, and the vegetables, from the many market gardens north of Bordeaux, are simple and allowed to remain so. Melons and soft fruit are offered for dessert, but the delight of visitors will probably be finding out that wild strawberries (*fraises des bois*) grow in the woods of Pessac, in the suburbs of Bordeaux, until the end of September. *Pruneaux fourrés d'Agen* (stuffed Agen prunes) and the *macarons* of St Émilion, small, lighter and more succulent than one had thought macaroons could be, are two sweet specialities. Otherwise the regional puddings are usually fruits in various forms.

I have said comparatively little about Bordelais cooking and it might seem that it was unimaginative; quite the contrary. Superbly plain it may often be, but transformed by a tradition of serious care into the sort of fare that is, often, remarkable simply because it is first class though never to the extent of obtruding on the dominant factor of the table in this part of France. This, of course, is the bottle, or bottles, of wine. For special occasions the host or the gourmet traveller will choose the wine first and fit the dishes to the bottle. And if, to the lovers of good food, this seems slightly exaggerated, I must beg leave to quote a great gourmet of our own times. 'For,' said he, 'good though it may be, you can't really discuss the day-to-day differences between one steak or stew or sauce and another. But every single bottle of claret is an individual.'

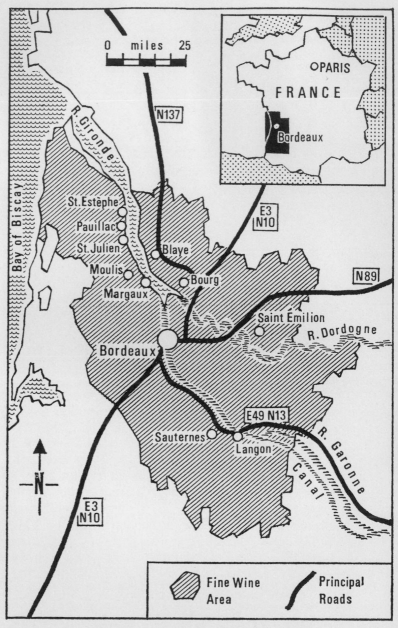

Outline of the Bordeaux vineyard which produces the greatest proportion of fine wines of any of the French wine regions.

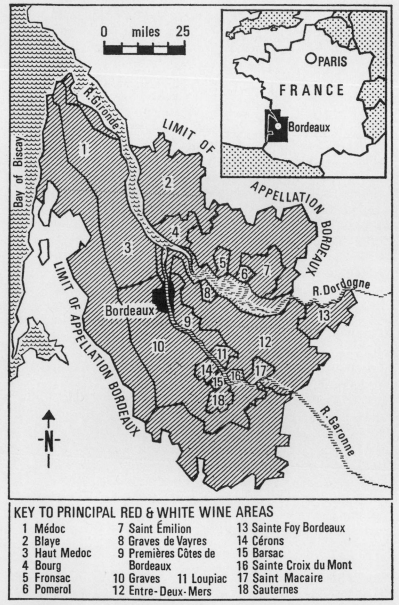

KEY TO PRINCIPAL RED & WHITE WINE AREAS

1 Médoc	7 Saint Émilion	13 Sainte Foy Bordeaux
2 Blaye	8 Graves de Vayres	14 Cérons
3 Haut Medoc	9 Premières Côtes de	15 Barsac
4 Bourg	Bordeaux	16 Sainte Croix du Mont
5 Fronsac	10 Graves 11 Loupiac	17 Saint Macaire
6 Pomerol	12 Entre-Deux-Mers	18 Sauternes

The Bordeaux region, showing the principal areas devoted to red and white wines. It will be appreciated that the outer limit, A.O.C. 'Bordeaux', contains the more specialised and superior A.O.C.s within it.

Specialities and dishes

Caviar de la Gironde Rather small-grained, but very good; perhaps, compared with Russian caviare of top quality, rather light in flavour.

Lamproie à la Bordelaise The lamprey is cooked in a sauce of red wine, with leeks and flavourings. It is not in the least fishy, and although this dish is certainly rich and rather expensive, one might describe the flavour as between turbot and rabbit, in a rich, dark (it is almost black) sauce. The lamprey has a poisonous vein running down its back, and it may have been this—or a creature that had 'gone off'—that was responsible for the death of Henry I, rather than the surfeit with which the poor man is credited in the history books. Lampreys are not in season all the year round, but with the arrival of the freezer even into the most august kitchens, I should not be surprised if it was obtainable (at a price, of course) in many smart restaurants. Lampreys are also found in the River Severn and other rivers with similar long estuaries, but apparently it is only the Bordelais who eat them.

Entrecôte à la Bordelaise A Bordelaise sauce is wine, butter, shallots, the marrow and flavourings, with possibly some tomato. But, as Mr Waverly Root has painstakingly worked out, it can also mean that the sauce is a Mirepoix, of rendered down vegetables—carrots, onions, celery—with ham, thyme and bay, or, simply, that the vegetable accompaniment to a dish so described will be potatoes and artichokes. *Entrecôte marchand de vin* is the *entrecôte* with a red wine sauce. It is worth noting that, generally, a French *entrecôte* will be the size and thickness of a tournedos or large rump steak, and an *entrecôte minute* the size of an ordinary, generous steak. Our 'minute steak' seems not to exist, except, as regards thickness, as *steak Diane*.

Grillé aux sarments This expression, which may be applied to meat, poultry and even fish, means that the object has been grilled over a fire made of vine wood. It imparts a delicious flavour. If you lunch with a member of the wine trade at his home or office and have a grill *au feu du bois*, this may mean that the grill has been made over wood from old wine casks—this is nearly as good as vine wood.

Soupe des vendangeurs The soup served out in the country to those making the vintage. It usually contains meat in generous quantities and lots of vegetables.

Faire chabrot A country expression and informal country custom, which means that, when eating soup, a glass of wine is poured into the last spoonful or so of liquid in the dish, which is then raised to the lips and drained.

Cèpes à la Bordelaise *Cèpes* are huge flat mushrooms, with a very definite and delicious flavour. They are cooked with shallots, a little garlic and, possibly, grape juice, and may be simmered in oil or grilled. They are definitely rich, and one large *cèpe* is usually enough for two people, if eaten after a substantial main course—it should certainly never be ordered when the diner wants something light and refreshing, such as a salad. But this is another of the great regional specialities and must be tried.

Foie de canard aux raisins Duck's liver, cooked, with various vegetables and flavourings, in a wine sauce, and served on *croutons*. Very good, but very rich, also very expensive.

Oie farcie aux pruneaux A very complicated dish, really from the Agenais, in which the goose is stuffed with plums, which have themselves been stuffed with a mixture of ham, olives and onions. It is often served with chestnuts. Again, rich and expensive, though excellent.

Tourin Onion soup, or onion and garlic soup.

Cheeses

Curiously there are no Bordelais cheeses. A good restaurant will be able to offer cheese from adjoining regions, but the cheese that is eaten everywhere in the area is the red-rinded Edam, known as *Hollande*. This is supposed to be because, in about the eighteenth century, the Dutch who were trading with the Bordelais persuaded the latter to take cargoes of cheese back to the Gironde in part payment for the wine. Nowadays the Bordelais affirm that the mild Dutch cheese perfectly complements the flavour of fine claret, and they are not entirely wrong, for a fine wine that may have a sort of nervous delicacy of taste would be overwhelmed by a very strong cheese, or a matured cheese, of the type of our Cheddar or Lancashire. A mildish blue cheese can partner a full-bodied claret, but my personal preference is for a really creamy cheese, as fresh as possible, with perhaps a small sliver of goat cheese (not too strong) as well.

Drinks

Apart from table wines there are a number of drinks made in Bordeaux. These include the white wine *apéritif*, Lillet (see p. 71),

Vieille Cure, originally made at Cénon and the wide range of liqueurs of the establishments of Marie Brizard and Bardinet. The last house also produces fine Martinique rums, of which the most famous is probably Rhum Negrita, widely used for cooking as well as for drinking. These rums are more delicate and, in the opinion of many, achieve a greater finesse than the heavier rums to which our naval traditions have accustomed us in Britain. A fine old Martinique rum—not, unfortunately, always to be found commercially—has the quality of a great liqueur.

For any detailed account of Bordeaux wines, the various books recommended on page 309 should be consulted. But the following notes may be useful for handy reference if you are on the spot without any of them.

The Bordeaux region produces about 10% of all the wines of France and at least 33%—possibly even more—of all the A.C. wines. Both red and white wines are made in fairly equal quantities, there is a little *rosé* and even some white sparkling wine, but this last is more of an oddity than anything else. The use of the word 'claret' for the red wines is a purely British idiom; the light coloured red wines of Bordeaux were called *'clairet'* in medieval times to distinguish them from the dark red wines from the south and centre of France that came through the port, and the name has stayed—and the British love of claret—ever since. The wine fleets would sail up the Gironde and rush the new wines—before wines were bottled the new vintage was, of course, better than anything old—to English ports, and in the Thames the king's butler (*bouteiller*) had the right of first pick of what was on sale. To show that a ship had paid the port dues, a branch of cypress would be hoisted on the mast, and at a certain point the sail would be dipped—which is the origin of the name of Beychevelle (*baisse voile*). In an attempt to give themselves a head start on the competing high country wines, the Bordelais did not permit any of these to be kept within the city wall, a rule that eventually reacted against them, for it was the establishment of reserves along the bank of the Garonne and the settling of all kinds of foreign firms of merchants here that produced the Quai des Chartrons; *'les Chartronnais'* today is a Bordeaux idiom signifying the ruling dynasties of the wine trade, *'la noblesse du bouchon'*.

Because of its long associations with England, the occupying power, Bordeaux was not a smart drink at the French court—they drank Burgundy after the duchy became joined to the crown—until the eighteenth century, when the Duc de Richelieu, Governor of Bordeaux, introduced it to Louis XV. This Duke's

Parisian architect, Victor Louis, had a pupil, Combes, who designed Château Margaux and many other beautiful buildings in this region. It was at this time, too, that many families from the British Isles settled in Bordeaux to found great wine concerns; the Johnsons and Lawtons are French now, but if there can be said to be such a thing as an eighteenth-century Anglo-Saxon look, as often seen in family portraits, many of the present-day members of these families perpetrate it. The Irish family of Barton, who are both shippers and proprietors (Langoa and Léoville Barton) has never become French in 300 years. After the Battle of Waterloo, one of Wellington's generals bought the Château de Gasq in the Médoc and retired to live there, giving the property his name of Palmer. Today there are several British firms who own or have considerable interests in estates in this area.

The properties in the Gironde are usually much larger than in Burgundy, and each vineyard is owned by a single individual or company. In 1855 a classification of the wines of the Médoc (and one wine from the Graves) was made and sixty-two of the best growths were listed in five categories; these *crus classés* are the aristocracy of Bordeaux red wines still, and although the first growths usually are the greatest, it is no longer true to say that, for example, a fifth classed growth is not as good as perhaps a third or second. Changes of ownership and methods may make the quality of one estate go up or down, but in general the classed growths are all fine wines. There have been classifications of the wines of other areas in recent times and the classification of a wine will be marked proudly on its label, but in general conversation the term 'classification' usually means that of the Médoc (see p. 178). Just below the classed growths come the *crus bourgeois*, which nowadays can achieve great quality, then the *crus artisans*, and the wines bearing the names of small properties or just the district from which they come. The four great first growths— Margaux, Latour, Lafite, Haut Brion—and Mouton Rothschild, which disdains classification—nowadays bottle all their wines at their estates, and so does Château Yquem, the great Sauternes.

Classed Growths

The sixty-two best red wines were classified in 1855 by an official committee into five 'growths' or 'crus', known collectively as the Classed Growths, or Crus Classés.
Other great properties sell a proportion of their wine château bottled, except for Pontet Canet, largest of all, which never does, and nor does Langoa-Barton.

Châteaux	District	Châteaux	District
Premiers Crus		**Quatrièmes Crus**	
Lafite	Pauillac	Saint-Pierre-Sevaistre	Saint Julien
Margaux	Margaux	Saint-Pierre-Bontemps	Saint Julien
Latour	Pauillac	Branaire-Ducru	Saint Julien
Haut Brion	Pessac (Graves)	Talbot	Saint Julien
		Duhart-Milon	Pauillac
Deuxièmes Crus		Poujet	Cantenac
Mouton-Rothschild	Pauillac	La Tour-Carnet	Saint Laurent
Rausan-Ségla	Margaux	Rochet	Saint Estèphe
Rauzan-Gassies	Margaux	Beychevelle	Saint Julien
Léoville-Lascases	Saint Julien	Le Prieuré	Cantenac
Léoville-Poyferré	Saint Julien	Marquis de Terme	Margaux
Léoville-Barton	Saint Julien		
Durfort-Vivens	Margaux		
Lascombes	Margaux		
Gruaud-Larose	Saint Julien		
Brane-Cantenac	Cantenac		
Pichon-Longueville	Pauillac		
Pichon-Longueville-Lalande	Pauillac		
Ducru-Beaucaillou	Saint Julien	**Cinquièmes Crus**	
Cos d'Estournel	Saint Estèphe	Pontet-Canet	Pauillac
Montrose	Saint Estèphe	Batailley	Pauillac
		Haut-Batailley	Pauillac
Troisièmes Crus		Grand-Puy-Lacoste	Pauillac
Kirwan	Cantenac	Grand-Puy-Ducasse	Pauillac
Issan	Cantenac	Lynch-Bages	Pauillac
Lagrange	Saint Julien	Lynch-Moussas	Pauillac
Langoa	Saint Julien	Dauzac	Labarde
Giscours	Labarde	Mouton-d'Armailhacq	
Malescot-Saint-Exupéry	Margaux	(now Baron Philippe)	Pauillac
Cantenac-Brown	Cantenac	La Tertre	Arsac
Palmer	Cantenac	Haut-Bages-Libéral	Pauillac
Grand la Lagune	Ludon	Pédesclaux	Pauillac
Desmirail	Margaux	Belgrave	Saint Laurent
Palmer	Cantenac	Camensac	Saint Laurent
Calon-Ségur	Saint Estèphe	Cos-Labory	Saint Estèphe
Ferrière	Margaux	Clerc-Milon	Pauillac
Marquis d'Alesme-Becker	Margaux	Croizet-Bages	Pauillac
Boyd-Cantenac	Margaux	Cantemerle	Macau

Visitors to the Gironde should take advantage of the fact that, although château bottled clarets of any kind are never likely to be cheap, they will be considerably cheaper than when sold abroad; there is no surer way of learning about fine wine than from trying claret, called by those who love it 'the most natural wine of all', on its home ground, straight from the property. There is certainly a claret for every kind of dish—the Borderlais will even drink it with plainly cooked fish—though straightforward grills and plainly roasted meat and poultry, or the more delicate sorts of game are probably the best possible accompaniments to the fine wines. The dry white wines (which are slightly soft and never as palate-scrapingly dry as some from other regions) are good *apéritifs* or with fish. The Sauternes and Barsacs

are delicious by themselves or with fruit, and in the area a glass of
a great sweet wine, well chilled, is often the accompaniment to
foie gras—it sounds an awful combination, but I was surprised
to find it good. The Sauternais themselves advocate Sauternes
with game or very spicy food, but this is rather a special taste,
though worth trying when on the spot.

White wines These are made from the Sauvignon, Sémillon
and Muscadelle varieties of grape. They come from Blaye, some
from Bourg, Graves de Vayres (on the Dordogne), some from the
Premières Côtes de Bordeaux (a region which is chiefly a red wine
area within the Entre-Deux-Mers), Entre-Deux-Mers; the Graves
region produces red and white wine, some properties, such as
Domaine de Chevalier, even producing the two kinds. These are
the finest of dry white Bordeaux.

The region of Sauternes, which produces the great sweet wines,
also includes that of Barsac, where the wines are equally great.
These sweet wines are made by allowing the grapes to remain on
the vines long enough to become shrivelled and with a bloom or
fungus forming on their skins; this is called *'pourriture noble'*
(*botrytis cinerea* is the scientific name) and it results in there only
being a drop of concentratedly sweet grape juice left. The vintage
in Sauternes can only be made by skilled workers, used to picking
grape by grape (with special scissors), when the degree of noble
rot is achieved. But until just over a century ago the wines from
Sauternes were dry, or at least not lusciously sweet (which may
be why some old cookery books advise Sauternes with oysters
and other fish), and the sweet wines evolved because the steward
at Yquem was ordered to wait to make his vintage until his
master's return; this was delayed by illness, but instead of the
wine being ruined it was a triumph. Recently several great properties have begun to make dry wines again as well, by picking
the grapes before the pourriture has started to form on them.

It is very difficult to describe in general terms the taste of great
wines, but whereas the Sauternes (such as Yquem, Filhot, Guir-
aud) are invariably sweet from the first taste to the after-taste, the
Barsacs (of which Coutet and Climens are two great properties)
have a curious dryish flavour at the end. The vineyards of Cérons,
which geographically lie between Graves and Sauternes, have the
dryness and refreshing quality of the former and something of the
sweetness of the latter. Across the Garonne, the wines of Sainte
Croix du Mont slightly resemble those of Barsac, and those of
Loupiac are a little like those of Sauternes.

Red wines These are made from the Cabernet Franc, Cabernet

Sauvignon, Merlot and Petit Verdot, and sometimes also from the Malbec and Carmenère grapes, used in different proportions. A fine claret of a great year can live longer than most other red table wines; I have had sixty- and eighty-year-old clarets that were still full of charm and forty-year-olds that were elegant and vigorous. At the other end of the scale there is a huge variety of differing wines for everyday drinking.

The red wines come from Bourg, where more red wine than white is made, and some from Blaye, where the reverse is true. There are also some from the Premières Côtes de Bordeaux, where *clairet*, a light pink wine, is still made. St Émilion, usually popular with British tourists, produces many fine and hundreds of good wines, ranging from the great Châteaux Ausone and Cheval Blanc to the everyday wines; they are usually very fragrant and rather full-bodied. Other good red wine areas in the St Émilion region are Pomerol (of which the great name is Château Pétrus) where the wines tend to be a little dryer than those of St Émilion, Néac, Lalande de Pomerol and, a little further away, Fronsac and Côtes de Canon Fronsac. The red Graves, of which Haut Brion (known to Pepys as 'Ho Bryen'), La Mission Haut Brion, Pape Clément, Domaine de Chevalier and Carbonnieux are notable wines just outside Bordeaux, are, as the name of the region implies 'gravelly' dry, delicate, sensitive clarets, with a most subtle spiciness about them in great years.

The Médoc, north of Bordeaux, produces a great variety of wines, all red (the two or three white wines that have been made from time to time are in the nature of curiosities) and regarded by many as the finest red wines in the world. Each commune or parish has its own individual character which is conveyed to the wines; there are, of course, infinite variations and exceptions, but it may be generally said that the wines of Margaux are flowery (some people think they smell of violets) supple and especially graceful; they often remind me of an old-fashioned fruit garden on a hot summer day. The wines of St Julien are very velvety, close-textured as regards fragrance, like a bunch of tiny choice flowers, with a silky flavour. The great Pauillac wines are supposed by some people to smell of cedarwood, or the inside of a cigar box, or have the '*goût de capsule*' (the metal covering for the cork of the bottle); I have occasionally noted the first two, but never the last, for to me the Pauillac wines have an essential fine fragrance that is dry, yet warm, and a flavour that contains so many shades of fascination that one seems as if one can never wholly determine the ultimate secret. The St Estèphe wines are quite different and tend to be rather slow to be ready for drinking and on the hard side before they are; when, however, they do come round they are very enjoyable, with an intensity of bouquet, elegant fruitiness and length. They, and possibly some of the great Pauillacs, are not wines with which I would advise a complete wine novice to begin his or her serious drinking, for they are of so definite and subtle a character that they can fail to be immediately appealing; like some people, they need knowing to be appreciated and enjoyed, though it is always possible for anyone informed to pick one of these wines that will possess the instant ability to charm anyone new to them. Other fine wines come from the parishes of Moulis, Listrac, Macau and Ludon, all of them different, of course, but generally light, graceful and elegant. Some of those that do not often get featured in Britain should certainly be tried when one is on the spot. There is also the point that a property that usually makes fine wine will make no less than a good wine even in a year that is generally poor. There have been several most enjoyable 1956s and 1965s that I can remember; if the wine of an estate with a high reputation is really unworthy of its name, for some reason, then the owner will usually refuse to put it out with the château label on it.

Visiting and touring the châteaux Ideally, the wine lover should arrange to see St Émilion, the Graves and Sauternais, and the Médoc, because the soil, the vineyards and the properties vary greatly in these fine wine regions. This could be done in two days, but to devote three to it would be less tiring. The Sauternais is well sign-posted so that, in about an hour, one can drive past most of the great properties. As St Émilion the vineyards are all comparatively close around the town. In the Médoc, however, the area is more extensive, and a wine map, such as may usually be obtained from either a shipper or proprietor (or the *Maison du Vin*) is helpful so as not to miss the narrow lanes and to find those properties that are not on the main roads. If at all possible an introduction should be obtained to either a shipper or the owner of a property, both to save time and to be sure of making the most of any visit.

For anyone in a great hurry, Châteaux Haut Brion, La Mission Haut Brion (with its fine garden and former priory), and Pape Clément are right at the gates of Bordeaux, in Pessac, and one could see one or even two in an hour. A short trip into the Médoc could take one as far as Margaux, where several very fine estates are grouped around Château Margaux, of which the chai, built, like the Château, by Victor Louis, is classically fine; this could take a couple of hours, slightly more if one went in and tasted in more than one property. Notices saying '*Visitez*', or '*Visitez les chais*' invite visitors to go in and have a look—there will generally be someone about, even should the estate not have anyone deputed to take charge of visitors and show them round. The usual procedure is to see the chai, where the young wines are stored, and either there or in a tasting room taste them if this is wished—though one is not invariably invited to do this, as it would obviously considerably deplete stocks. Should you be absolutely set on tasting a particular great growth, the only way of assuring this is to go accompanied either by another owner or a shipper, or representative of the trade who will have arranged that this facility is offered to you. The same applies should you wish to see a property that is not generally open. Visitors are sometimes surprised that they never get a chance of tasting any old wine at a château, but once the wine goes into bottle it is then either sold, sent into cellars in Bordeaux belonging to members of the trade, or simply put into the private reserve of the property, so it just will not be available.

Tasting is done from glasses in Bordeaux. The Bordeaux taste-vin, now not used, is rather like a plain saucer with a bulge in the middle (see p. 152). Wines offered for tasting in the office of a shipper or owner may be already in bottle or young wines still in wood from which tasting samples have been taken. Remember the sacred lunch hour (mid-day until 2 p.m.), shake hands when arriving and leaving with whoever shows you round and never even think of tipping the *maître de chai*.

Things to see and do

Arcachon In the Aquarium et Musée, one section is devoted to oysters, and there are comprehensive exhibits of many kinds of fish.

Aubeterre-sur-Dronne In the fourteenth- to fifteenth-century Château, visitors see the kitchen and other rooms in which a variety of domestic utensils are on show.

Blaye In the Citadelle, from which an excellent view may be had of the Médoc across the river, the Maison du Commandant d'Armes contains a small museum devoted to local history and art.

Duras The kitchens of the Château are on view to visitors.

Mortagne-sur-Gironde The Ermitage Saint Martial, 3 kilometres outside the town, the hermitage comprises a kitchen, refectory, cells and the chapel.

Villandraut   There is a small Musée Régional, including exhibits to do with local folklore.

Le Prieuré   In the kitchen of the Château, which is in the parish of Margaux, there is the complete equipment and furnishings of former times.

La Brède   The Château, open at certain times to visitors, was the home of Montesquieu and many of the rooms, including the dining-room, are furnished as in his time in the seventeenth century.

St Émilion   This is possibly the most picturesque wine town in France. From the terrace below the belfry there is a good view of the vineyards, and the Château du Roi, from the top of which the '*Ban des Vendanges*' is proclaimed each autumn. In the vineyards behind the town may be seen lines of stone emplacements, in which the Romans planted vines. The refectory in the cloister of the Collégiale may be seen. In the Musée Gaudet there are exhibits relating to the history of the town.

Cadillac   The impressive Château des Ducs d'Épernon is open to visitors, who may see the sumptuous chimney-pieces, some of them showing fruits and grapes in relief. The local association of white wine growers has a tasting room and information centre in the Château, which can usually receive visitors.

Pauillac   The small Musée du Vin is in the former Château du Grand-Puy Ducasse. Visitors may see a variety of exhibits relating to the wines of the Médoc and the Confrérie du Bontemps du Médoc, whose ceremonies are frequently held here.

Mouton-Rothschild   The chai and impressive dining-room adjacent to it are usually open to visitors. The Musée in the Château itself can only be seen if written application is previously made, but it is very well worth while doing this, as the museum not only contains an unrivalled collection of works of art—pictures, tapestries, glass and china—to do with wine, but the way in which these are displayed is remarkable.

Bordeaux   The Maison du Vin can provide information about all the regional wines and contains many exhibits of interest concerning them. There are numerous monuments in the city showing the preoccupation with wine, including various ornamental heads on the Hôtel de la Bourse crowned with vine leaves. The Quai des Chartrons and Quai de Bacalan show typical houses of the seventeenth- and eighteenth-century wine trade, with the cellars below them and the doors opening on to the quayside so that the wine could be loaded direct on to the vessels in the port. The Rue Xavier Arnozan is particularly beautiful and typical of rich town houses of the wealthy merchants. In the Hôtel de Ville the dining-room is especially fine. In the Musée des Arts Décoratifs, in what formerly was the Hôtel de Lalande, there are numerous exhibits relating to the history of Bordeaux, fine china and some glass, Palissy ware and many objects to do with wine, such as the stove in porcelain, with the chimney represented as a post wreathed with vines and tended by cherubs. The liqueur establishments of Marie Brizard, Bardinet, responsible for Rhum Negrita, and that of Millet are well organised to receive visitors.

Brittany

Ars Mor or Armorica is the old name for Brittany, meaning 'the country of the sea', and many of the foodstuffs are affected by the proximity of the ocean, the slightly salty butter, the lamb from the tide-washed pastures which is entitled to the description *pré salé*, and the huge variety of fish of all kinds, with the 'white butter' that accompanies many of them. The style of cookery is not elaborate and some gastronomic writers have tended to consider Brittany a poor region, but the very fact that first-class ingredients, cooked in simple ways, characterise the Breton table will appeal to the visitor.

Food in general

Shellfish, sea and freshwater fish, including carp and salmon are plentiful everywhere. As well as lamb, Morlaix ham is famous, and there are many sausages and pork products, which appear as *pâtés* or hard, cold sausages, rather like salami.

Vegetables are produced in market gardens and include new potatoes, artichokes, carrots, cauliflowers and the famous onions, which come mostly from around Roscoff and St Brieuc, and which are sold in quantities to Britain by the travelling 'Roscoff Johnnies'. The onions vary slightly according to where they are grown, but are pinkish when ripe and remain hard and firm for many months when stored. There are also the strawberries of Daoulas and Plougastel, where there is a strawberry feast on the third Sunday in June, and also walnuts, pears, grapes and melons. Claude of Brittany, who married François I of France, and who was fond of gardens, gave her name to the greengage: Reine Claude.

Canned foods, in addition to meats, include fish. The first cannery was started at Nantes in 1824. Brittany is the biggest producer in France of canned fish, chiefly sardines, mackerel and tunny. Peas and French beans are also important in the canning industry.

Biscuits and sweets include the biscuits and wafers from Nantes, and a type of bon-bon also from Nantes called a *berlingot* (similar to satin cushions), caramels from Rennes and also *Pralines Duchesse Anne*, which are sugared burnt almonds, and angelica from Châteaubriand. Probably the most famous of biscuits are the *crêpes dentelles*, very light and fragile coffee-coloured wafers, rolled like small flat cigars, which come chiefly from Quimper, and are served with ice-cream and compôtes.

Specialities and dishes

Cotriade   Described by some as a northern version of bouillabaisse. This is either a fish stew, with potatoes served on a separate plate, in which there may be a variety of fish, but not lobster, and there is aslo a cotriade made with mackerel alone.

Palourdes farcies   Clams stuffed with shallots, herbs and put under the grill.

Brochettes de coquilles Saint Jacques   A type of scallop kebab.

Homard à l'Armoricaine   This is one of those controversial dishes. The recipe, involving herbs, tomatoes and garlic, suggests the south of France, and some authorities hold that the dish was created in Paris and became *à l'Américaine* by a mistake in the writing of the menu.

Andouille   A type of sausage made from pork intestines, poached, then fried and served with potatoes.

Courraye   Cabbage stuffed with a mixture comprising hare or rabbit, and often served with quails or other small game birds.

Bouillie   Very much a peasant dish, this is a type of porridge made from buckwheat flour. It can be served *à la crème*, or with cider.

Beurre blanc   A speciality around Nantes, but as it is also a Loire speciality, it will be found described on p. 260.

Sauce bretonne, à la bretonne   This term may mean several different things. A dish with this description probably means that the meat, usually lamb, is accompanied by white haricot beans. The original sauce bretonne is a derivation from sauce espagnole, a game sauce base with butter, browned onions, chicken essence, but the simpler version more frequently met with, is composed of onions, carrots, leeks, butter and either cream or white wine, according to what it is to be served with.

Galette bretonne   A flattish, round cake, rather like gingerbread without the ginger, or a maid of honour without the almonds.

Gâteau bretonne A flattish fruit cake.

Far breton A batter mixture with raisins in it. The first time that it was described to me, with much elaborate detailing of the recipe, I disappointed my kind Breton hosts by remarking that it was merely a sweet Yorkshire pudding but in fact that is exactly what it is, made at the bakery and served hot if it comes home in time, otherwise cold.

Farsac'h This is claimed to be the ancestor of Christmas or plum pudding, but many things might be that. It contains raisins and plums and, probably, apple brandy or rum as well in the mixture.

Bigoudens Almond paste biscuit-like cakes.

Beignets de Mam-Goz One gourmet guide rather neatly calls these 'granny's fritters'. They are potato cakes, made sweet with peel and fried crisp, served with jam.

Maingaux Rennais A combination of thick and fresh cream, whipped together, served with strawberries or raspberries, and a speciality of Rennes.

Crêpes These are certainly the most widespread Breton speciality, though rather curiously they are not often featured on the menu in ordinary restaurants. To eat them you must go to a *crêperie*, an establishment which sells nothing else, which may be like a small, smart restaurant or a snack bar or even a travelling barrow-cum-stall. There are two kinds, those made of *froment*, or wheat flour, which are sweet, served with sugar and/or jam, jelly or honey. They are the closest to the ordinary pancake. Then there are the *crêpes* of *sarrasin* or *blé noir*, which is buckwheat, rather like wholemeal flour, which are salted and served, if desired, with such things as ham, cheese, tomatoes, rather like a savoury omelette. The Breton *crêpe* is a very large, extremely thin pancake, made on a special griddle called a *galettière*, on which the batter is spread with a *raclette*, which is like a rake without prongs. *Crêpes* are usually good value and one can make a good meal, at little cost, by having a savoury one followed by a sweet one. The accompaniment is usually cider, served in a *bol* or *bollée*, which looks like a tea-cup without a handle.

Cheese

In view of the good Breton butter, it is somewhat surprising that cheese is not a great speciality.

The Véritable Nantais is a small, square mild cows' milk cheese, originally made about seventy years ago by a priest in the Vendée, hence the name by which it is sometimes known—*Fromage du Curé*.

Saint Agathon is a small, round flat goat cheese, chiefly produced in the region of Guinchamp.

The Crémet Nantais is a small fresh cream cheese, only made in the summer. Cheeses with the names of *Sainte Anne d'Auray*, *Ferté Bernard*, and *Conerré* are mentioned in books, but seldom found nowadays.

Drinks

Wine   Wine has been produced in the Rhuys region, though I have never tasted it and it cannot be considered a commercial article. It is said of this particular beverage, that to drink it requires four men and a wall; one man to hold the glass, another to do the drinking, two men to hold the drinker up and a wall to support him.

Although there are no vineyards within the Breton peninsula, the great wine of the region is Muscadet. This has nothing at all to do with Muscat or Muscadelle. The wine has proud traditions; it is supposed to have been drunk by Abelard, who was a Breton, and it is mentioned by Rabelais in 1530. But the Muscadet vineyards were totally destroyed by severe weather in 1709, and the despairing vignerons travelled to Burgundy, where they obtained fresh vines, of a type called Muscadet de Bourgogne or Melon. The very dry white wine produced in these vineyards was mostly consumed on the spot, but in 1929 the sommeliers of Paris were taken round the vineyards and were impressed to the extent of beginning to recommend it, especially in establishments serving shellfish and other fish. Today Muscadet enjoys great popularity throughout France, especially since the terrible frosts of 1956 did such havoc in the Chablis vineyards and because the price of the white Burgundies has risen so steeply in recent years.

Muscadet is made from just the one grape and Bretons will tell you that it is the only French wine to be named in this way. (Remind them of the nomenclature of the Alsatian wines and they will reply that Alsace is not really France.) There are three kinds of Muscadet entitled to an appellation: Muscadet, Muscadet des Coteaux de la Loire, and Muscadet de Sèvre et Maine. The fattish, sloping shouldered Burgundy bottle is used, and the wine is considered at its best when drunk young and very fresh. It gains enormously by being bottled on the spot, so that those who have not been especially impressed in Britain should try it when visiting the region, but it is definitely very dry, excellent as a first-course wine or with shellfish.

A V.D.Q.S. wine also worth tasting on the spot is the Gros Plant, again made from a single grape. It is dry, slightly full, and usually comes in a tall green bottle, rather like an Alsace or Moselle bottle. If you intend trying both the wines at a single meal, drink the Gros Plant first, as otherwise it will seem rather indifferent after Muscadet.

Cider This is probably the 'beer' of Brittany, although you will not find it available in most restaurants, it is served in bars and *crêperies*. There are two main kinds, the 'hard' or dry cider, and the sweet kind, and it can be sparkling or still. *Cidre bouché* undergoes its fermentation in bottle, like wine, with the cork held down by a metal clamp. As in England, there is ordinary bottled cider of various kinds, and draught cider. Some can be little more than faintly alcoholic apple juice, other kinds are definitely in the 'hard liquor' category, so, especially if you are ordering it by the 'bol' in a *crêperie*, where the little pottery cup seems to hold so little that one is tempted to consume it in quantity, ask in advance as to the type you are drinking.

Eau-de-vie-de-cidre is made, but nowadays tends to be a personal, farmhouse produce. I have never tasted it, but imagine it as a really tough apple brandy.

Things to see and do

The oyster nurseries in the Gulf of Morbihan It will come as a surprise to most lovers of oysters to learn that the majority of all the flat oysters (*ostrea edulis*) enjoyed in Europe probably start their existence in this part of Brittany, especially around Locmariaquer. The oyster is curious in that it requires a certain type of water in which to live and develop, both the tides and the degree of salt affecting its health and fattening, and very seldom does it grow satisfactorily for the table in the same place in which it has been born. In recent years, several unusually hard winters and the increase of industrial waste affecting the quality of the sea have virtually destroyed the traditional old oyster beds, and nowadays the 'spat' or tiny oyster is reared by attaching it to tiles, which are whitened, curved like those in roofs in the south, and held together in bunches by wire. At various stages in its growth it is put into deeper and deeper water and eventually it is brought to be 'finished', as it were, in certain special areas already famous for oysters, such as, in Brittany, Cancale. The tiny oyster is almost invisible, like a crumb, when first attached to the tile, at six months it is taken off its first tile and, looking now rather like a cornflake, attached to another one, ready to be put into deeper water in the oyster park in the spring. The ridges on the shell indicate its age, though an oyster that grows up naturally, possibly attached to a huge bank of other oyster shells, sometimes grows two coats to its shell in a year. The oyster buyers can rear their oysters elsewhere until they are five years old, but by this time they are about the size of a fried egg and oyster eaters do not want them any bigger in Europe. Older oysters mature on shallow trays in the oyster parks. It is, throughout, a skilled business to care for them, especially when they are small, as an error with the knife when removing them kills the oyster.

The Cancale oysters are sometimes known as *pieds de cheval* because of their shape, and they have a pinkish tinge.

There is nothing spectacular to see at Locmariaquer, but the people are courteous and willing to show the oyster parks to the interested visitor. Anyone seriously concerned with shellfish or marine biology may care to write to Dr Louis Marteil, of the Institut Scientifique et Technique des Pêches Maritimes, at Auray, the great local authority on the subject.

Lobster pens are open to the public at Audierne.

The Charles Pérez Aquarium at Roscoff is one of the foremost establishments of its kind in Europe and the most important French marine laboratory. You can see most of the Channel fish in their natural state.

The great fig tree at Roscoff is near the station, in an enclosure to which the public are admitted if they ring the bell at the lodge. This tree is said to have been planted by Capuchin monks in 1625. It is now propped up, covers an area of about 600 square yards and some years, yields as much as 1000 lb of fruit.

Circuit of the Muscadet country The Comité Interprofessionel des Vins d'Origine du Pays Nantais, whose offices at 12 rue de Strasbourg, Nantes, will provide full information about the wine and directions as to how to make a comprehensive tour in the region.

At Nantes, in the Natural History Museum in the Place de la Monnaie, there is an especially fine collection of shells and even a specimen of the extinct Great Auk, scarcely gastronomic, but at least very remarkable.

The Salorges Museum, also at Nantes, contains a room devoted to the food industries of the region such as canning and preserving.

At Morlaix there is still a large tobacco factory, where cigars are made. This is not generally open to the public, but visitors may be interested to know that Morlaix has been a centre for tobacco trading since the eighteenth century, when the Compagnie des Indes founded a factory there, and also a farm. It was, as might be expected, a great centre for the smugglers who were engaged in running cargoes of tobacco over to England, and the local producers often kept bands of smugglers in their employment for this trade.

Château des Rochers, south of Vitré, was the home of Madame de Sévigné, where she stayed especially when she wanted to economise after the extravagances of her husband and her son. Occasionally she and her friends would visit Vitré, and of the official banquets that were held there the Marquise remarks, 'As much wine passes through the body of a Breton as water under the Bridges'.

At Rennes the imposing Courts of Justice were literally built on wine and cider and staffed on spices, because funds for them were found by levying a tax on both wine and cider, and the judges received payment from clients in the form of the then rare and precious spices from the east.

At Quimper, the statue of King Gradlon stands between the spires of the cathedral. Until the eighteenth century it was the custom, every 26 July, for a man to climb up to the statue, tie a napkin round the King's neck from behind, then offer him a glass of wine. The climber would then drink the wine himself and throw down the glass into the square; anyone who caught it unbroken received a huge money prize, but the rumour was that the thrifty Town Council always made a few cuts in the glass stem before the ascent. King Gradlon's bishop and adviser was the saintly Corentin, who was said to exist solely on a single miraculous fish, which appeared each day in the river, offered itself to him to cut up, on which he would cut away half and fling the rest back. The following day the whole fish again appeared in time for the saint's meal. It was King Gradlon who reigned over the vanished kingdom of the bay of Cornaille, of which the capital was the town of Is; it was so beautiful that Bretons think that when the Lutetians sought a name for their own chief city, they called it 'Par—Is' meaning 'like Is'. The city came to destruction because of Gradlon's daughter, the beautiful but wicked Ahès (her name is sometimes given as Dahut); the Devil, in the guise of a handsome youth, tempted her to get from the chain round her father's neck the golden key that unlocked the gate in the sea-wall protecting the town. Gradlon and Corentin fled on horseback before the invading sea, with Ahès behind her father, but Corentin, looking back, saw the Devil riding the waves to overtake them, and called to Gradlon to fling his daughter into the water, at which the sea retired, although the city of Is had vanished and Gradlon chose Quimper as his new capital. Ahès became a mermaid, luring sailors to destruction at the bottom of the bay.

Museums of Breton art and interiors

The Château de Dinan   Exhibits include an old corn mill and washing-up equipment, most interesting wooden and pottery utensils, including braising pots and a *plat à galette*, jugs and cider cups, and huge salt and tobacco jars in the room with the collection of Breton coifs.

Château de Vitré   In the Tour de l'Oratoire the reconstruction of a Vitré house, collection of china and pottery, perforated dish covers, a cider press and all the hearth utensils.

Château de Kerjean   This is south of Plouzévedé, and contains a small museum of Breton art and the old kitchens, with their huge chimneys.

Château de Nantes   There is a very comprehensive collection of popular art with Breton interiors reconstructed, wooden articles, pottery, also the 'Cellier' of the Chevaliers Bretvins, with an old wine press.

Burgundy and the Lyonnais

Burgundy has been a rich region for centuries. As an independent duchy it was prosperous and influential; its dukes lived in great state and its merchants prospered. As a religious centre, with the concomitants of scholarship, healing and hospitality, in addition to the arts fostered by the church, it was unparalleled; Cluny in its great days was the most important religious foundation in Christendom, and the network of monasteries and abbeys linked to it throughout Europe were so active in running hospitals, arranging pilgrimages and acting as advisers in various matters concerning local economy that Sir Stephen Runciman has neatly described the monks of Cluny as 'the American Express of the Middle Ages'. The natural resources, too, are great: the fertile Champagne region marks one of the boundaries of Burgundy and to the east there are the great butter and cheese mountain pastures. Even in the Morvan, the wilder region, the Burgundians have managed to produce superb hams (*jambon de Morvan* is one of the great raw hams of France), the great white Charollais cattle thrive in the lush meadows, game abounds in the forests, fish in the streams and, in the only regions where crops might fail to flourish because of the poorness of the soil, the vine has, for longer than records exist, produced wines famous far beyond the comparatively small districts where they are made. The only possible drawback to Burgundy, from the visitor's point of view, is that there are too many tempting good things! But one can, if strong-minded, avoid cream sauces at every meal, and as great wines can be taxing to the mind as well as to the palate, it is fortunate that there are plenty of 'little' ones in the area as well.

The Beaujolais is the southern part of Burgundy—even more jovial people in beautiful country. The food is as would be expected similar, though perhaps generally more inclined to be true country cooking rather than haute cuisine, and very welcome on that account. Lyon, strictly not in Burgundy, has been included here, both because of convenience and because the dishes for which it is famous are closer to those of Burgundy than Provence. The Lyonnais think that their city is the centre of French

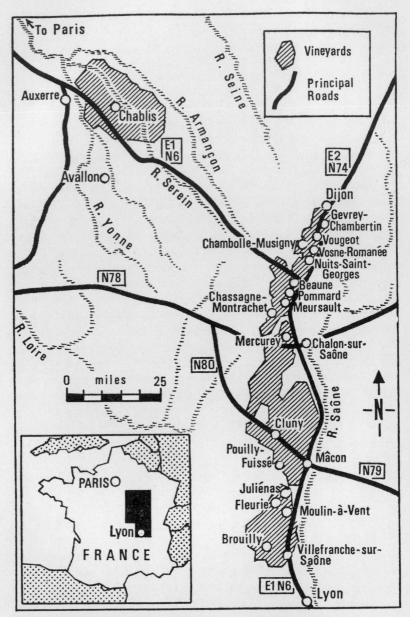

General map of the whole Burgundy region, including Chablis and the
vineyards of the Côte Chalonnaise, and the Mâconnais and Beaujolais.

gastronomy and certainly there are many excellent restaurants, but the visitor on holiday may prefer to keep away from this essentially industrial region.

Food in general

Burgundian cooking is ideally suited to the needs of people who work very hard physically and who are jovial by temperament. It is high in protein—lots of meat, and many fine cheeses—with wine and cream coming into many of the special occasion dishes. Some writers describe Burgundy as being famous for beef, mustard and wine; the Dijon mustard is world famous and is available in many varieties. It is made from *verjus*, the juice of un-ripened grapes and the mustard seed, and certainly accords well with many of the beef-based dishes and specialities such as *lapin à la moutarde*. The beef will be noted specially on a menu when coming from Charollais cattle. The spiced honeycake (*pain d'épice*) of Dijon is as famous as the mustard and it is made into fantastic shapes for different public holidays: a large fish for the *'poisson d'Avril'* (1 April), bells, snails—which are also made in chocolate—and toy animals. The cassis liqueur (see p. 197) which is the other great speciality is used as a filling for chocolates and other sweets, and to flavour all kinds of cakes and ices. The num-ber of different kinds of *pâté*, ballotines, galantines, brioches and pastries stuffed with different meat fillings, and variations on the famous *jambon persillé* (ham in parsley-flavoured jelly) that are to be seen in the charcuteries at the times of any of the big festivals is astonishing; in addition to the ordinary types of sausages such as the *cervelas*, which may also contain *pistaches*, and *andouilles* (tripe sausages or chitterlings), there are the cheese puffs known as *gougères*, *feuilletés* (flaky pastry cases), with *morilles* (a type of mush-room), the fat Burgundian snails, ready to re-heat and serve, and poultry, game and meat joints prepared with aspic and truffles, looking like the glittering illuminated pictures in old manuscripts showing ducal banquets. Brillat-Savarin did not think much of Burgundian truffles, but they are used in many regional dishes, notably the *poulet demi-deuil*, famous speciality of the Lyonnais, in which the chicken is given a 'half mourning' appearance by having its breast threaded with slices of truffle. The kind of elaboration found in recipes throughout this area is exemplified by the *saulpiquet*, a ham dish with a spiced cream sauce, delicate to taste and difficult to make (in fact impossible in small quantities), therefore another good dish to try in a restaurant; this name has its origin in '*sau*', the Latin for salt, referring to the seasoning and spicing of the meat and sauce. As well as the *quenelles de brochet* (what may be described as the apotheosis of fishballs made with pike), there are *quenelles de volaille*, sausages of chicken meat, light and delicate.

Plenty of good vegetables make the local markets fascinating and colourful; artichokes and pumpkins are perhaps the most noticeable, and a *gâteau de courges*, a pumpkin tart, is sometimes found on menus. The nursery gardens abound, and the orchards, which make the region very beautiful in the spring, yield fine fruit. *Bugnes*, a type of doughnut, *rabotte* (apple dumpling), cakes and tarts filled with *groseilles* (redcurrants) or other fruit, are in all the pastryshops.

Specialities and dishes

Pouchouse A stew of freshwater fish, with white wine. (See p. 237 for *meurette*, which is a similar thing, only made with red wine.)

Jouée A type of pasty with bacon.

Oreillons de veau farcis Calves' ears, stuffed with pike pounded as for quenelles, and cooked with white wine.

Fressure de porc, or ferchus Pig's fry, cooked with red wine, onions and herbs.

Oyonnade A type of goose stew.

Bœuf à la Bourguignonne Beef cooked in red wine, with onions, mushrooms and diced bacon. One of the great dishes, and excellent with fine wine.

Rable de lièvre Saddle of hare, usually accompanied by wine, onions and mushrooms.

Œufs à la Bourguignonne Eggs poached in red wine and, sometimes, a rich stock, and served on *croutons*. This is rich and you either like it very much or else you find the combination of ingredients far too much.

Gras double Lyonnais Tripe, with onions and parsley.

Pommes à la Lyonnaise Potatoes with onions—the expression '*Lyonnais*' usually means that the recipe contains onions.

Gounerre A type of *pâté* of potatoes.

Tabliers de sapeur A colloquial name for a dish of grilled tripe with a Béarnaise sauce.

Tourte Charollaise An open tart with pears covered with cream.

Rigodon A type of fruit and walnut custard.

Cheeses

Epoisses A soft cheese, made from the milk of cows of a breed called the Pic Rouge de l'Est. It comes in two sizes, either *'entier'* or *'demi'*. *Aisy Cendrée* is a type of Epoisses, dried under the ashes of vine wood.

Saint Florentin A cow milk cheese, which is also sometimes called Soumaintrain. The real Saint Florentin is white and is eaten while fresh, the Soumaintrain has an orange rind and is yellow inside, and it gets quite strong in flavour as it matures. (A strongish, creamy cheese is the best accompaniment to red Burgundy, perhaps with a slice of goat cheese or blue cheese as well.)

Mont d'Or A cow milk cheese, made in the Lyonnais.

Claqueret Another Lyonnais cheese, fresh and soft, mixed with onions and chives.

Chevrotins de Mâcon Small goat cheeses of the Mâconnais. They may, according to where you find them, also be called *Beaujolais*, and sometimes, colloquially, *Boutons de Culotte*.

Thoissey A goat cheese, rather like a large cork in shape.

Citeaux A cow milk cheese, originally made by the monks. The actual name of Citeaux itself derives from the place where the abbey was founded, which is slightly marshy, with many bull-rushes—citeaux.

Vézelay A small goat cheese, made in the Morvan.

Cabrion A Saône-et-Loire cow milk cheese, wrapped in plane leaves.

Fromage des Laumes I have never seen this cheese, but it sounds very special, as it is washed in water containing coffee, which is said to give the rind a dark brown colour.

Rigottes Small goat cheeses. **Rougerets** are similar.

Drinks

Crème de cassis, blackcurrant liqueur, is one of the great regional specialities. Combined with white wine, it makes a *vin blanc cassis*, a popular light, refreshing apéritif, sometimes known in the region as *un Kir*, after Canon Kir, the Mayor of Dijon, who was famous as a lover of good food and drink.

Marc de Bourgogne, distilled from the residue of the grapes after they have been pressed, is regarded as one of the best marcs in France; it can be fiery, but when thoroughly matured can be wonderfully mellow and subtle. However, it is definitely strong.

197

Fine bourgogne is a distillate of Burgundy wine. It is curiously light and delicate, more so than marc. It is a comparative rarity and it has an *appellation controlée* to itself.

The Hospices de Beaune consist of the Hôtel Dieu founded in the fifteenth century by Chancellor Nicolas Rolin and his wife, Guigonne de Salins, and the Hospice de la Charité. They were then endowed and have been subsequently enriched by gifts of vineyards, and the produce of these (which often bear the donor's name) is sold for the upkeep of the establishment. In 1859 these wine sales were made a public auction, at first held in the cellars of the Hôtel Dieu, and since the centenary of the auction in 1959 in the covered market of Beaune, always on the third Sunday in November. The wines are available for tasting before the auction, and buyers come from all over the world to bid. The auction is conducted by means of two tapers burning down; when the second taper goes out, the last bid wins. Although the wines of the Hospices are not representative of all the wines of Burgundy, the prices they fetch—and the quality they show at this first tasting—indicate the situation as regards the other wines.

The sale of the Hospice wines is the occasion for many other tastings to be held in Beaune. There is a range of the Beaujolais and other wines in the Hotel de Ville, and the House of Patriarche traditionally holds a tasting of '*grands millésimes*' (great vintages) of wines dating back forty or more years in their cellars at the convent of the Visitandines. Entry to this last is on payment of a small sum. For the other tastings it is necessary to obtain a ticket or be the guest of someone in the wine trade. During the weekend of the sale too, are held *Les Trois Glorieuses*, the three great feasts. The first of these is a dinner on the Saturday night at Clos de Vougeot, when the guest of honour presiding over the sale and other celebrities are made honorary Chevaliers du Tastevin, and songs are sung during the long meal. On the Sunday after the sale there is a *dîner aux chandelles* (dinner by candlelight) in the cellars of the Bastion de Beaune. On the Monday, there is a lunch, called *La Paulée*, at Meursault; this was originally a meal for the different vignerons, who brought their own bottles of wine. Guests still do this and exchange bottles, as well as singing songs (songs accompany most Burgundian activities) and usually a guest of honour is presented with an award. It is necessary to have tickets for all these functions—and even then, if you come late you may find your place taken. The whole occasion, or series of occasions, are very much the concern of the wine trade and their guests, and hotel accommodation for miles around is booked months in advance, so it is highly advisable to have some kind of personal introduction if the tourist is to enjoy the visit.

Tasting in Burgundy is done, when it takes place in a cellar, from a *tastevin*, or flattish cup of either silver or glass, with irregular indentations on the inside of the bowl, and a thumb piece by which it is held. The reason for this is that Burgundy cellars are dark and the colour of the wine cannot easily be seen in the dim light of perhaps one candle or faint electric bulb. As the wine is run over the indentations in the tastevin it can be noted more clearly, and many members of the wine trade find that the use of the tastevin, with which the wine makes immediate contact with a greater area of the mouth than when a glass is used, enables tasting to be more definitive. Most members of the wine trade carry their own personal tastevins with them when tasting. If you see one on a table in an office, do not assume that it is an ash-tray! The thumb piece may look like a cigarette-rest and there are some ornamental tastevins used for ash-trays—but to use a real one for such a purpose would be a real gaffe. (See illustration page 152).

Beaujolais   Nearly all the wine is red, a beautiful bright ruby, though a very little white Beaujolais is nowadays made. The grape of the Beaujolais is the Gamay, and the inhabitants of the region usually prefer to drink their wine young, even within a few months of its vintage. The *vin de l'année*, as it is called, is often served cool, either being brought straight up from the cellar or else even being put in the ice bucket for a short time. All Beaujolais is a wine to quaff generously—the Compagnons du Beaujolais have as their motto '*Vuidons les tonneaux !*' (Empty the casks!) The wine of a great year can, to my way of thinking, improve marvellously if kept for a few years, but this is often put down as '*le goût anglais*' (English taste). The wines of the different regions vary in character and anyone on the spot should take advantage of the well-organised *Route du Beaujolais* and the tasting rooms in the towns to note the subtleties of the wines. You are not charged for what you drink but you can contribute anything you wish to the wine growers' association which runs these establishments. One of the greatest charms of the Beaujolais region and its people is that somehow they are exactly and delightfully as one expects a wine country and its inhabitants to be—straightforward, sturdy and always ready to laugh.

The *Pinot Chardonnay* and the *Pinot Blanc* are the grapes used for the finest white Burgundies.

The *Pinot Noir* is the grape used for the finest red wines.

Aligoté is the name of a grape used for many white wines of every-

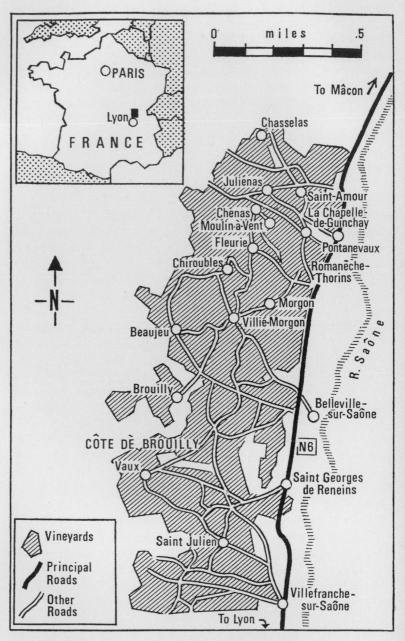

The Beaujolais vineyard, in hilly undulating countryside, with an eastern aspect. In good weather the Mont Blanc range in Switzerland is clearly visible across the river.

day quality. It is the sort of wine that can be enjoyable at luncheon in the sunshine, dry and refreshing, and it is the grape used for White Beaujolais and usually *vin blanc cassis*.

Bourgogne-Passe-Tout-Grains is the name that must be applied to red wines in which the Pinot Noir and the Gamay groups have been mixed. It can be a pleasant everyday wine.

The **Côte Chalonnaise** and the **Mâconnais** produce both red and white wines, mostly of a quality that may be described as everyday to good.

Chablis is the region where some of the finest white Burgundies are made, but the vineyards are so tiny—allotment size, often—that visitors will soon see why it is impossible that all the wine sold is Chablis can be the genuine article. True Chablis—which is never cheap, even when it is sold without the name of one of the vineyards attached—is very pale in colour, with a slight greenish tinge, and very dry indeed, even when it is a big wine. It is in fact too dry, almost in a 'minerally' sense, for many people, but can be incomparable with fish and shellfish, and even if, eventually, you decide that it is too dry for you, do not miss trying the real thing when you are on the spot.

The Côte d'Or is the great wine region that stretches from just south of Beaune northwards to Dijon. It is divided into the Côte de Beaune, around the town, and the Côte de Nuits, both producing red and white wines. The majority of the finest white wines come from the Côte de Beaune and the finest red wines from the Côte de Nuits, though there are certain notable exceptions. The properties in Burgundy are much smaller than visitors usually expect, and a single vineyard may be divided between a large number of owners; this is why Burgundy cellars usually contain—as far as wines kept at the property are concerned—far less than the tourist imagines he will see. In Beaune and the establishments of Nuits Saint Georges, where large general stocks are held by the shippers, the cellars are of course enormous. The fact that, with these small, sub-divided properties within vineyards, each owner will make a slightly different type of wine, complicates matters for the wine lover wanting to learn; it is important, as far as fine wines are concerned, to know not only the vineyard within the parish, but the owner, and, if the owner does not bottle his wines (few small proprietors do) then the shipper who has handled it. Because estate-bottled Burgundy is so expensive in Britain the visitor to Burgundy should seize the chance to try some of these great wines if possible, though even there they will not be cheap. But wines sold to a restaurant by one of the great Burgundy

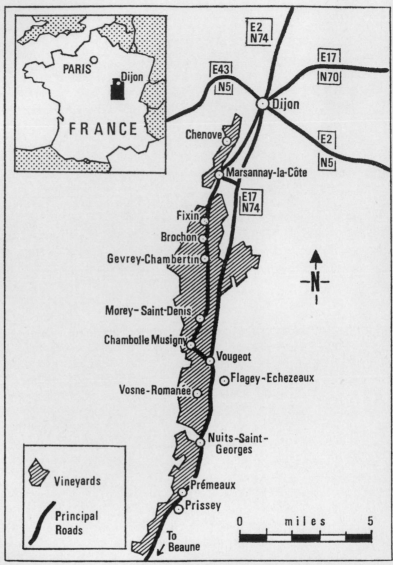

Sketch map of the Côte de Nuits, showing the principal villages with names in general use on wine labels. It should be remembered that, in addition to the actual vineyards, with their own *Appellations Contrôlées* which are shown on large-scale wine maps of the area, there are also many fine vineyards which, for economic reasons, merely use the words *'premier cru'* plus the name of the village, because a more detailed nomenclature would increase their tax rating.

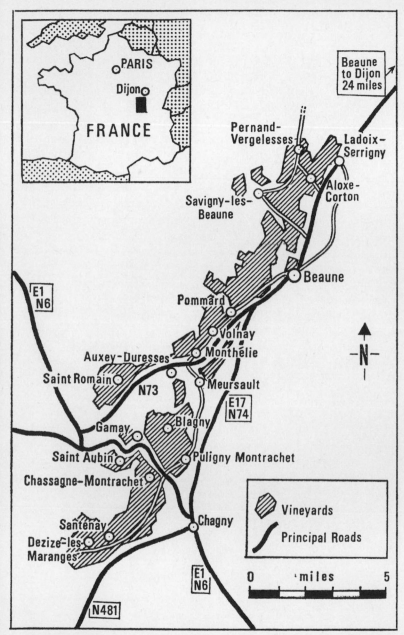

Sketch map of the Côte de Beaune, showing the principal villages. The wines of the Hospices de Beaune, both red and white, come from this region.

houses will usually be named in detail, and interesting comparisons may be made; sometimes, too, a restaurant will buy direct from the property and establish a reputation both for the man who made the wine and for the establishment who bought it. All this makes Burgundy endlessly fascinating for the lover of fine wine.

The way Burgundies are named is rather complicated. The enthusiast is urged to read one of the books recommended on p. 309 to clarify matters, but in general among the fine wines the wine that just bears the name of a vineyard, such as Corton or Chambertin, is a step up from the wine that bears the name of the village made famous by those vineyards, such as Aloxe-Corton or Gevrey-Chambertin. Sometimes, however, the name of another vineyard is attached to that of the great vineyard (such as Charmes-Chambertin), which means usually that the wine will rank just below that of the great vineyard and above that of the wine bearing the name of the village of Gevrey. This means that it is at least useful to know the villages of the Côte d'Or, as opposed to the vineyards. At Corton, however, the white Corton-Charlemagne is a finer wine than the plain white Corton, though this is easy to remember, as the wine from Corton is mostly red.

It is obviously not possible for the small-scale proprietors out in the country to be ready to receive visitors at all times, but the larger establishments, both at Beaune, Nuits-Saint-Georges and Meursault are usually very willing to show tourists their cellars.

The Burgundy bottle is fattish, with sloping shoulders. Even if they should throw a deposit, Burgundies are seldom decanted, except in the most particular restaurants. For the finest wines, enormous glasses are often put on the table—those vaunted as suitable for the great Romanée-Conti wines hold a bottle or more of wine if filled. Personally, although one gets a great puff of fragrance from swirling the wine around in such a glass, I dislike having to plunge my face into it and grope for the liquid rather like an ant-eater going into a jar; the balance of the bouquet and the flavour of the wine seems, to me, to be upset by such a procedure, and I prefer an ordinarily generous glass. Try both and make up your own mind. A wine that merely smells and does not taste is not worth whatever you paid for it.

The taste of red Burgundy is velvety and can be full of fascinations. The smell should be sweet, deep, rich—but the treacly taste and vulgarly scented wines that sometimes get sold as Burgundy have nothing in common with the aristocracy of the real thing. Fine Burgundy should never be a great big fat, obvious wine; it is delicate, supple, sleek, with a concentrated bloom to it like a flower border at twilight. It should charm, never overwhelm. But it can never be cheap and both the red and white wines of the finest Burgundies are among the most expensive on the market—some authorities admit to finding white Burgundy the most fascinating of all wines—and therefore, if at all possible, the wine lover is urged to be extravagant whenever it is possible to taste these great wines at their nearest to a bargain price on their home ground.

Things to see and do

Burgundy is so rich in treasures of the arts that it would be diffi-cult, without devoting a book to the subject, to list everything that may be associated with food or wine—as the grape is por-trayed in every type of Christian art, Christ being 'The True Vine', there are numerous representations of grapes and vintage scenes, as well as other examples of food and drink in art. The great abbey churches throughout the region entertained vast numbers of pilgrims and distinguished guests, and their cellars, refectories and food stores, and the pharmacies attached to the hospitals of such establishments, bear witness even today to the way in which Burgundian life comprehended all aspects of good living, as far as the merchants and small proprietors were concerned, not merely from the point of view of the nobility.

Autun The Musée Rolin, formerly the house of Chancellor Nicolas Rolin, contains fine exhibits of Burgundian art and general souvenirs. The Musée Verger-Tarin contains the reconstruction of a nineteenth-century bourgeois interior, with furnishings and utensils from earlier centuries in addition. There are vintage scenes on the great door of the cathedral and an old-fashioned butcher's shop on the road up to the cathedral.

Auxerre The Musée Leblanc-Duvernoy contains regional china and furniture. It was to Auxerre that Alexandre Dumas came to recuperate, after having narrowly escaped cholera, and where he ate snails at the Auberge du Léopard. Subsequently he paid regu-lar visits to conduct a type of 'cure', consisting of cherries and white wine.

Beaujeu There is a tasting room here, and the town gave its name to the region. The Musée Folklorique et des Traditions Populaires contains most interesting exhibits of local crafts, especially cooperage and sabot-making, and there is a complete room devoted to dolls dressed in local costumes.

Beaune There are numerous wine houses open to the public in this town and signs are displayed inviting visits. The Syndicat d'Initiative, behind the covered market, where the wine sales are now held, can usually provide information as to opening times of the different establishments. Visitors who go round the Hôtel Dieu are shown the great kitchen, which is very well kept and beautiful in appearance, and the pharmacy, also outstanding for the tourist. The cellars of the Hospices are not usually open to the visitors on the routine guided tours, but can be seen if special application is made—though it must be admitted that they resemble many other Burgundy cellars. The Musée du Vin de Bourgogne is installed in the former Hôtel des Ducs de Bourgogne, and is very well laid out, showing every aspect of wine production in the region, from ancient times to the present. There are interesting collections of tastevins and coupes de mariage—the chalices in which a newly-married couple would pledge each other immediately after the marriage ceremony—and a magnificent Lurçat tapestry, showing wine, the source of life, triumphing over death, in the room where the Ambassade des Vins de France has its meeting.

Brançion The Confrérie des Vignerons de Saint Vincent come to the church each Christmas in procession and during the midnight mass the best wines of the year are blessed.

Chalon-sur-Saône In the refectory of the Hôpital the ancient tableware and equipment may be seen.

Dijon In the Ancien Palais des Ducs de Bourgogne, now the Musée de Beaux Arts, there are numerous art treasures to see, and also the enormous ducal kitchens, dating from 1435, and with six chimneys. In the same museum there is a beautiful Hebe, by Rude, and a fine bas-relief by Attiret of Autun, with cherubs making the vintage. The Musée Perrin de Puycousin contains a collection of objects relating to local life in Dijon and Tournus, and there is the reconstruction of a local inn, with various scenes of regional activity, with wax figures carrying on everyday occupations. The Cellier de Clairvaux, built in the thirteenth century by the monks of Clairvaux, who were forbidden by the rules of the order to drink wine, but who made a good thing out of producing and selling it, has now been transformed into a regional tasting room. Since 1920 in November each year a Food Fair is held at Dijon. The town was once actually saved by its wine; in 1513, when it was besieged and obliged to sue for surrender terms, the governor had the idea of sending out his envoys to the enemy preceded by wagon-loads of wine. The besiegers drank—and easy peace terms were soon negotiated.

Flavigny The Ursulines of the local religious establishment invented a type of aniseed sweet in the seventeenth century, and the town is still famous for them.

Fontenay The great abbey, founded by Saint Bernard in 1118, is very well worth seeing, and the monks' bakehouse and dovecote are on view.

Joigny The inhabitants are known locally as 'Maillotins', because in 1438, the vignerons revolted against their overlord, and killed him with their '*Maillets*'; these utensils are still seen in the arms of the town.

Louhans In the Hôtel Dieu, dating from the eighteenth century, the pharmacy may be seen by visitors.

Mâcon The dispensary, in the Hôtel Dieu, is especially fine in the style of Louis XV and there are collections of china well worth seeing.

Montréal The stalls in the church are remarkable for their carvings, which include scenes from Burgundian life, and show, among other things, wine merchants drinking.

Marcigny In the Tour du Moulin there is a museum of local life and history.

Montbard This is the town of the great naturalist, Buffon, who enjoyed fame throughout Europe in the eighteenth century. His house may still be seen, and '*truite farcie caprice de Buffon*' pays tribute to his memory by being a stuffed trout, accompanied by banana. It is as delicious—properly made—as it sounds exotic.

Montargis During the reign of Louis XIII, the chef of the Duc de Plessis-Praslin created a new sweet—roasted almonds covered in sugar. They were such a success with the ladies of the court that the Duke gave his name to them. Pralines are still made today, in a shop opposite the Church of the Madeleine.

Nevers The Musée Municipal Frédéric Blandin contains a very important number of collections of china, glass and enamels. It is at Nevers that is supposed to have lived the celebrated parrot Vert-Vert, the property of the Visitandine Convent. His fame spread until the sister convent, at Nantes, asked the Visitandines to send him to them for a few days. Unfortunately on the way the parrot was taught a disgraceful vocabulary by the rivermen and the horrified sisterhood at Nantes sent him back, to be punished. He seems to have expiated his bad language and was henceforth so spoiled that eventually as an eighteenth-century song says, he was positively stuffed with sweets and fiery with liqueurs, so that when he found a pile of *dragées*, he died of a surfeit of sweetmeats.

Juliénas The tasting room here is in a church that was deconsecrated at the time of the Revolution. The murals which have been added since are rather crude in style but, more important for tourists who may be travelling with friends easily shocked, they are extremely uninhibited in subject.

Pontigny The Abbey, built by Cistercians in the twelfth century, is still occupied by the Séminaire de la Mission de France. The former cellar is now the refectory, which may be seen.

Chenôve The fourteenth-century pressoir des Ducs de Bourgogne may be seen.

Vougeot Clos de Vougeot is now the property of the Chevaliers du Tastevin, and is usually open to visitors, who may see the former huge cellar, used for ceremonies of the order and banquets, and the enormous fourteenth-century presses.

Vézelay There are scenes of vintaging on the door carvings of the church.

Villié-Morgon The tasting room is very well arranged, with exhibits and carvings, including one showing the artist's idea of the first press—a Gaul squeezing a bunch of grapes into a wooden bowl.

Vincelottes There is a fine twelfth-century cellar, formerly used by the monks of the Abbey of Reigny for storing their wine, as it is near to the Yonne, a river highway much used by producers of wine.

Vaux en Beaujolais This village is both picturesque and famous as being the original of Clochemerle, the Beaujolais village described in several novels by Gabriel Chevallier, who lived in the region during the war. The tasting room has murals of the various incidents in the first book—and, once again, is not for the prudish.

Belleville-sur-Saône The Maison du Beaujolais is both a tasting room and the central office for information about the whole region. Visitors who have any time to spend should inquire about visiting the house of Raclet, 'saviour of the vine', which is still preserved as an old Beaujolais country house, with the kitchen as it was in the last century when Raclet, trying to find a remedy for a pest attacking the vines, noticed that the vine outside, which was watered by the hot water coming from his sink, was healthy—and used hot water against the particular caterpillar. The Maison de la Dîme, out in the country, is another place of reunion for the Compagnons du Beaujolais. The Hôtel Dieu in Belleville has a pharmacy that is worth visiting.

Tonnerre In the ruins of the Abbaye Saint Michel may be seen the remains of the cellars, with vaulted roofs supported by pillars.

Tournus The Hôtel Dieu is staffed, like that at Beaune, by the Sœurs Hospitalières de Sainte Marthe. The seventeenth-century pharmacy is very fine, and the kitchen is also worth seeing. In the Musée Perrin de Puycousin there are most important collections of scenes from Burgundian life, with wax figures in costume engaged in their everyday occupations, and there is also a reconstructed cellar.

La Puisaye Colette was born in the region, at Saint Sauveur in the Rue des Vignes. The pottery of the district is famous and tourists will find many shops specialising in it, especially at Saint Amand, Saint Sauveur and Ratilly. The owners of the Château de Ratilly have even opened a studio for students of pottery in the Château and this may be visited by tourists.

La Rochepot The kitchen-cum-dining-room of this picturesque castle is on view.

Saulieu This has been a gastronomic town for centuries. Rabelais praised the fare and in 1677 Madame de Sévigné stopped there and admitted that, for the first time in her life, she got tipsy. In the present century Saulieu was renowned for the cooking of Alexandre Dumaine at the Côte d'Or; after the death of Fernand Point of the Pyramide at Vienne, Dumaine was generally admitted to be the greatest chef in France. He recently retired, handing over his establishment to a trainee of his own.

At **Fleurie, Saint-Amour** and **Moulin-à-Vent,** in the Beaujolais, the tasting rooms provide a good opportunity of tasting the local wines.

Lyon The Musée Lyonnais des Arts Decoratifs has exhibits of furniture and silverware, and a seventeenth-century dining-room and kitchen. The Hôtel Dieu, where Rabelais practised medicine, contains the Musée des Hospices, with its pharmacy. The Palais des Arts has fine collections of china and glass. The Musée du Vieux Lyon in the Hôtel de Gadagne has exhibits showing the history of the city. Although cloth is only indirectly to do with food and drink, the Musée Historique des Tissus at Lyon is probably the finest in the world and should certainly be seen if possible.

Champagne and the Ardennes

'La Champagne' is the region, 'le Champagne' the wine. The region as its name implies, is open countryside, really includes Sainte Ménéhould, which I have put into Lorraine (p. 163), and is much influenced by the rich butter-based cookery of the Ile de France and surroundings of Paris, and also the pork and game products of the Ardennes and the Belgian border. Few people think of staying long in this part of France and indeed, from the big main roads, it looks rather uninteresting, but there are beautiful woods and stretches of peaceful countryside for anyone who goes away from the big *routes nationales*, and the Ardennes are spectacular. Superb churches and cathedrals abound and are often decorated with carvings or windows showing the activities of *vignerons* or *tonneliers*.

Food in general

The rivers and streams provide carp, salmon and trout, but for the tourist the fish that will crop up most often is probably the pike (*brochet*). This is in fact often rather a dreary fish, and certainly a hideous one, but when its flesh is made into delicate, lightly seasoned fishballs, or sausages, called *quenelles*, and when these are served in a superlative sauce, the fish deserves its renown. *Quenelles de brochet* are featured in Burgundy too, but those of Champagne are very good indeed.

The smoked ham of the Ardennes and the Reims hams in pastry are famous, and thrushes (*grives*) are another Ardennes speciality, sometimes made into *pâtés*; the Ardennes are also a region for wild boar (*marcassin*) and pork products such as *andouillettes* and *petits pieds* (stuffed trotters) are widespread throughout the whole district.

Vegetables include cabbages, vast quantities of which are grown for *choucroute* and dandelions (*pissenlits*) which are made into a salad with bacon. Beets are also served with many of the pork and game dishes.

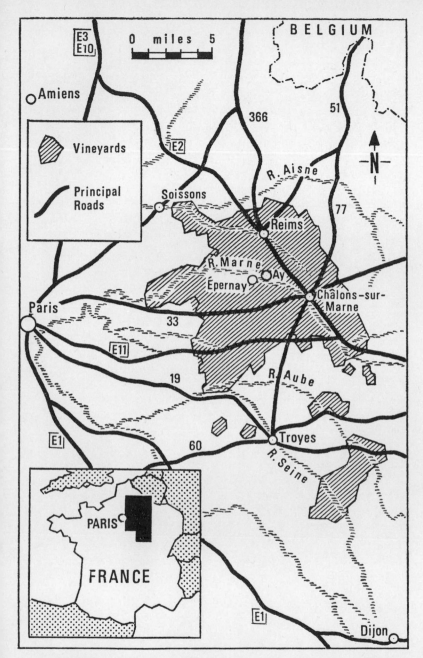

Outline of the Champagne vineyard. The limits of this are nowadays strictly controlled, but in the nineteenth century a much larger area was under vines and the resulting wine was not prevented from calling itself 'Champagne'.

Reims and Provins are famous for a special kind of pear, called the *rousselet*, which is so juicy and rich that it is quite impossible to send it away to market; the pears are a traditional gift offered by Reims to any visiting celebrity or monarch (the Kings of France were always crowned in the cathedral), and are known as *poires tapées*. Walnuts come from Saint Gilles and an apple called the *croquet des Ardennes* from that area. Strawberries and cherries are also plentiful.

Specialities and dishes

Pieds de porc à la Sainte Ménéhould Poached, grilled pigs' feet, from the Lorraine border.

Andouillettes de mouton A version of chitterlings but made with mutton. A Troyes speciality, as are the ordinary *andouillettes* or tripe sausages. They are rather rich. The *andouillette* is the only sausage that can claim to have saved a town, for during the religious wars of the sixteenth century the troops besieging Troyes happened to get into the part of the town where the *andouillettes* were made and, being hungry, they devoted so much time to feeding that the defenders were able to bring up reserves and drive out the invaders.

Cervelas de brochet A pike and potato sausage.

Pain à la reine A type of fish mousse, with pike a main ingredient.

Cailles sous la cendre Stuffed roasted quails, in vine leaves.

Gougère de l'Aube A small cheese *brioche* or puff.

Biscuits de Reims Small oblong macaroons, traditionally served with Champagne.

Massepains de Reims Reims marzipan. There is also *pain d'épices*, a sort of honeycake, from Reims.

When dishes are described as being cooked with Champagne, it is usually the still wine that is involved, though occasionally there will be a note that the *vin rouge* of Bouzy or Ambonnay, the red still wine, is used.

Cheeses

Brie The Province de la Brie is to the east of Paris, along the lower valley of the Marne, the chief town being Meaux, from which the best cheeses come. The descriptions *'fermier'* and *'laitier'* differentiate the farm-made from the creamery-made cheeses. Brie de Melun and Brie de Montereau are slightly thicker cheeses, Brie de Provins is smaller and thicker.

Brie is acknowledged the king of French cheeses and has been famous since the thirteenth century at least. The poet duke Charles d'Orléans sent presents of Brie to his friends, Henry IV said it was the best cheese he knew of, Condé celebrated the victory of Rocroi with red wine and Brie, Queen Maria Leczinska had Brie in her *bouchées à la reine*, Rabelais praised it and Saint Amant wrote a whole poem to it. Even the wretched Louis XVI asked for some red wine and Brie when he was captured at Varennes, and the cheese triumphed over the tables of Talleyrand and his colleagues of the Congress of Vienna, for one day the diplomats had a discussion as to which was the best cheese known to man and when Talleyrand presented them with a Brie, they unanimously elected it as supreme. Talleyrand never ate any other kind and cynics said that 'King Brie' was the only monarch to whom he had ever remained faithful. Large, thin and, at its best, unctuous without being actually runny, Brie is a cheese that combines richness with delicacy, and when good it is difficult to think that any cheese of this kind could be better.

Coulommiers or **Brie de Coulommiers** This is, as its name implies, a type of Brie and is slightly cheaper. *Macquelines* is a type of Coulommiers and a little also like Camembert. *Fromage à la pie* is a very fresh version of Coulommiers, *Riceys Cendré* another type.

Soumaintrain A strong cheese, rather similar to Munster, made in the Aube and Yonne regions.

Langres A cheese seldom encountered far away from its town, but rather like Livarot (see p. 278).

Chaource and **Ervy** These are both Coulommiers-like cheeses, mainly produced around Troyes. Chaource is the smaller kind, creamy and rich. *Boursault* is similar to Chaource.

Barberey or **Fromage de Troyes** Soft, Camembert-like cheese.

Boursin A lightly creamy fresh cheese, sometimes having herbs and garlic incorporated—it is then described as *'à l'ail et aux fines herbes'*.

Wines

The traveller driving down the main road through Reims may well wonder where the vineyards are. They can be picked out in the distance if you know where to look, but generally you do not see any vines. But the great chalky undulations of the 'champaign' give the quality to the fine wines, and the miles of cellars cut into the chalk are the perfect places for bringing the wine to maturity. Nowadays the majority of Champagne wines are white and sparkling, but the region has been under vines since at least Roman times and many kings have appreciated the still wines, including our own Charles II, in whose reign it became very smart in England, because of the visit of St Evremond, friend of the Marquis de Sillery, who had quantities sent over to him. The wines were even bottled in England, but later in the same century the cellarmaster at the Abbey of Hautvillers, Dom Pérignon, discovered that the charming vivacity of the light wines of Champagne could be preserved if they were put into a bottle stoppered with a cork. Prior to this, bottles had been more in the nature of carafes, and corks more like bungs. Dom Pérignon did not invent the sparkle that already existed in the wines, but he harnessed it within the bottle, and just as important, evolved the system of blending the wines so as to produce a product of quality.

Today, most Champagne is made from a mixture of black and white grapes, the Pinot noir and the Pinot chardonnay, although some Champagne houses produce a *blanc de blancs*, which is a wine made entirely from white grapes; (the term, used by itself, does not mean that the wine concerned is Champagne. It can be used of any white wine—still or sparkling—made entirely from white grapes); this is very light, delicate and, what some people would call a 'morning' Champagne, the perfect *apéritif*. There is also a *blanc de noirs*, but this is rarer; it is a wine made only from black grapes. In general terms, the white grapes give the wine its finesse and delicacy, the black grapes body and fragrance, so that the combination is ideal, both for vintage and non-vintage wines. Although there are plenty of small owners of vineyards in Champagne, these proprietors do not make their own wine as a rule, but sell it to the large houses, some of whom own vineyards as well, but who must also buy in enormous quantities to keep up both their stocks for current demand and the reserves from which their blends of non-vintage wines are made.

Each house has its own detailed way of making Champagne, but in general the procedure is as follows. The wine goes into bottle the spring after its vintage, when it has already been subjected to the most careful processes of selection and blending, according to the districts from which it comes and the grapes from which it is made. It is then bottled for the *prise de mousse*, or sparkle, which is a form of secondary fermentation, captured and scientifically controlled to take place in the bottle, where the carbon dioxide remains within the wine, instead of fermenting in a vat and giving off carbon dioxide into the air. The wine spends the rest of its life in bottle, at first with a temporary cork, held down with a metal clip called an *agrafe*. During this time any sediment in the wine is brought to where it can be removed by an ingenious procedure: the bottles are ranged in racks, called *pupitres*, with the neck pointing slightly down. Every day, a man called a *remueur* gives each bottle a shake and a slight turn (these men shake tens of thousands of bottles daily, up to 60,000 even), so that after several weeks the bottle is standing almost upside down, with any sediment having gradually slipped down onto its cork. This position is known as *sur les pointes*. The bottles can remain like this for years looking most strange, stacked upside down, resting on their corks in the cellars, and some wines of a fine vintage can live way beyond the seven to fifteen years that is the general lifespan of a good Champagne. The real ageing starts with the second corking that makes the wine ready to drink, after a process known as the *dégorgement*. This involves the cork being taken out with the accumulated sediment, a *dosage* of any sweetening put in, with wine to replace any that has been lost, and the second cork (composed of many sections and so large it is difficult to imagine it as ever going into the bottle) being put in and wired down. This used to be a delicate operation that was carried out by real sleight of hand, but which is now generally achieved by the necks of the bottles being frozen, so that the sediment comes out with the little lump of ice and the bottle can be recorked without danger of much of the wine being lost.

The dosage of sweetening varies according to the type of wine that is to be made: *brut* or *nature* implies very little or no dosage; *extra dry*, *très sec*, *extra sec* mean that a little sweetening has been put in, *dry* or *sec* will definitely be slightly sweet, *demi-sec* is a really sweet wine and *doux* (beloved of the Russian Court before the Revolution, when it was often combined with Chartreuse) too sweet for most people. The British have always liked a rather dry wine; indeed, some Champagne houses quarrelled bitterly with their British customers in the nineteenth century about making it so dry, and the head of at least one famous Champagne house refused point-blank to make a completely dry wine in his lifetime, but Britain has always, after France itself, been the biggest customer for Champagne, so that the dry drinkers prevailed. But there is a definite place for slightly sweet Champagnes, either at the end of a meal or perhaps as an *apéritif* when one is feeling a little tired and does not want a very crisp, dry wine, but rather something gentler, with a scrap of sugar for instant energy.

Each of the Champagne houses has an individual style of wine, and it is worth sampling as many as possible to see the shades of differences. There is a Champagne hierarchy of what are called the *grandes marques*, some of the houses that are both the most important and most famous for quality, but there are plenty of good Champagnes outside these.

The expression 'B.O.B.' stands for 'Buyer's own brand' and is the brand that a restaurant or wine merchant will have made up specially by a Champagne house to suit a particular clientele; the wine can be identified by a code number, in tiny figures, on the label, so that the Champagne authorities can refer to the source of supply. Although the great names of Champagne will be familiar to most tourists, it is worth their while trying some that may be unfamiliar when in the region, either because these are the product of small houses that do not make enough to export (there is one very famous and expensive one), or because they send their wines to markets outside Great Britain. Champagne is not cheap, even on its home ground, but it is a wine of great fascination and many people swear by its therapeutic qualities; Hilaire Belloc said, 'Champagne is not a wine but a drug . . . I pant for it when I am tired . . . I only drink Champagne to raise me from the dead—a thing I constantly need.' The carbonic acid gas in the wine makes it absorbed into the bloodstream faster than with a still wine, which is why Champagne makes a party go quickly, and why an invalid or convalescent can often take a little Champagne to stimulate the appetite.

Champagne rosé is simply Champagne in which the black grapes have been left for long enough at the time of the first fermentation to give their colour to the grape juice, or a careful blending of the red wine of the region to the white wine at the time of bottling. **Vin nature de la Champagne,** or, as it is sometimes (but incorrectly) called, *Champagne nature*, is the still white wine of the region. For various complicated reasons, this is hardly ever seen outside the district (it cannot be exported at the time of writing) and is therefore well worth trying, though it too is never cheap. A good still Champagne can be delicious and very fine (it happens to be something I am personally very fond of), but an indifferent one is rather like indifferent perry or even flat beer.

Bouzy rouge is the best-known red wine of the region, fresh and enjoyable, without any pretensions to being a great wine but it

CHAMPAGNE AND THE ARDENNES

can be a very pleasant one, especially if you are of those who do not always take kindly to an all white wine meal. **Cumières** is another red wine with an agreeable fragrance.

The terms *crémant* (not to be confused with the place Cramant in the region) and *perlant* are sometimes found and imply that the wine so described is not as fully sparkling as those produced by the *méthode Champenoise*. This is the means by which the finest sparkling wines are made anywhere, though they must say they are produced by this method and never imply that they are actually Champagne. As will have been appreciated, the degree of sparkle can be controlled, and the slightly sparkling wines are delightful.

Champagne should never be served in the flat *coupes* so often used, especially in Britain, both because these are mean in size and because their flatness makes the wine go flat quickly. Ideally, the bubbles in a fine Champagne should be tiny, swiftly and steadily rising and should continue to do so for some while, and they will both do this and appear more attractive if the wine is served in a tall glass. This may either be the isosceles triangle-shaped *flûte*, or an elongated tulip-shaped glass or goblet. Some very old Champagne glasses, either the *flûte* shape, or fairly deep saucers or tulips, have hollow stems, so that the wine goes right down into the foot of the glass and the bubbles rise from there. These are very charming, though abominable to clean. Champagne served as a *vin d'honneur* (mark of welcome to someone) or as a refreshment between times is usually accompanied by little biscuits.

Ratafia is a Champagne apéritif of grape juice and brandy, again seldom found outside its place of origin. Moët et Chandon make a good one. *Marc de Champagne* is the brandy distilled from the residue of grapes after the pressing and *fine de la Marne* another, as it were, Champagne brandy, distilled from the wine (see p. 76).

Things to see and do

The Champagne houses The three centres of Champagne are Reims, Épernay and Ay, and the great houses in each have arrangements for showing visitors through the *caves*. Some houses are only open in the high season, but the larger ones can receive visitors all the year round, and many have multi-lingual guides to escort them. Visitors should be advised to wear coats, as it is really cold deep underground and the visits usually last at least an hour. Any detailed information about them may be obtained from the *syndicat d'initiative* in Reims and Épernay, or from the C.I.V.C.

(Comité Interprofessionel du Vin de Champagne), 23 Rue Henry Martin, Épernay. The size of even quite a small Champagne cave has to be seen to be believed, and the largest, Moët et Chandon in Épernay, has over sixteen miles of underground galleries, while Pommery and Greno in Reims have at least eleven miles. The establishment of Mercier at Épernay even has small trains in which to take visitors around—something useful to remember if a party of visitors includes anyone unable to walk far. Car rallies are held in many cellars. Abel Hugo, Victor Hugo's son, warned visitors in the nineteenth century of the danger of visiting Champagne cellars without the protection of a wire mask against flying glass from exploding bottles, but nowadays bottles seldom break in this way.

The vineyards may be seen by following any of the routes du Champagne, which are: the *route bleue*, covering the Montagne de Reims and Ay; the *route rouge* follows the Marne from Épernay to Dormans via Hautvillers and Châtillon, and the *route verte* south of Épernay shows the Côte des Blancs, where the white grapes are chiefly grown.

The Abbey of Hautvillers, where Dom Pérignon worked, is not generally open to visitors, as it belongs to Moët et Chandon, but if application is made to this house, arrangements can usually be made to show seriously interested visitors the remains of the Abbey and the memorial to Dom Pérignon. The church, with Dom Pérignon's grave, is open from the road at any time.

Musée de Vin de Champagne at Épernay This shows the different stages of the making of the wine, with all the equipment, including old presses, bottles and glasses, and a model of the Abbey of Hautvillers.

Troyes *The Hôtel Dieu le Comte* contains an exceptionally fine medieval pharmacy, with jars, pestles and mortars and the complete equipment and setting for an apothecary of former times.

The Hôtel de Vauluisamt has a fine set out museum of furnishings and folklore of Troyes and the Champagne region.

The Church of St Urbain has a particularly beautiful statue of the Virgin and Child, with the Baby preoccupied by a large bunch of grapes.

Soissons *Abbey of Saint Jean des Vignes*, now a ruin. Visitors can see the refectory and sometimes the great cellar is also shown.

Reims As well as the sweets and biscuits that are specialities of the town, a great deal of Champagne-based mustard is made, and this is often sold in containers shaped like Champagne corks or bottles.

The Maison Vergeur contains a museum of old Reims through the ages. In *the Musée des Beaux Arts* the tapestries of the life of St Rémy show the saint blessing an empty cask, which became full of wine.

Bar-sur-Aube In the museum, two very fine drinking goblets, and in St Peter's Church, the Chapelle des Vignerons or St Paul's Chapel, in which the walls and roof are decorated with vine branches and pruning knives. Some of the tombstones in the church represent the trades of those buried, a butcher and a fishmonger among them.

Other things to note

On the last day of the vintage, the Fête du Cochelet celebrates the end of the harvest, with a garland presented to the head of the firm, and a feast, also called the cochelet. St Vincent is of course the patron of all vignerons, but at Reims St Jean is the patron of the cellar staff and those engaged in work connected with Champagne.

Cognac and the Surrounding Region

It is difficult to define this area, as considered for the purposes of this guide, but I have tried to cover the districts between the Loire region, Auvergne and the Massif Central and Périgord, and the Bordeaux country. Although the Atlantic coast is very popular with those who like informal holidays, especially if they sail, and the inland part of this area contains many treasures of art and architecture, it is not, as a district, often sufficiently spectacular to tempt those going to the south to break their journey. But the food can be very good and it is said, probably with great justification, that the two French words known throughout the world are the names of Paris and Cognac. The names of some regions within the provinces which may not be familiar to visitors and which are sometimes applied to dishes, are: the Angoumois, Aunis and Saintonge, which together form *'les Charentes'*; then there is the province of the Vendée, south of the Loire on the coast, part of Poitou (with the region of Gatine) further to the east, and the Limousin and its northern part, the Marche, south of the Loire and around Limoges. The Creuse is in the Marche, the Corrèze in the Bas Limousin and the Deux Sèvres roughly in the region bordered by Niort, Poitiers, Parthenay and Fontenay-le-Comte. The Vienne (a confusing name to find on a menu if one has been accustomed to think of schnitzels and Austrian food) and the Haute Vienne are the regions approximately around Poitiers and Limoges.

Food in general

The cooking medium is butter, for which the Cognac region is noted, and although plenty of onions and shallots appear in dishes, the use of garlic is sparing. Various types of casseroles are typical of the cooking in this region. Curnonsky said that it abounded in true country cookery. The *coup du milieu* is a Charentais custom still followed at country feasts: a glass of Cognac is served as a digestive in the middle of the meal. The salty marshes of Poitou, now mostly drained, and the coastal pastures produce the fine *pré salé* lamb, also small game birds, and there is more game inland in the forests, and plenty of freshwater fish of all kinds, including eels, in the streams. Limousin beef is highly esteemed and also the pork. On the coast there is a vast quantity of first-rate fish; oysters, lobsters, mussels, a clam-like shellfish, called *lavignon*, sardines, tunny, shrimps, plaice and skate among the range. The big snails that feed on the vines are known here as *cagouilles*—there is a stew of them called a *lumas* made in the Deux Sèvres region—and the inhabitants of the Charente are sometimes scornfully referred to as '*cagouillards*' on account of their supposed sluggishness. The Charentais melons, of course, are very famous, and there are plenty of *cèpes* in this region; cabbage is the great vegetable of the Vendée and white beans, called *mojettes* are found in many districts. There is a lot of general market gardening too.

There are many sweet biscuits, such as the *macarons* of Thouars and Dorat, the meringues of Uzerches; *massepain* (marzipan) and a type of pancake called a *flognard* are general regional specialities. Niort is famous for angelica. *Tertous*, which are flattish cakes made with buckwheat flour, and *tourteaux fromagers*, open tarts filled with cream cheese, are other delights. Chocolates called *marguerites* and *duchesses* are specialities of Angoulême and *nougatines* of Poitiers and Nevers.

Tobacco is also cultivated, mostly in small family plots, and the tourist may often see huge leaves of it hanging up to dry outside a house.

Specialities and dishes

Andouilles limousines   Tripe sausages, usually served grilled.
Farcidure de pommes de terre   A type of potato and vegetable dumpling, usually served with the *andouilles*.
Farcidure   This is a type of dumpling, usually a cabbage leaf stuffed with sorrel, beets and buckwheat flour, sometimes with bacon added. It may be put in soup or served as an accompaniment to meat. Occasionally it is called *poule sans os*, but this is a very colloquial name for it.
Broccana   Veal and pork meat, finely ground and served in a pasty.
La chaudrée   This is a soup made of tiny sea fish. It is something of a La Rochelle speciality. The name, which occurs in other parts of France as well, refers to the archaic word for cauldron, in

which the stew is cooked. Lovers of chaudrée are said to stipulate that it should be made in a cauldron hung over a fire of vine shoots (*sarments*), ideally from vines of the islands off the coast, which have acquired a slight flavour of seaweed (*varech*).

La mouclade A stew of mussels, made with either cream or white wine and shallots.

Bréjauda A soup made with bacon and cabbage.

Lièvre en chabessard, or en cabessal, or chabessal The *cabessal* or *chabessard* is the round pan which country women put on their heads when they are going to carry a load. The dish gets its name because the hare, stuffed with spices and pork, ham and veal, with shallots and garlic, then cooked in wine and blood, is tied into a round shape, to fit the round dish in which it is traditionally served.

Lièvre à la royale This is cited as a regional dish by many authorities, although Miss Elizabeth David quotes *Le Temps* of 29 November 1898 as giving an article by a M. Couteaux, who invented the recipe, having spent a week hunting the special type of hare he required 'with red fur, killed if possible in mountainous country, of fine French descent (characterised by the light nervous elegance of head and limbs)'. M. Couteaux' recipe takes from midday until seven in the evening to prepare and cook. Whoever actually invented the dish it is probably impossible to say, but it is very rich, involving the hare being stuffed with *foie gras*, shallots, its liver and lights, parsley and truffles and several bottles of wine and glasses of brandy. Not the sort of thing to undertake in the majority of homes, so definitely a dish to sample if it is featured, or can be ordered when one is on holiday.

À la limousine Any dish described in this way is likely to be accompanied by cabbage with chestnuts.

Clafoutis Black cherry custard tarts.

Pâté de fromage A sweet ewe milk cheese tart.

Cheeses

Aunis A ewe milk cheese, triangular in shape, made in the Charente-Maritime.

Petit pot de Poitiers A small fresh goat cheese.

Jonchée A fresh cheese, either cow milk or goat milk, so called because it is put to set in a rush container.

Mothe Saint Héray This is rather like a small Camembert, often dried between plane leaves.

Tomme de Brach A ewe milk cheese made in the Corrèze.

Ruffec A thick cylindrical cow milk cheese.

Trois cornes A cow milk cheese with, as its name implies, three 'horns'.

Caillebotte Associated specially with Parthenay, but found elsewhere in the Cognac area, this is rather like a cheesy form of yoghourt.

La brique, or **Chevrotin cabion** Mixed cow and goat milk cheese, brick shaped, but smaller than a real brick.

Bleu de Laqueuille From the edge of the Auvergne, this blue cheese, made from cow milk, is round and about 4–5 inches thick. If allowed to mature for a length of time, it becomes reddish-orange on the outside, and eventually quite white, dotted with reddish streaks. It was evolved about 1850 by Antoine Roussel, to whom there is a statue at Laqueuille.

Saint Loup A cylindrical goat cheese. **Sauzé** is another of the same type.

Chef Boutonne A square or round goat cheese.

Drinks

There are local wines throughout this region, but most of them are only worth trying as pleasant holiday drinks. The *rosé* of Verneuil is well spoken of, and so are the vins gris of the Vienne area.

Pineau des Charentes is the regional *apéritif*. It is grape juice and Cognac and the only *apéritif* to have an *Appellation Contrôlée*. There are several establishments producing pineau and it is a drink that should appeal to many visitors, as it is not very dry, yet has a pleasant toughness and body to it on account of the Cognac.

Cognac, the supreme brandy, is made in a strictly limited area of the region; this area is sub-divided (in ascending order of quality) into *bois communs, bois ordinaires, bons bois, fins bois, borderies, petite champagne* and *grande champagne*. These names refer to the districts from which the brandies come and, as will be noted, are vaguely descriptive of the type of countryside. Only spirit distilled in a pot still according to the regulations in the actual Cognac area has a right to the name of Cognac, although brandy can be, and often is, made in many other wine-growing regions. 'Brandywine' or *brantwijn*—literally 'burnt wine'—is said to have been first made in Cognac at about the beginning of the seventeenth century, when the trade with the Low Countries in wine had suffered a severe setback and the Cognac wine makers had a glut on their hands. The spirit, distilled, was not only very acceptable but required far fewer vessels of transport.

The wine from which Cognac is made would not be enjoyed by the average wine drinker; it is thin and harsh. Some of the vineyards are owned by various great Cognac houses, but many are the property of small-scale peasant owners, from whom the big establishments buy the wine for distilling. This process is carried out twice, the first liquid to be produced being known as '*brouillis*'; this is then distilled again in what is known as the '*bonne chauffe*' and the result (minus, each time, the 'heads and tails' of the distilled product, which are impure) is Cognac. Then the Cognac goes into wood—ideally, into casks made of Limousin oak, which are unrivalled for producing fine brandy, but which are becoming both scarce and expensive—and there it matures. During this time a considerable amount evaporates, and the Cognac makers say ruefully that the sun is their best customer. A black deposit forms on the roofs of warehouses where the Cognac is kept during this time, so that one can usually see, from the outside, where it is. Cognac matures only in wood—though not indefinitely—and when the time comes for the brandy to be bottled it will, from then on, cease to improve or change. Visitors to Cognac may see some of the oldest bottled brandies in *tierçons*, which are containers of 120 gallons, smaller than an ordinary cask. The word may be translated as 'puncheon'. The brandy is usually drawn for testing from the cask by means of a device resembling a test tube suspended from a wire and called *une preuve* instead of the *velenche*, used in other wine regions.

Today all brandy from Cognac is non-vintage, though it may be graded according to its quality; it is important that both the Cognac for brandy and water, or the liqueur brandy of the great houses should maintain its quality always, which is why the constant blending is necessary. If, however, while you are in the region you visit a Cognac house or are entertained by friends, you may get a chance to taste a real vintage Cognac, which will not have been blended. It will not be a century old, because, after a certain point, brandy begins to decline and deteriorate, but it may be thirty or forty years old. According to French law a vintage Cognac cannot now be labelled as such, therefore, although there will be a high proportion of old brandy in a fine and expensive blend, this is probably the only chance the ordinary person may get of tasting a vintage Cognac—unless one is found in the reserves of a British wine merchant. The curious thing is that Cognac described as 'old London landed', which means that it will have spent the period of its maturation in cask in a London bonded warehouse, without ever being 'refreshed' by being topped up and in the damp, even wet atmosphere of our dock cellars, will be quite different from exactly the same Cognac that has matured in the region of its making. Cognacs of this kind are rare, and will become rarer, and are very dear and yet, for the connoisseur, they are great treats; the thing to look at, if you are ever offered such a Cognac, is for evidence on the label as to when it was bottled; if it was only ten years old when it went into its bottle, even if this was fifty years ago, it will still only be a ten year old Cognac. Elaborately be-cobwebbed bottles can be a great disappointment when opened.

In case the visitor encounters a wine waiter too accustomed to playing up to customers who do not know anything about Cognac (or any other good brandy), it is worth stating firmly that the enormous balloon glasses sometimes used are detested by the real brandy lovers. A brandy glass should be like an ample wine glass, but never so large that it cannot be cupped partially and comfortably in the hand so that the spirit can be gently warmed by this contact. If a brandy glass is heated by artificial means, the beautiful fragrance of a liqueur brandy will be thrown off too soon for the drinker to enjoy it, a nasty burnt smell will result and possibly even a burnt hand.

The word *fine* is sometimes used to signify brandy, as in the expression *fine maison*, or *une fine*, but although a waiter may understand either of these, they are not, strictly, legal in France as indicating Cognac brandy. 'Fine' is merely the brandy distilled from wine (see p. 76).

Things to see and do

Angoulême A collection of Charentais china is in the Musée Municipal. The Chapelle des Cordeliers was the church of the monastery of Jean Thevet, who, in 1556, before the more famous Nicot, brought to France from Brazil what he called *l'herbe angousmoisine*, which was in fact the tobacco plant.

Aubusson The Maison du Vieux Tapissier contains the reconstruction of the interior of an old house with local historical exhibits.

Bassac At the Abbaye de Bassac, 6 kilometres east of Jarnac, the abbey kitchen is open to visitors. It dates from the seventeenth century, although the establishment was founded in the eleventh century.

Celles-sur-Belle   The seventeenth-century kitchen and refectory of the abbey church—7 kilometres north-west of Melle—are open to visitors.

Cognac   There are some exhibits connected with folklore in the Musée. The principal brandy houses are open to visitors, the largest being Martell and Hennessy; that of Otard is installed in the Château de Cognac. As in the other wine towns, the ideal plan is to arrange to see one large and one smallish establishment if possible.

Dissay   At the Château de Vayres, 9 kilometres outside Dissay, there is an interesting seventeenth-century dovecote for 2,620 birds.

Fontenay-le-Comte   The ground floor of the Musée Vendéen contains exhibits to do with the folklore of the region.

Guéret   The Musée Municipal contains exhibits covering folklore and china.

Maillezais   The salt store, cellars, refectory and octagonal kitchen of the fourteenth-century monastery are open to visitors.

Montmorillon   There is a Romanesque kitchen attached to the Church of Saint Laurent.

Nieul-sur-l'Autize   In the cloisters of the abbey of this village, about 10 kilometres south-east of Fontenay-le-Comte, may be seen the refectory and cellars, dating from about the seventeenth century.

Noirmoutier-en-l'Île   In the small museum in the Château, visitors can see exhibits connected with local history and a collection of Jersey pottery.

Poitiers   The Grande Salle, or waiting room, in the Palais de Justice, although nothing directly to do with eating and drinking, is nevertheless one of the most remarkable and beautiful rooms built for the purpose of giving parties, for it was originally the place where the Courts of Love, presided over by Eleanor of Aquitaine and her daughter, were held. The great fireplaces, on the dais, were a later addition, but give a clear impression of what the great hall of a castle or seat of government was like in the Middle Ages.

Pons   The Hospice des Pèlerins, a pilgrim shelter, is on the Bordeaux road. The stone seats, on which pilgrims might rest, some of their graffiti on the walls, and the doorway to the sick-room may still be seen.

Rochecorbon   In the Château visitors may see a room furnished in Saintonge style, and the kitchen, dating from the seventeenth century, with a spit installed.

La Rochelle In the Musée Lafaille, the Cabinet Lafaille, just as it was in the eighteenth century, is on view, with an exceptionally fine collection of shells. In the Musée d'Orbigny there is an important collection of china, together with a pharmacy from the military hospital, with many local exhibits.

Sablonçeaux The gothic cellars of the abbey may be seen.

Saint Martin de Ré The Musée Cognacq, in the Ancien Hôtel des Cadets de la Marine, contains local china and utensils.

Saint Michel en l'Herm The huge banks of oysters (*buttes huîtrières*) may be seen. It is not known whether they were formed naturally or were due to some shipwreck or other accident.

Saint-Vincent-sur-Jard Clemenceau's house has been preserved as a museum, and visitors may see the kitchen-dining-room, which contains a copper watering-can that belonged to Marie Antoinette.

Saintes In the Musée Mestreau there is the reconstruction of a Charentais room and a fine collection of regional china, including Palissy plates.

Limoges In the Musée Adrien Dubouché the china collection is one of the finest in France and shows the evolution of all kinds of china ware from the earliest times. In the Musée Municipal, in the former Archbishop's Palace, there is a fine collection of enamels and some regional exhibits. Visitors can see round a porcelain factory and an enamelling establishment, many of which are open all the time. The Rue de la Boucherie is famous for the seventeenth-century stalls and shops of the butchers, whose church, that of St Aurélien, is also in this street.

Jarnac This is smaller than Cognac, but there are several important brandy establishments in the town. The house of Hine may only be seen if application is made in advance, but it is of particular interest to British visitors, as the house was founded by an Englishman who came out as a student at the beginning of the nineteenth century and eventually married his master's daughter and took over the firm.

The Dordogne, Lot, Quercy and the Limousin

The valleys of the Rivers Dordogne and Lot have recently become very popular with those holiday-makers who want quiet, beautiful countryside, delicious food and interesting things to see. It is not a region for people who want large hotels, night life and sophistication, but it is a part of France where, as someone has said, one finds every charm of country life, plus a wonderful climate. In the spring the flowers in the road verges are like garden borders, the castles are romantic in a way that the smart 'country house' châteaux of the Loire never seem to be—and the food is superb. The majority of the hotels are small and comfortably 'family' in style, and I can, in fact, more easily recall the few establishments where I have had an indifferent meal rather than all those in which even the most inexpensive lunch has been a delight. This is an area of country cooking, practised by those who are happy in their smiling surroundings, and just that bit better in consequence (it has been said with some truth that the way to cook well is to make one of the ingredients love), and enhanced by two great natural riches—truffles, 'the black diamonds' of Périgord, and *foie gras*.

The area dealt with in this region includes part of the Limousin in the north, Périgord in the centre, Quercy, between the Rivers Dordogne and Lot, the Agenais (after Agen, the plum town) to the south-west and the Rouergue to the south-west. My excuse for making this extension of the region is that the traveller has got to get there—presumably from the north—and that many people will also wish to come through the district from the south or from Spain.

Food in general

The description '*Périgourdine*' applied to a dish usually means that it contains truffles—and possibly *foie gras* as well. The Périgord truffle is black and, although attempts are made to increase production by encouraging it to form, it still grows, as it were, wild, often near or beneath oak trees, known as *chênes truffiers*. Pigs, usually females, are trained to sniff out the truffles and root them up when the person in charge of this animal (which is known as a *chercheuse*) grabs the precious object before the pig can eat it. Sometimes dogs are used, as in Alsace (see p. 155), but the traditional *chercheuse* is a young sow. The geese, whose fat supplies the chief cooking medium, are a special kind that can be made very fat for *foie gras*; they are seldom served as roast goose, simply because they are too big and with too fat a flesh. The merits of Périgord *foie gras* as against that of Strasbourg are debated by gastronomic pundits; that of Périgord is sometimes said to be more unctuous, but I have never had the chance to make a direct comparison.

Walnuts are produced in huge quantities, the two chief types being the Corne and the Grandjean; this last grows chiefly around Sarlat and, as well as being good to eat fresh, it yields a delicious oil (*huile de noix*). If you see this marked on a menu as being available for a dressing to a salad, at least try it, even though it is usually more expensive than ordinary oil. The flavour is one that I find exceptionally delicious whether served neat or as a cooking medium—but as some people are thought not to like it restaurateurs sometimes hesitate to offer walnut oil to foreign tourists. There are a variety of vegetables, many of which go into the thick soups typical of the area, and which include *cèpes*, asparagus and salsify, and haricot beans locally called *mounzettas*, and there is an abundance of fruit; in addition to the plums previously mentioned, there are cherries, greengages, peaches, pears and strawberries. The markets (*halles*) seen at Caylus, Auvillar, Martel and Villeréal testify to the established traditions for plenty of good local produce. Table grapes, the *chasselas doré*, are especially prized and there is a fair lasting a week, the Semaine du Chasselas, each September. The streams yield crayfish, salmon, carp and *barbeau* (barbel). The woods—the whole region is much wooded—provide game, and hare and rabbit become more than country makeshifts when served with truffles. Although goose is seldom served roast, it is often presented in the very rich *confit d'oie*, in which it is cooked and preserved in its own fat and juices; a little of this confit goes a long way, and the same may be said of *confit de canard*, *confit de dinde* and *confit de porc*. *Confit d'oie à la sarladaise* also involves potatoes—a lot of potatoes are eaten in this district, presumably necessary as blotting paper for some of the richness—with truffles lightly fried in goose fat. Chicken is a frequent dish also often served with truffles, and the *boudin blanc*, white tripe sausage, also contains them. Guinea fowl (*pintade*) is

229

featured on menus and may well be truffle-packed. Sucking pig (*cochon de lait*) will almost certainly include truffles in the stuffing, so will partridges and quails and sometimes the dish of vegetables that accompanies meat will contain chopped truffles, cooked with potatoes, onions and tomatoes and anointed with goose dripping.

Sweet things, in addition to the usual items, tends to be of the sweet bun or cake type. The *fougasse* is a big, light, rich bun, *jacques* are apple pancakes and *pascades* pancakes from the Rouergue that may be made with walnut oil. *Milliasses* are cakes of flaky pastry made with corn meal, and *mique* a type of dumpling of corn meal and wheat flour, served sometimes with a rich stew, as well as being a cake when made with sugar. Candied walnuts and sweets made of chestnut flour—there are many chestnut trees as well as oaks and chestnut flour is sometimes referred to as *pain des paysans* —are two other regional specialities.

Specialities and dishes

Truffles Truffles can appear in salads, stuffings and in scrambled eggs, when they are referred to on menus as *brouillade Périgourdine*. But the most famous presentation is when they are served whole, lightly seasoned and sprinkled with brandy and then wrapped in a layer of salt pork, or dough, and cooked *sous la cendre* (in the ashes of the fire, rather like potatoes). This dish may be elaborated by having *foie gras* put in with the truffle. It is always expensive, very rich, but one of the great regional dishes, so worth trying even if you have to share a truffle between two or more people.

Tourte de truffes A type of tart of truffles and *foie gras*, served hot.

Truffes en pâté Truffles enveloped in *foie gras* and baked in a crust, a slightly smaller scale and lighter version of the sous la cendre dish.

Cou farci Goose neck, stuffed with pork, truffles and *foie gras*.

Pommes sarladaise A potato pie of potatoes and truffles baked together.

Crispés de Montignac Small egg croquettes, with tomato sauce.

Enchaud Périgourdin Roast rolled fillet of pork.

Anguilles au verjus Eels grilled and sprinkled with the juice of unripe grapes.

Tripou Rouergat Lamb's tripe, baked in a caul.

Sabronade A soup made with pork, ham, beans and other vegetables and so thick that it is really more of a stew. Typical of the very substantial soups that characterise country fare for working people.

Purée au marrons A chestnut *purée* combined with herbs and potatoes and possibly other vegetables, and served on a *croûton*.

Gougeas de Quercy Small baked pumpkin puddings.

Tourteaux Maize flour pancakes.

Friands de Bergerac Small potato cakes, sweetened.

Cheeses

Rocamadour A small goat cheese.

Cabecou A small, flat goat cheese, made in the Lot Valley.

Bleu de Quercy A cow milk cheese with blue veining, resembling the Bleu d'Aveyron (see p. 252).

Fromage de la Trappe d'Échourgnac A fresh cow milk cheese.

Petits Fromages de Thiviers, Cujassou and **Lagniole** are all small goat cheeses.

Roquefort, from the Rouergue is the cheese served when something extra-special is required, even though it is a neighbour rather than a local cheese (see p. 252).

Drinks

The Bergerac region, touching that of Bordeaux, produces a variety of wines, of which the sweetish white Monbazillac can be very good to drink as a between times wine or *apéritif*, as well as at the end of a meal. There are also the white wines of Montravel, light and dry, Rosette, which in spite of its name is also a white wine, and Pécharment, which is down in all the reference books as producing pleasant red wine, though I have several times enjoyed the white as well. The other Bergerac wines are dry white and red. The Côte de Duras also makes light wines, mostly white. All of these are definitely in the 'holiday' wine category, often delightful to drink in the region, but only a very few of them— Château de Panisseau being a marked exception—really having much character when they are exported. The Gaillac wines, however, can be very pleasing; they are all white—as far as I know —and may be dry, medium dry or sweet. The crisp quality of all these dry white wines is excellent for balancing the richness of a regional meal.

A most extraordinary wine, however, is made in the region of Cahors. It used to be known as black wine, because of being so dark red in colour, and it enjoyed fame for many centuries—at worst, being mixed with the Bordeaux wines in a bad year in the Gironde, at best being enthusiastically praised by a variety of visitors, including Rabelais (though one tends to fear that he enjoyed almost anything as long as it was drinkable) and Arthur Young. It was a vigneron of Cahors who was sent for by François I to found the royal vineyard at Fontainebleau. The black wine was remarkable for lasting many years in cask and was supposed to have great therapeutic qualities, but the phylloxera hit the Cahors vineyards hard and today only a small proportion of the formerly renowned wine is made in the traditional way. If, however, you find a bottle that bears the name of a proprietor still making wine as—it is said—it has been made for about a thousand years, the wine will surprise you. It is far more than a holiday wine; without having infinite subtlety, such as is found in the great clarets, Cahors has a wonderful warming appeal, a comforting quality and an amazingly tonic effect. The vines, of the Malbec variety, may go on yielding for up to 100 years, and the wine may stay in its cask for—in certain fine vintages—forty or fifty years. It never seems to get tired or weakened by this process. Of course, this type of Cahors is not a commercial wine and only a small quantity is produced—but it is well worth while going on trying to find a bottle that, by its very quality and not necessarily the fancy label or name, will assure you that it is 'the real thing'. Cahors was only a V.D.Q.S. wine, but, as a dedicated proprietor said, 'We prefer to be the first of the V.D.Q.S. for the present, rather than just among the lower ranks of the A.C.' In 1971, however, red Cahors got its A.O.C. Some white wine is also made in the region, but although Warner Allen praised this some years ago, I have not yet found one of special quality.

The region's walnuts are used in producing various types of nut liqueur. *Eau de noix* is what may be described as a nut brandy, *crème de noix* a sweet liqueur.

Things to see and do

Agen This is the great plum and prunes town and is surrounded by fruit trees. The Musée contains some fine examples of Palissy ware and other china.

Autoire The Manoir d'Autoire is a small house, furnished with eighteenth- and nineteenth-century furniture and furnishings, worth seeing by anyone who has only been able to see huge and splendid châteaux or reconstructions of peasant dwellings.

Azay-le-Ferron The Château has several good collections of china and a fine dining-room.

Bergerac The Musée du Tabac, in the Hôtel de Ville, is the only one of its kind in France and shows in detail the history and economic significance of tobacco. In an adjacent room there is a regional museum.

Brantôme The Abbaye de Brantôme was founded by Charlemagne, but has been considerably rebuilt and restored since the eighth century. Visitors may see the refectory, the bakehouses and cellar of the foundation.

Brive-la-Gaillarde In the Musée Ernest Rupin there is a section devoted to the folklore and industry of the region.

Cahors The Musée Municipal contains rooms devoted to the history and famous personalities of Cahors.

Issoudun In the Hôpital of the Hôtel Dieu there is a fine collection of seventeenth-century Nevers jars.

Lanquais Visitors to the Château see the fine dining-room and old kitchen.

Meillant The large dining-room in the Château is particularly worth seeing.

Moissac In the Musée Moissagais there are collections of regional china and furniture and the reconstruction of a Bas Quercy kitchen in the nineteenth century.

Noirlac Visitors to the Abbaye de Noirlac may see the twelfth-century refectory and cellar.

Toulouse The Musée Saint Raymond contains collections of china, bronze ware, clocks and other applied arts. The Musée Paul Dupuy contains examples of Languedoc popular art and there is a reconstruction of the pharmacy in the Jesuit College.

Villefranche-de-Rouergue In the Chartreuse Saint Sauveur, the huge refectory, formerly the great chamber of the hospital may be seen.

Biron In the Château, dating from the sixteenth century, the enormous kitchen, said to be the largest castle kitchen in France, may be seen.

Montaigne The Château is a nineteenth-century reconstruction of former buildings made after a fire, but Montaigne's own tower, with his study and bedroom, were preserved and are well worth seeing. The great essayist was interested in food as in everything else; he preferred his baker to make his bread without salt, he did not much like salads or fruit, except for melons, but was greedy about fish. He invariably dirtied his table napkin and would have liked to have had a fresh one with each course of the meal and although he thought that 'the exercise of shouting and arguing before a meal' was probably good for the digestion, afterwards he liked to rest 'and to hear other folk talk, provided I have nothing to do with it'. Visitors are usually admitted to Montaigne's apartments, but it is wise to apply in advance.

Castelnau This feudal castle used to pay rent in the form of a new laid egg. In the twelfth century the lord of Castelnau fought fiercely against his immediate overlord of Turenne. King Louis VIII, as arbiter, gave judgment in favour of Turenne but imposed a purely symbolic tribute—the fresh egg. Annually, four oxen bore this in state to Turenne.

Franche Comté and the Jura

Some writers describe Franche Comté as the lowlands of the Jura, but even the rocky peaks that rise above the numerous winding streams seem quite high; the Jura in general is a most varied and unspoiled mountainous region. The forests are very beautiful, that of Joux especially. The district is ideal for a quiet holiday, the food good, not elaborate, and the wines and cheese most interesting. Franche Comté belonged to the Duchy of Burgundy, then to the Empire, was briefly Spanish (1556–1598), and then again was the property of Austria, only becoming permanently French after numerous campaigns and prodigies of resistance in 1674. There are a few dishes and one wine that may be due to Spanish influence and the 'Free Country' also claims to have introduced the delights of grilled sweetcorn to the United States, by means of Comtois settlers two and a half centuries ago. The numerous salt deposits made the region of great importance in the days before salt became cheap and plentiful.

Food in general

The high pastures are rich, providing both excellent dairy products and good meat. Pork products of all kinds are served, as in many other mountainous regions, ranging from the *cochonnailles* (assorted pork) of an *hors d'œuvre*, *jambon droz*, a type of specially cured and smoked ham, and *Jésu de Morteau*, which is a large smoked sausage, flavoured with aniseed. *Brési* is smoked beef, also sometimes added to a stew. Besançon is known for *langues fourrées* (stuffed tongues). Sometimes rather unusual soups of frogs, or cherries (it is a great cherry district) are found, and there is a great range of different types of mushroom which accompany fish and meat dishes: *cèpes*, *mousserons*, *oronges*, *morilles*, *bolets*, *craterelles*, *lépiotes*, *russules*, *chanterelles* and *jaunottes*. The streams and rivers provide an abundance of fish—it is a very popular fishing area—including, as might be expected, trout, but also pike (*brochet*), carp and salmon. Nantua, on the edge of the lake of the same name, is credited with the invention of the delicious sauce that often accompanies fish dishes, and *gratin de queues d'écrevisses* (gratin of crayfish tails). In Jura cooking, butter—usually good in the mountains—is the cooking medium and salads may be dressed with *huile de noix* (walnut oil) which gives a most delicious flavour. Kid (*chevreau*), squirrel (*écureuil*) and many other game birds appear on menus, but although books mention the possibility of bear being served, I have never seen it and should imagine that, as in the Pyrenees, it is now an archaism. Cheese is an ingredient in many recipes, and there is a local fondue.

The sweet dishes are numerous and many appear to have originated in the religious houses in which the area is rich. Two of these, Baume-les-Dames and Baume-les-Messieurs, were so exclusively for the very aristocratic that they acquired their suffixes '*dames*' and '*messieurs*'. A minimum number of quarterings was essential before one could even be considered for admittance, royalty and nobility using the establishments rather like luxury hotels. *Craquelins des Chanoinesses de Beaume-les-Dames*, *gaufres* (wafers rather like waffles), and *pets de nonne* (a little doughnut, like a fritter) from the same establishment, *pain d'œuf au caramel* (which may be described roughly as a superlative crème caramel) from the Abbey of Château Chalon, are some of the sweets that may have been invented to please the noble ladies in retirement. *Galette de goumeau* is an open tart filled with a cream and egg mixture, *flan au fromage* a short crust case with cheese and eggs, rather like a *quiche*, *unchères* small tarts flavoured with lemon and vanilla, *sèches* small biscuity cakes, and *roncin aux cerises*, a Montbéliard speciality, is a moulded baked pudding, composed of eggs, crumbs soaked in milk, sugar and cherries. Various *beignets* (fritters) are found, including a type that contain acacia flowers, quince and apple jelly and different sorts of jams and biscuits.

The Jura is also famous for making pipes, especially at St Claude, where an important industry was established by the local craftsmen, adept, like many in the mountains, at carving, in the eighteenth century. It was in 1854 that a Corsican asked a man of St Claude, Daniel David, to make pipes with the briar that he could provide, and the St Claude briars enjoyed world fame as the result, holding a monopoly of the production until 1885. Even to-day St Claude is still known for briar pipes and many other accessories for smokers.

Specialities and dishes

Les Gaudes This is the most celebrated local dish, but one is unlikely to find it in a smart restaurant, as it is really a type of corn-meal porridge, or very thick soup.

Croustade or **croûte Comtois** or **Jurassienne** Toasted cheese, onion and chopped bacon.

La craiche The melted butter which rises from *les gaudes*, which is often served on toast.

Féchum or **féchun** Cabbage stuffed with bacon and vegetables and, sometimes, eggs, served by itself or with boiled beef. The name recalls the Provençal '*fassum*'. It is a speciality of Mont-béliard.

Les rôts Grilled maize.

La panade A type of bread broth.

Matefaim A thick pancake, supposed to be originally Spanish.

La flamusse A dough made with maize.

La meurette This is a dish that is also found frequently in Burgundy, and is a stew of freshwater fish. What distinguishes it from the *pouchouse* (see p. 196) is that red instead of white wine is used in the *meurette*.

Quenelles de brochet These, which are found in Burgundy, the Lyonnais, and many other parts of France, are so often served with a *Sauce Nantua* that I have included them here. They are, essentially, fishballs (made with pounded pike flesh) and should be very light and delicate. They are regarded as one of the great tests of a chef by some authorities and good ones can certainly be delicious. It is only fair to say, however, that, as with many other masterpieces of *haute cuisine*, they are not the sort of dish that one would order day after day, and though they are light the sauce is —or should be—rich.

Cheeses

This is a famous cheese region and some of the cheeses are produced in co-operatives which have the rather confusing name of '*fruitières*'. This is because many farmers only possess a few cows and vast quantities of milk are required for the big cheeses— 600 litres for a 50 kg Gruyère, for example. The *fruitières* have existed at least since the thirteenth century. Tourists are often allowed to visit the cheese-making chalets and inquiries about this should be made on the spot. There are two nationally famous

237

institutions where cheese making is taught and studied, at Mamirolle and Poligny. They are not generally open to visitors, for reasons of hygiene, but anyone specially interested in cheese production can be shown round if previous application is made.

Comté The great cheese of the region, this looks almost exactly like a wheel of Swiss Gruyère, but has straight sides. It is made from cow milk, and has very few small eyes or none at all. It is excellent for cooking as well as eating raw.

Morbier A cow milk cheese, round, and about the size of a Camembert. It is made in two moulds and when the two pieces of cheese are stuck together, their edges are rubbed with charcoal, which makes a black line in the cheese, visible when it is cut through. It is made up in the mountains and gets its name from the Morbier Fair, at which it was originally sold, when the animals were brought down from the high pastures.

Gex A large cow milk cheese made in the high pastures. It is a *fromage persillé* (see p. 53) and is also called *Bleu du Haut Jura*.

Septmoncel Made in the mountains near St Claude, and similar to Gex, except that it is made from a mixture of cow and goat milk.

Saint Claude A small goat cheese, which may be served fresh or matured.

Vacherin Not to be confused with the meringue and cream sweet, this is a soft milk cheese which, in the Jura, may be wrapped in pine or cherry bark.

Croix d'Or A small goat milk cheese.

Mamirolle A cow milk cheese rather like a St Paulin, but oblong.

Cancaillotte A very strong cheese—it is sometimes called *fromage fort* or *fromagère*—which looks deceptively like a mild cheese spread. It is a cow milk cheese, made from skimmed milk, which is then partially cooked with butter, seasoning and wine or brandy. It is presented in little tins or cartons. Sometimes beaten eggs are added to the cheese.

Drinks

As in Alsace, many fruit brandies are made, especially kirsch—the cherry trees in the river valleys are spectacular when in blossom. *Mirabelle* (brandy from small plums), *prunelle* (sloe brandy), and *gentiane* (the bitter herby digestive, of which Suze is the best-known branded make) are all widely made and there is even a liqueur made from the buds of fir trees, rather strongly piney. *Macvin* or *Macquevin* is a curious concoction not usually found outside the cellar of a family native to the region; it is white wine, boiled up with brandy, spices and sugar and bottled. It is strong, warming and pleasantly aromatic. *Hypocras* is a spiced red wine mixture, often served at country christenings.

The wines of the Jura are said to have won fame as far back as Roman times. Certainly the vineyards flourished under the supervision of the numerous religious establishments and that vaunted connoisseur, Henry IV, used to send 'barils' of Arbois wine to special friends. When Franche Comté belonged to Burgundy and while Burgundy was the smart drink at the French court (Bordeaux was still associated with the English and their occupation), the Jura wines were royal tipples as well and the Emperor Maximilien accorded them the right of free entry to all his lands in 1493. Celebrities such as Rousseau, Voltaire, Alexandre Dumas enjoyed them; Prince Metternich, ingratiating himself with Napoleon (who cared so little about food and drink that he left most entertaining to Talleyrand and his other ministers and is supposed to have tackled all the dishes set before him simultaneously) remarked, on being complimented on his Schloss Johannisberg, that the Emperor had a finer wine in France; this was Château Chalon. Metternich was, in fact, being fairly sincere, for his family had been buying quantities of it since 1780. The proudest thing in the history of Jura wines, however, is the work of Pasteur, and it was largely due to the peculiar nature of these wines that the existence of bacteria was discovered by him.

Red, white and *rosé* table wines are all made, the latter sometimes being described as '*vins gris*'. Some sparkling wine is also made by the Champagne method. The '*vin fou*' of the Jura is made by bottling either white or rosé wine at the peak of its first fermentation. The house of Henry Maire own the largest single vineyard in the Jura—that of Françoise de Montfort, which makes a vin *rosé*—and make a complete range of all the Jura wines, but although visitors should certainly not miss a visit to the Henry Maire establishment at Arbois, it is also advisable—as in any wine region—to try and see something of the smaller producers and sample as many different wines as possible for purposes of comparison.

Some of the grapes used in the production of Jura wines are not likely to be familiar to wine lovers; the red wines are made from the Poulsard and Trousseau, also the black Pinot, the whites from a grape called the Melon, which is a type of the Pinot Chardonnay. The Poulsard is sometimes called the Plant d'Arbois and makes wine often described as '*pelure d'oignon*' (onionskin) because of its pinkish-brown colour; this term is also sometimes applied to wines from the south of France, again because of their colour.

The two extraordinary wines of the Jura are the *vins jaunes* and *vins de paille*. It has been suggested that a Spanish abbess, during the occupation by Spain of Franche Comté, planted vines from the sherry region to make the first 'yellow' and 'straw' wines; certainly these wines have some traits in common with sherry, but the most complicated thing about them is differentiating the method and type of each.

Vins jaunes are made solely from the Savagnin grape. They stay in cask, like sherry, and remain in wood, in cool cellars, for at least six years, during which time they cannot be topped up, so that the wine evaporates considerably. On the surface, during this time, forms a covering of fuzzy whitish stuff, called '*le voile*' (the veil), which is the same sort of thing as the '*flor*' that forms on the surface of a fine sherry. (The technical name is *mycoderma vini*.) The yellow wines that result after the curious and lengthy period of maturation in cask, do in fact taste slightly like sherry, though as they are not fortified in any way they can still be described as table wines. The *vins jaunes* coming from the Château Chalon region are considered the finest—this name refers to an area and not a single property. They must, according to the A.C. regulations, attain a minimum strength of 12 % of alcohol by volume, if they are to have the A.C. Château Chalon, while the other yellow wines require only 11 %. Château Chalon wines are bottled in a curious dumpy bottle, called a clavelin; they are never cheap—nor are any *vins jaunes*—and perhaps the visitor might enjoy them best when drunk as an apéritif and with the first course of a meal, though they can accompany any main dish.

Vins de paille are so called because the grapes from which they are made—Poulsard and Trousseau—are dried, either on straw mats, or, as happens occasionally, by being hung up, so that the grapes shrivel to raisin-like blobs, containing a very little extremely sweet juice. They are not pressed until as late as the February after being vintaged, and then the fermentation takes a long time, because of the high sugar content of the must. They also remain in cask for many years, sometimes as much as ten, before being bottled. The A.C. regulations require *vins de paille* to attain a strength of 15 % of alcohol by volume (one reason why they are seldom seen in Britain is because 14 % is the Customs limit for table wines), and as a certain amount of sugar remains in the wine it is not suitable to drink a *vin de paille* throughout a meal, though it is agreeable with fruit or after dinner. *Vins de paille* are white, like *vins jaunes*, and some people think that their name refers to their golden straw colour. They are very fragrant and, taken in small quantities, most delicious; it is therefore an idea for a small party to share a bottle, rather than for two or three people to struggle through several glasses of a wine that is anyway expensive and may be only enjoyable for them in small quantities.

L'Étoile, a name that puzzles some people, is the name of a region, producing white, yellow and straw wines. The white wines go very well with fish.

It is said of the *vins d'Arbois* (Côtes du Jura is a lesser appellation) that '*Plus on en bois, plus on se tient droit*' (the more you drink, the more upright you stand)—implying that they don't affect head or gait; but there's another saying

> *Le bon vin d'Arbois*
> *Dont on ne boit*
> *Qu'un verre à la fois*

(The good wine of Arbois, of which one drinks merely a glass at a time.) The Fête du Biou, which takes place the first Sunday of September, is the great vintage celebration of Arbois, when a gigantic bunch of grapes—the '*biou*'—is carried in procession to the church and after a service hung up as an offering to Saint Just, the patron saint of Arbois.

On the last Sunday of July, there is usually a sale and exhibition of Jura wines in Arbois, accompanied by a procession.

Things to see and do

Arbois The house where Pasteur grew up, which remains furnished as it was, may be visited and the laboratory, with the remains of some of his experiments, is open. The Musée Sarret de Grozon contains furniture and china and the reconstruction of a middle-class nineteenth-century room. Pasteur's vineyard, which still produces wine, is 4 kilometres outside the town. Pasteur brought the property in 1874 and it was here that his great work on fermentation was begun in 1878. The establishment of Henri Maire, in the centre of Arbois, is open to visitors, who can taste the wines and obtain information about them.

Arc-et-Senans The Saline Royale de Chaux, the royal salt works, where a complete town was planned in the eighteenth century solely round the production of salt, may be seen.

Baume-les-Messieurs In the Abbey, the eleventh-century cellar is open to visitors.

Besançon In the Palais Granvelle the Musée contains exhibits relating to the region. In the Hôpital Saint Jacques there is a fine collection of pharmacy jars. The Château de Moncley, 36 kilometres from Besançon, is a very fine example of Louis XVI architecture, and contains the original furniture and furnishings designed for it.

Dôle The house in which Pasteur was born, in the Rue des Tanneurs, has been made into a museum.

Lons-le-Saunier The eighteenth-century Hôpital, with its pharmacy and kitchen, with all their equipment, may be seen.

Montbenoît The kitchen of the fifteenth-century abbey may be seen.

Neuchâtel The historic section of the Musée des Beaux-Arts et Musée d'Art et d'Histoire contains furniture and costumes relating to local life.

Pérouges The entire town has been most carefully restored to give an exact impression of what it was like in the sixteenth century. Shops of the various tradesmen and craftsmen may be seen, a wine press, of the type known as a 'squirrel press' (*à l'écureuil*) or treadmill, operated by a wheel in which men walked round to turn it, and the village inn, now a restaurant with a hotel.

Salins-les-Bains The saltworks are open to visitors. In the seventeenth-century Hôtel Dieu the pharmacy has a fine collection of jars and equipment.

Poligny The pharmacy and vaulted kitchen, and the refectory of the seventeenth-century Hôtel Dieu may be seen if application is made to the nuns.

Île de France (and Paris)

It is not possible, for reasons of space, to include a detailed account of Paris in this book, but the Île de France region, surrounding the capital, has contributed greatly to the fine cooking in the city, and many dishes have been evolved there that are now famous throughout France and the world.

Food in general

The vegetables are especially famous and are rushed to the great markets of Les Halles: asparagus from Argenteuil, Laon and Lauris, peas from Clamart, beans from Arpajon, carrots from Crécy, lettuce from Versailles, and mushrooms either from the woods surrounding Paris where there are *morilles* as well as field mushrooms, or, as with the *champignons de Paris* (the white, button type), from the mushroom caves that are extensive around the city. Potatoes are also plentiful and the description *Parisienne* applied to a dish may often mean that potatoes are included. Game is supplied from the various forests that were once the hunting grounds of the sovereign and nobility and fish of various kinds from the many rivers, including the Loing, whose pike (*brochet*) is well known, and a *matelote*, the type of fish stew, is supposed to have first been made in Paris.

Specialities and dishes

Potage St-Germain   A thickish pea soup, actually first made at St Cloud.
Sauce béarnaise   Invented about 1830 at the Pavillon Henry IV at Saint Germain. It is made with egg yolks, tarragon, white wine, vinegar and shallots.
Sauce Robert   An onion sauce made with mustard.
Sauce gribiche   A vinaigrette with chopped hard-boiled egg in it, but some authorities give this recipe as a type of mayonnaise with tarragon.

Sauce ravigote A type of vinaigrette, plus chopped herbs, anchovy and pickled cucumber or gherkins.

Sauce Bercy A sauce made with white wine, meat gravy and shallots.

All these sauces are supposed to have been, if not evolved, at least perfected in Paris. Sauce Bercy is named after the huge area at Bercy where all the wine comes in and is held for bottling, or kept in bond. Anything described as '*Bercy*' refers to this; and the dish is usually substantial and able to be prepared quickly for the workers there.

Œufs Bercy Eggs with pork sausages.

Entrecôte Bercy Steak with watercress and Bercy sauce.

Foie de veau Bercy Grilled calves' liver with Bercy sauce.

Merlans Bercy Whiting with white wine, shallots, and butter.

Haricot de mouton A stew of mutton, turnips, potatoes and onions. The bean does not appear, because the title of this dish derives from 'halicot' an archaic word that just meant 'stew'.

Sauce marchand de vin This is supposed to be another Bercy speciality, and the white wine in the Bercy sauce is replaced by a red one. But the term '*marchand de vin*' as applied to a steak can sometimes mean the meat grilled with shallots and a piece of marrow on the top as it might have been done in a cellar by a head cellarman or tonnelier (but see p. 174), and without the sauce, except for a little red wine added to the meat juices.

Miroton de bœuf Boiled beef with onion sauce.

Crème Chantilly Whipped sweetened cream.

Gâteau Saint Honoré An elaborate and very rich creamy dessert cake.

In addition, there are the various dishes that have been composed by the chefs of famous restaurants, bearing either the names of their inventors or of the establishments: Marguéry, Dugléré, and so on. These are mostly 'chef' creations, however, rather than direct adaptations of regional cooking.

Cheese

Brie and **Coulommiers** are the chief cheeses, but as they are on the outskirts of the region, they are dealt with elsewhere (pp. 212–213).

Fontainebleau is a very light cream cheese, often eaten with sugar and/or pouring cream.

Things to see and do

In Paris

The markets Les Halles and the *entrepôt* region of Bercy. The markets are best seen in the small hours of the morning, when the produce comes in from the country, and the sheer beauty of the fruit and vegetables is striking. To see the Bercy region, one should try and get an introduction to someone in the wine trade and see round an establishment, such as one of the huge wholesale establishments, who blend market *vins de consommation courants* as well as fine wines. It is impressive, although perhaps not very picturesque as compared with sight-seeing in the wine growing regions. Les Halles are now sited at Rungis.

Musée des Arts et Traditions Populaires, Palais de Chaillot French folklore.

Musée Carnavalet, 23 Rue de Sévigné In Madame de Sévigné's house, this is a collection showing the history of Paris and life in the capital over four centuries.

Musée de Cluny, 5 Rue Paul Painlevé As well as medieval arts and crafts, the great tapestries *La Dame à la Licorne,* two of which show the senses of taste and smell.

Musée des Archives Nationales, Hôtel de Soubise, 60 Rue des Francs Bourgeois This is the museum of the history of France. Among other great treasures, it contains a letter from Parmentier suggesting the possibilities of cultivating the potato.

Musée de la Conciergerie, 19 Quai de l'Horloge The kitchens of Saint Louis.

Arpajon Market gardening centre, where a *Foire aux haricots* is held every September. The special type of bean is called *chevrier,* after the man who evolved it in 1878.

Foire aux jambons Held, since 1222, from the evening of Palm Sunday to Easter Day, in the Boulevard Richard Lenoir (home of Maigret) in Paris.

Foire au Pain d'Épice Held for a month after Easter in the Avenue de Trône, Place de la Nation, Cours de Vincennes.

Auberge du Père Ganne, Barbizon This inn was frequented by Rousseau, Millet and many other artists who made the region famous.

In the cellars of the Tour d'Argent restaurant there is a wine museum with a spoken commentary.

Musée Municipal, Coulommiers Includes a folklore section.

Épernon The old cellar, formerly belonging to the Priory of Haute Bruyère, is called Le Pressoir.

245

Rambouillet Marie Antoinette's dairy is open to visitors.

Abbaye de Royaumont The thirteenth-century refectory and kitchens are on view.

Thomery This is a centre of grape cultivation. It has been estimated that there are more than a hundred miles of trellises of vines in it. The preservation of the grapes for some time is due to the discovery of Lapenteur, a vine grower who, in 1848, gathered such fine Chasselas grapes from his vines that he vowed to give them to Saint Vincent whose day is 22 January. He managed to keep the grapes by putting the stem of the bunches in water, and since that time table grapes have been preserved in bunches in exactly the same way.

Musée Alexandre Dumas, Villers Cotterets The novelist was born and spent his youth here, and it is worth noting that he hoped to be remembered more for his *Dictionnaire de Cuisine* than for his other bestsellers.

Fontainebleau The Treille du Roi (the King's Trellis), in the Park, is a great vine of Chasselas table grapes that are auctioned annually. The vine is said to have been established in 1730, but the first vines planted at Fontainebleau are recorded as having been set by François I, in the middle of the sixteenth century, when the King sent for a grower from Cahors to start a royal vineyard. It is also thought that this may have been an early instance of grapes being cultivated for the table and not just for wine.

Other things of interest

It was at Chantilly that Vatel, supervising the reception of Louis XVI and his court as guests of Condé, had the terrible experience of finding that three days of entertaining 5,000 people were getting too much for him. He did not sleep for twelve days before the King's arrival, and then, while coping with sixty tables, each for eighty people at each meal, was told that the roast ran out on the first evening. Vatel worried about this all night. When told next morning that the fish had not arrived, in despair he rushed up to his room and committed suicide—and the fish was delivered almost immediately afterwards. Culinary historians have dealt harshly with the poor man, describing him as a caterer rather than a cook. A real cook, they say, would have invented something wonderful and made a victory out of a catastrophe.

At Rosny-sur-Seine the Duc de Sully commanded the great horticulturalist Olivier de Serres (most appropriately named

246

'Olive tree of greenhouses') to lay out the nursery garden, which included 8,000 mulberry canes. It was Serres who pronounced the famous phrase, 'Tilling and pasturing are the two nipples of France'.

It was in the kitchens of the Pavillon Henry IV at Saint Germain en Laye that *pommes soufflées* were first made. A dinner was being held for the inauguration of the railway from Paris and the train was late. The chef took out the potatoes he was frying and eventually put them back into the hot oil to be finished, at which they puffed up surprisingly and a new dish was born.

Shops in Paris of interest to the gourmet

Hédiard, 21 Place de la Madeleine, 8, and 70 Avenue Paul Doumer, 16. For all luxury produce, including wines.

Paul Corcellet, 46 Rue des Petits Champs, 2. Coffee, exotics, vinegar.

Chez Kitai, 12 Rue de Surène, 8. Sells only tea of all kinds.

Balestié, 2 Avenue des Gobelins, 5. Coffee specialists.

Creplet-Brussol, 17 Place de la Madeleine, 8. Cheese specialists.

Androuët, 41 Rue d'Amsterdam, 8. This is also a restaurant in which you can taste wines with the cheeses in which the house specialises. M. Andronët has written a fine book on cheese.

Courtois, 11 Avenue de la Grande Armée, 16. Cheeses.

Tachon, 37 Rue de Richelieu, 1. Cheese and wines.

Maisonnette du Caviar, 13 Rue du Colisée, 8. Different kinds of caviare and smoked salmon.

Pétrossian, 18 Boulevard de la Tour Maubourg, 9. Caviare and Russian specialities.

Dominique, 19 Rue Bréa, 6. Caviare and smoked fish.

Prunier-Duphot, 9 Rue Duphot, 1, and *Prunier-Traktir*, 16 Avenue Victor Hugo, 16. As well as being specialist sea-food restaurants, these houses also sell caviare, including that from their own establishment in the Gironde.

Poilâne, 8 Rue du Cherche-Midi, 6 and 49 Boulevard de Grenelle, 7. The best bread in the city.

Spécialités de France, 44 Avenue Montaigne, 8. Chocolates, sweets, fruits and similar delicious temptations.

Battendier, 8 Rue Coquillère, 1. Luxury foods and wines, but also specialists in charcuterie and foie gras of different kinds.

Maison de la Truffe, 19 Place de la Madeleine, 8. Foie gras and truffles.

Fauchon, 26 Place de la Madeleine, 8. Luxury foods and wines.

ÎLE DE FRANCE (AND PARIS)

WINE MERCHANTS
J.-B. Besse, 48 Rue de la Montagne Sainte Geneviève, 5.
Brossault, 22 Rue des Capucines, 2.
Nicolas, head office 2 Rue de Valmy, Charenton, and 396 shops.
   The Nicolas establishments are reliable and the wine lists
   especially attractive. Stocks vary according to where the shop is,
   but those in the smart quarters carry a wide range. Nicolas are,
   in fact, the biggest wine buyers in the world and greatly influence actual production.

Languedoc and the Tarn

The food of this very varied region is robust rather than delicate and around the Mediterranean coast anyway, is supposed to show Roman and Arab influences. The great bean dishes may be due to the former, the numerous sweet things and pastries to the latter; there was a considerable spice trade from the east through Montpellier from very early times. The small lordships of the various parts of the country remained comparatively isolated from the outside world until fairly recent dates in the Middle Ages and consequently there seems to exist a greater degree of what may be called village independence; I remember how, when I was visiting wine establishments in and around Tuchan, I was told that many of the peasant proprietors never bothered to set their clocks or watches to national time—they kept to what they considered was their own time.

There are several curious things about the gastronomy of parts of this region. The large Spanish colony in Toulouse makes the cooking of many homes and small restaurants in this city quite unlike that of any other French town; an Englishman was responsible for the great speciality of Pézenas and another Englishman for the exploitation of one of the best-known mineral waters in France (see pp. 255–256). In the latter part of the twentieth century it may well be that a number of rice dishes, formerly associated chiefly with Italy or Spain, will develop in the area, for the salty pastures of the Camargue (strictly in Provence) and surrounding regions are being prepared for crops by large-scale rice sowing, and this cereal is therefore being increasingly used.

Food in general

This is a region in which oil, garlic and, in the mountains, pork fat are important ingredients. In the mountain streams of the Tarn region trout, eels, shad (*alose*) and other freshwater fish, including crayfish, are plentiful and good, and I have never elsewhere tasted a *poulet aux écrevisses* (chicken with crayfish), which must have evolved locally rather like the famous poulet Marengo. *Frétins* (small fry, rather like whitebait), are also served from the river, and on the sea coast there are *poulpes* (small octopus) and *seiches* (cuttlefish). Snails are also plentiful here and there are many different ways of presenting them (see p. 251).

Grives (thrushes) are a speciality of the causses, or high pastures in the Tarn, and small game birds, including *cailles* (quails) and ortolans are esteemed because of the flavour the juniper and thyme of the garrigue, the stony moors, gives to their flesh and to that of the hare (*lièvre*).

Pignons (pine nuts) are often served with trout and also as a sweet, for example in an omelette. *Châtaignes* (chestnuts) are served, especially in the Cévennes, as a vegetable, generally in *purée* form. Artichokes are abundant, truffles are also found and Nîmes olives are renowned. There is plenty of fruit.

Pork products are also plentiful: *fritton d'Albi* is a type of pork brawn, the *salaisons des Corbières* are sausages, the *saucisses d'Arduze*, which may be grilled or stewed, are other kinds of sausage and the Saint Gaudens raw ham is famous.

Sweets and sweet things include the *gratin du Vivarais*, which might be described roughly as a pumpkin meringue pie, the *marrons glacés* (candied chestnuts) of Carcassonne, and the candied violets (*violettes pralinées*) of Toulouse, and honey (*miel*) from Narbonne. Jams include *confiture de figues* (figs) and *pastèque* (water melon). *Touron Languedocien* is a type of soft nougat, and a speciality of Carcassonne and Limoux. *Biscotins*, hard little biscuits, are special to Montpellier, and *réglisse du Vivarais* (stick liquorice) is made in Uzès and Bagnols-sur-Cèze, and bonbons called *minervas* in Nîmes. *Flaunes de Lodève* are light buns, made with ewes' milk cheese, and the *fouasses* of Millau are sweet pastries.

Specialities and dishes

Cassoulet This is one of the great dishes of the south-east and Castelnaudary, Carcassonne and Toulouse each claim to make the best. There is no definitive recipe for each kind, however fiercely the locals may opine that theirs is the only true and original type, but the dish, which consists of white beans, pork and sausage, cooked for a long time and, according to tradition, the crust being broken up and stirred in seven times, usually contains goose if it has the name Toulouse attached, mutton if Carcassonne, and pork only if Castelnaudary. But this is only a generalisation—many variations are possible. The *cassole*, for which the dish was named, is an archaic term for the cooking pot, and ideally the cassoulet should go on endlessly cooking; Anatole France wrote that the cassoulet in his favourite Paris restaurant had been on the stove for twenty years—but that was before gas or electricity and when fuel was cheap. It is a very substantial dish indeed, however it is made.

Snail recipes The snails sometimes facetiously referred to on menus as *rapides* are generally cooked in a court-bouillon, but the accompanying butter or sauce can vary as follows:

Li cagaraulo à l'ailloli With the garlic mayonnaise of Provence.

Escargots au beurre de Montpellier Butter with lettuce, herbs and pounded anchovies and gherkins.

Escargots à la Languedocienne With a sauce based on goose dripping, flavoured with ham, garlic, saffron and other herbs.

Escargots à la Lodévoise With a sauce made of onions, ham, garlic, herbs, egg yolks and walnuts.

Escargots à la Narbonnaise With a mayonnaise mixed with milk and pounded almonds.

Escargots à la Nîmoise With a sauce containing ham, herbs, garlic, vegetables and pounded anchovies.

Escargots à la Gayouparde With a sauce containing diced ham, browned in walnut or olive oil, containing garlic, pounded green walnuts and parsley.

Escargots à la Sommiéroise With a court bouillon containing orange skin, and then served with chopped bacon, pounded anchovies, walnuts and garlic, and accompanied by spinach. Sommières is near Nîmes.

Grives à la Cévenole Roasted thrushes on croutons, accompanied by a sauce made with the wine of Frontignan.

Ouillade or **oulade** Soup made with beans and cabbage cooked separately in two pots and only mixed before serving. In the Cévennes it is called *oulade* and contains potatoes and possibly sausages. *Aigo bouillado* of the Basses Cévennes also contains garlic.

Mourtairol A Rouergue region dish, or a chicken boiled with saffron.

Alicot or **alicuit** A Rouergue dish of goose or duck left-overs, served with *cèpes* and chestnuts. (There is also a local cheese called aligot.)

Sauce aux briques Stew made with sausages, black pudding and *confit* of goose or poultry, cooked with garlic, tomatoes, peppers and herbs.

251

Les Manouils Ham mixed with garlic and herbs, rolled up in tripe and cooked in a pot-au-feu.

Le gras double A stew made with tripe, vegetables, ham, garlic and herbs. A speciality of Albi.

Anchoïade Fresh anchovies, soused in milk and fried in oil with garlic and bay, served hot with chopped onion.

Brandade Dried salt cod, made into a creamy consistency with milk, oil, garlic and lemon juice. A Nîmes speciality.

Tripes de thon Unless you go out on a boat you are unlikely to get the 'real thing', which is tunny fish cooked in white wine, with vegetables and herbs, plus a ladleful of sea water, or sometimes, rum. A speciality of Palavas-les Flots, and Agde.

Féche sec Pig's liver, lightly pickled, served either hot or cold.

Fouace de gratillons salées Small hot tarts, made with *gratons* or *gratillons*, which are scraps of fried lard or bacon. Served as an *hors d'œuvres*.

Cheeses

Small goat cheeses, both fresh and matured, are found in the region, but its great glory is **Roquefort,** the only cheese made from ewe's milk to come into the category of the great cheeses of the world. The milk is collected during the lambing season and mixed with rennet from the lamb's stomachs after being heated; the curd coagulates and is drained, then interspersed with crumbs of bread on which the culture of *Penicillium glaucum Roqueforti* are growing and which make the blue veining. The cheese is then salted, pressed and brought to the Roquefort caves for maturing in the cool humidity. It cannot be made anywhere else, even though the milk can be taken from ewes throughout the region and even from the Pyrenees and Corsica. Tradition says that Roquefort was discovered by a shepherd who left a piece of bread and ordinary cheese forgotten in one of the caves and, coming on it later, ate it and found it delicious.

Bleu d'Aveyron or **Bleu des Causses** is a cow milk *fromage persillé* (see p. 53).

Wines

The Hérault region is that which produces the largest quantity of wine in France, but a great deal of it is either wine intended for making into vermouth, or else into the various vins de consommation courants, or everyday wines, usually sold under brand names. The V.D.Q.S. wines, however, are worth trying when you visit the region and the A.C. wines are briefly described as follows:

In the valley of the River Aude, a very beautiful drive for the tourist, are made the white wines of Limoux, the most famous of which is Blanquette de Limoux; this is a sparkling wine, made by the Champagne method, but there are also still wines. The name Blanquette, which is applied only to the sparkling wines, comes from the pale underside of the Mauzac grape used for this wine. Visitors can see round the Cave Co-Operative at Limoux.

Several *vins doux naturels* (wines in which the fermentation has been stopped by the addition of alcohol) are also made in the Roussillon region and in the south-east of Languedoc. They are sweetish and can achieve great fragrance and real charm, but although they are drunk in France as apéritifs and in between meals, the British taste has so continuously been for dry wines before food that the traveller may find them strange; they are, however, well worth trying while on holiday, when a sweetish drink in the sunshine is often very acceptable. The poet Géraldy wrote some lines which are pertinent:

> *Aujourd'hui, des Messieurs austères*
> *Boivent des vins secs en grognant;*
> *C'est un goût qui vient d'Angleterre . . .*
> *Le vin qui réchauffait Voltaire*
> *C'est le Muscat de Frontignan.*

In the Roussillon, the best known are those of Rivesaltes, Maury and Banyuls—the Cave Co-Operative at Maury can offer visitors a tasting, and the word *'rancio'* on the labels of any of them implies that they are matured in cask (though this only applies when concerning these particular wines). The Muscats of Frontignan and Minervois are other well-known vins doux naturels, from the south-east of the area, some of them attaining a great sweetness that is very popular with people who are not hide-bound by thinking that they ought somehow to prefer a dry wine; they are not, however, wines to accompany food, except perhaps fruit or sweetish things. Some of them are put into curious, rather contorted bottles, rather like twisted sticks of barley sugar.

The general Languedoc wines such as Côtes du Languedoc, Minervois and Costières du Gard are V.D.Q.S., except for one called Fitou, a soft, rather full-bodied red wine, worth trying, which has an A.C. Clairette du Languedoc is a fullish white wine, made from the Clairette grape, and often used for making vermouth, though it has an A.C. also. The Costières du Gard red and rosé wines from Château Roubaud have recently become known in Britain, but a white wine is also made which is well worth trying.

From the vineyards around Sète a huge quantity of wine is produced for making into vermouth—which some people do not realise is itself a wine, to which herbs and spices are added and which is matured in wood. There are numerous small tasting rooms out alongside the roads where one pays to sample the wines—these are really more like drink kiosks. Vermouth itself is made in slightly different ways according to the practice of the different houses, but Noilly Prat, the largest French firm, mature the wine in a special way. It is made from several different grapes, including the Clairette, Picpoul and Bourret, plus some from Muscat grapes, the fermentation of which has been stopped by the addition of brandy; this last is called mistelle. The casks of wine are then put out into open-air enclosures at Marseillan, where up to 10% of the contents will evaporate, or up to two years, after which the wines are brought round to Sète for blending and then sent to Marseilles, their headquarters, where the herbs and other ingredients are added (see p. 274).

Things to see and do

Agde The Musée Agathois contains a collection of folk-lore exhibits and reconstructions of rooms furnished in regional style.
Alès The Station Séricole and its experimental annexe contain data on mulberry cultivation and, as would be expected, everything to do with silk-worms. The establishment is closely connected with the work of Pasteur, whose researches saved the silk industry in the nineteenth century.
Béziers Musée du Vieux Biterrois et du Vin contains exhibits concerning local history and a reconstruction of a room in a mid-nineteenth-century inn, with special exhibits relating to wine. Wine sales are held on Friday afternoons in the town.
Mas Soubeyran In the Musée du Désert, the section in the Maison de Roland is exactly as in the seventeenth and eighteenth centuries, with the kitchen and its equipment.
Montpellier The Wine Fair is held annually in October. The École d'Œnologie is not usually open to casual visitors, but

applications made by anyone specially interested can usually result in a visit being arranged, and the same applies to the École de Viticulture and the École National Supérieur Agronique. The old name for Montpellier was Monspistillarius, Mount of the Spice Merchants, and the town was the capital of Languedoc and for centuries a port. The medical properties of spices led to the foundation of a school of medicine, now the university, where Rabelais took his doctor's degree.

Nant In the Church of Saint Pierre the finely decorated choir stalls, with fishes, bunches of grapes and olive branches, should be seen.

Nîmes The Musée de Vieux Nîmes contains a collection of household utensils and pottery.

Roquefort-sur-Soulzon The Société des Caves, where the cheeses are matured, arrange visits to the caves (on Saturdays and Sundays only during the winter, otherwise every day).

Sainte Enimie The small folk-lore museum in Le Vieux Logis is a room of former times, reconstructed with the furniture and equipment of everyday life. The Halle au Blé displays an ancient grain measure.

Pézenas Visitors to this delightful old-fashioned town will certainly be encouraged to taste the *petits pâtés*, which are a speciality, and the local people who make them will say that they were the invention of the chef of Lord Clive, who stayed at the nearby Château de Larsac in 1753, convalescing from his Indian campaigns; they make out that this man, an Indian, adapted an Indian recipe, but the fact is that the *petits pâtés* are composed of mincemeat, made as it originally was in England, with fresh meat and spices and peel (being neither wholly sweet nor entirely savoury) put in a pastry crust, so that they are rather like a variation of an old-fashioned Banbury cake. It therefore seems more probable that Lord Clive's chef had been taught to make them from an English recipe.

Vergeze Fifteen miles from Nimes, this is the site of the Perrier spring. It had been known to the Romans, but was rediscovered in the nineteenth century by a Doctor Perrier. He chanced to meet A. W. St John Harmsworth, brother of the future Lord North-cliffe, who was touring France with his tutor after coming down from Oxford, and who, on being shown the spring, was so impressed that he bought it but promised the Doctor that it should always bear his name. Because Mr Harmsworth was partly paralysed as the result of a motoring accident, he used to exercise with Indian clubs, and this is why Perrier bottles have been made in their distinctive shape. Visitors are welcome to see round at the spring and bottling plant.

Sète This curious, canal-divided little town is the centre of many of the vermouth establishments, who obtain most of the wine for making vermouth from the surrounding districts. Many houses are open to visitors, and if possible it is a good idea to see a large establishment, such as the impressive Noilly Prat installation, plus one of the smaller houses where traditional quality is still maintained in a different way—the Déjean establishment, which can receive visitors if application is made in advance, is highly recommended. Noilly Prat keep their strange 'maturing parks' of hundreds of casks out in the open, on the Bassin de Thau, at Marseillan; this is not usually open to the casual visitor, but if application is made in advance, it may generally be seen.

Frontignan Many establishments making the sweet wine of the same name offer facilities for tasting, but, to the best of my knowledge, there is no central, non-commercial tasting room and visitors are therefore expected either to buy wine or else pay for anything consumed in quantity.

Albi The Verrerie Ouinère, founded in 1896, is one of the first factories to be managed by the employees. Visitors may see the glass-works by appointment.

Toulouse The Musée Paul Dupuy contains a collection of regional art and includes a pharmacy of the seventeenth century and various domestic utensils (see also p. 233).

Carcassonne Birthplace (in 1856) of the great chef Prosper Montagné, who had hoped to be an architect but who was apprenticed as a kitchen boy at the Hôtel des Quatre Saisons.

Saint Guilhem-le-Désert On the evening of the Thursday before Good Friday, there is a procession to the church to adore the relic of 'The True Cross', in which the pilgrims carry snail shells transformed into tiny oil lamps—hence the name of the event, *La procession des escargots*.

The Loire

The Loire is the longest river in France and it would require a book to deal even moderately comprehensively with the food and wines of the environs of the river and its various tributaries. Perforcedly considering the matter from the point of view of the tourist visiting a region vaguely determined as 'Loire', I have outlined the district for the purposes of this section round Laval, Le Mans and Chartres to the north, Pithiviers and Sancerre and Pouilly-sur-Loire to the east, Ancenis and Cholet to the west, and Thouars, Levroux and Bourges to the south.

This area is curious gastronomically. It gave England the Plantagenet kings and then, from the time of Jeanne d'Arc to the reign of Louis XIII, was constantly visited for long periods by the monarch and—sometimes separately—by the queen and her court. The local products, cooked and served by the chefs to the king and nobility for both private and public meals therefore underwent a refining process, especially as the area also received a great deal of influence from Italy during the time of the Renaissance when many Italian artists came to work there. The sweet things, the cakes, delicate sauces, fruits and rich but somehow light pork dishes are all things that could be summed up by describing them as the sort of foods wealthy people like to indulge in when on holiday. The Duc de Guise was eating sweets when he was murdered at Blois, Catherine de Medici (who brought her cooks with her when she came as a bride from Italy) compounded lotions and comfits, probably more than the poisons with which she has been associated, in her secret cabinet at Chaumont, Rousseau, tutor to the children of Madame Dupin, owner of Chenonceaux in the eighteenth century, admitted to getting 'as fat as a monk, the cooking was so good', and then there is Proust with his madeleine and Rabelais with his *fouaces* and countless feasts, as well as the string of poets who have chanted the praises of the wines. The region might be personified by an elegant lady or gentleman, stretching out a hand for a sweet or cake, with a tall glass of a light, fragrant wine at their elbow, or mazagran still used for coffee or chocolate.

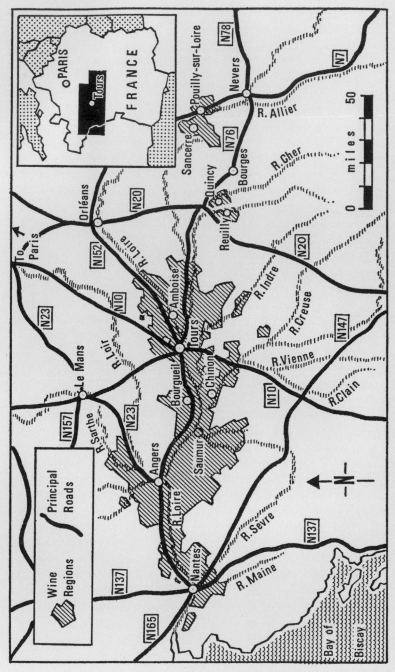

The vineyards of the Loire and its tributaries, with the principal towns associated with wine.

Much of this area is known as 'the garden of France', and it abounds in nursery gardens and the cultivation of fine vegetables and superlative fruits. The religious establishments created the tradition of gardens and cultivation of this kind and naturally established many of the vineyards. The hospitable instinct was encouraged because of Chartres, Orléans, Vendôme, Tours and Châtellerault being on main pilgrim routes.

Often the various dishes of the region bear the name of a special area within the district; as these are not always as clear as *Sancerrois* or *Orléanais*, here are some that may frequently occur:

La Beauce The great plain around Chartres.
Gâtinais The region to the west of Montargis.
Perche-Gouët Between the rivers Loir and Huisne, this area is famous for apple trees (and cider), and the great dappled horses known as percherons.
Sarthe The region of the river of that name around La Flèche.
Blésois The Blois region.
Les Mauges South of the Loire between Nantes and Anjou.
Véron North of Chinon.
Poitou The former province of pre-Revolutionary France south of Thouars and Châtellerault.
Berry The ancient province south of Bourges.
Maine The province around Laval and Le Mans.
Vendée South of Cholet.

Food in general

Fish from the rivers are plentiful and good, including carp, *brochet* (pike), *alose* (shad), *anguille* (eel), and *saumon* (salmon), as well as smaller fish. There are even *lamproies* (lampreys) at Vierzon. Often the fish are made into a *matelote*, or type of stew, or, if small, fried and served as *friture*.

Pork dominates the meat course, and as well as there being all kinds of sausages and potted meats, pork is sometimes combined with the fruits of the region in a way that is not often found outside it—*noisettes de porc aux pruneaux* (pork with prunes). There are also many chicken dishes, some of which include the *géline de Touraine*, a smallish black fowl, very tender and succulent, and for game, from the Sologne especially, including a number of dishes for rabbit or hare (*lapereau* is a young rabbit, and *lièvre* a hare), and *chevreau* (kid). Pastry is used in different kinds of *vol-au-vents*, and there is a great variety of different kinds of *pâté*.

259

Asparagus is plentiful and around Tours there is a vegetable called a *cardon*, which has no exact English translation though it may be termed 'cardoon' and is rather like large-scale celery. There are also beans and excellent mushrooms from the local mushroom caves; a salad of raw sliced fresh mushrooms, with a delicate dressing, is delicious.

Fruits are a source of great pride: peaches, pears of several kinds, including one called Bon Chrétien, apples called Reinette de Mans and Crat Vert, Saint Catherine plums (also called *Petits Damas*), quinces (*coings*), a curious fruit that is like an apricot-peach, called the *alberge de Tours*, melons, cherries called *guignes* around Angers (hence the liqueur called *guignolet*), and dessert grapes, which are picked and then hung with their stems in water in special temperature-controlled rooms, so that they stay fresh for months, are all regional specialities.

The sweet things are infinite: *sablé biquette* is a sort of goat cheese biscuit, a *Vouvraysien* an almond cake; *fouaces* are sweet buns, *cassemusses* somewhat the same. The *macarons* of Cormery are particularly famous; they have a hole in them, made, so the story goes, after the vow made by the Abbot of Cormery who, wishing to make the macaroons distinctive, prayed for guidance and was told to put on the cakes whatever he first saw when he opened the kitchen door. As Frère Jean, the cook, had just dropped a coal on his habit and it had burnt through the cloth, the first sight the Abbot saw was the worthy brother's navel. Honey from the Gâtinais is also famous, and *cotignac*, a stiff jelly of quinces and apples, and *pâté de coings*, which is a thick quince jelly, like the Spanish *membrillo*, is another regional speciality. A type of tart made with pumpkin and called *citrouillat* is a Berry speciality.

Specialities and dishes

Cerneaux au verjus   Green walnuts, in grape juice, with salt and pepper, which are sometimes served as a first course.

Jambon de volaille   A dish from Richelieu, which is stuffed chicken legs.

Beurre blanc   A sauce which accompanies fish the whole length of the river. It is basically composed of butter, shallots and vinegar and should be fairly thick and creamy.

Rillettes, rillons, are types of potted pork, though sometimes they may also contain rabbit, in which case there will usually be '*de lapin*', or the adjective *solognote*. *Rillauds*, an Angers speciality, are pieces of breast of pork, cooked and served hot, rather like an *andouillette* out of its skin.

Poulet en barbouille   A Berry speciality, in which the blood of the chicken is added to the sauce. It is rich and delicious.

Carpe or **saumon à la Chambord**   Involves the fish being cooked in red wine, which is far more delicious than it sounds.

Pâté de Chartres   Dumplings of stuffed partridges.

Pâté de Pithiviers   A lark pastry, which has been made at the same shop in the town, Gringoire, for two centuries. It is supposed originally to have won fame by being eaten by Charles IX, in an impromptu meal out hunting, after which the king made the cook a royal pastry-cook, a title that remained in the same family for 300 years. The *pâté* should not be confused with the *Gâteau de Pithiviers*, which is a rich almond paste tart.

Quiche Tourangelle   An open tart made with *rillettes*.

La chouée   A cabbage and butter dish.

Truffiat   A potato cake.

Poire belle angevine   Usually stuffed with an ice-cream, this is a pear in syrup, with liqueur.

Tarte des Demoiselles Tatin   Apple or peach slices, caramelised and covered in pastry.

As Orléans vinegar is famous, vinegar made from wine is often used in the various dishes of the region and is especially good in the dressings for salads. Mustards in great variety are another Orléans speciality and mustard is often used in the regional dishes.

Cheeses

Sainte Maure   A goat cheese, like a small cylinder, made mostly in the regions of Sainte Maure and Loches. It is sometimes referred to as *chèvre long*. *Villebarou* is like a Sainte Maure, but round. *Ligueil* is similar.

Crottin de Chavignol   A small, round, rather tall goat cheese, made in the upper Loire, round Sancerre it is also called *Sancerre*, and *Saint Amand Montrond*. The word *crottin* means 'droppings'.

Crémets   Little fresh goat cream cheeses, or goat and cow mixed. Speciality of Anjou.

Gien   A squat cylindrical cheese, mixture of goat and cow milk.

Olivet   A factory-made cheese, rather like Coulommiers. *Olivet bleu* is in season from October to June, and *Olivet cendré* from

November to July. *Vendôme*, which also may be bleu or cendré, is rather similar, and so are *Frinault affiné* and *Villiers*.

Saint Benoît Another soft cheese, the surface of which is rubbed with salt and charcoal. It also resembles Olivet.

Pithiviers au foin Like Coulommiers, with the surface sprinkled with grain.

Valençay and Levroux Goat cheeses, in the shape of a pyramid, fairly firm and medium strong. *Chateauroux*, *Pouligny Saint Pierre* are other goat cheeses, *Tournon Saint Martin*, flat and round in shape, *Chabris*, which has been described as 'the Camembert of goat cheeses', and *Lormes*, are others.

Thénay A soft, cow milk cheese, matured for about six weeks, is rather like Camembert.

Sainte Marie A white, fresh, cow milk cheese.

Chabichou A Poitiers cheese, made from goat milk, squat and cylindrical in shape. There are various different kinds—*Chaunay*, *Civray*, *Couché* and *Saint Gelay*. The origin of its name is obscure, but at one time it was also called *fromage cafioné* because, during the winter, it was kept in small baskets called '*coffins*' or '*coffineaux*'.

Mothe Saint Héray A cheese looking rather like a small Camembert, often dried between two plane tree leaves. It comes from the Deux Sèvres region, and *Fromage de chèvre à la feuille* is a similar type of goat cheese, usually dried on chestnut leaves.

Drinks

Cider is made in the Perche region, and there are also many different fruit liqueurs, such as the *guignolet* (from a type of cherry) of Angers, and the vast range of fruit liqueurs produced by the Cointreau establishment at Angers. But fruits of all kinds are used to make liqueurs, and the lucky traveller may get the chance to try *eau-de-vie de coings* (quinces) or one of the liqueurs made from the local plums, as products of a restaurant or a friend's house, for everyone in this part of France goes in for bottling, potting, preserving and distilling.

The wines of the Loire present a complete range, from the very dry to the luscious, and although the majority nowadays are white and *rosé*, there are still some excellent red ones. They have been praised for centuries; Alcuin, who was brought from York by Charlemagne to be the imperial tutor, and who ended his life as Abbot of St Martin, at Tours, is probably the first Englishman to write on wine, in a letter addressed to a friend in France while he was on leave in England, and it is the Loire wines that he praises and orders to be sent over to him. Charles d'Orléans, Rabelais, Ronsard, Joachim du Bellay, Jules Lemaître all wrote about the wines, and references to them occur in a wide variety of works. It would be impossible to note each one separately and there are many which qualify only for the description 'strictly local', especially the V.D.Q.S. wines, which should be tasted and enjoyed on the spot, but the principal regions in the area may be generally noted.

At the top of the region taken as 'Loire' in this section, are the Pouilly and Sancerre vineyards. The wines of Pouilly and Chavignol are sometimes described as having a 'gun flint' flavour, but how many of us have tasted gun flints? Anyway, they are white, dry and can be very good. Wines entitled to the A.O.C. Pouilly-sur-Loire are made from the Chasselas grape, those entitled to be called Pouilly Fumé or Blanc Fumé de Pouilly (the *blanc fumé* part of the name is not to do with the flavour but the grape), are made from a type of white Sauvignon. Sancerre is a wine that can attain great finesse, being dry without pronounced acidity, and full-bodied without losing its crisp appeal; a good Sancerre can smell like a mountain meadow when the snows are melting, cool, but with a floweriness in the background. Sancerre is also made from the Sauvignon grape.

The small areas of Reuilly and Quincy produce dry white wines, that of Reuilly being very dry, slightly 'minerally'. Like the white wines of Cour Cheverny, Azay-le-Rideau, Chaumont, Beaugency and Saint Jean de Braye, near Orléans, these are all refreshing 'little' wines, to be enjoyed on the spot. Some red wine is made near Orléans, notably that of Meung, but these red wines will be thin and lacking in character for most people accustomed to the classic red wines that are worth exporting. The red Touraine wines, however, are very well worth consideration; Chinon (the wine of Rabelais), Bourgueil, and Saint Nicolas de Bourgueil are excellent, fragrant, supple and capable of true finesse. If a restaurant has thought it worth while letting any of them grow to a benign old age in bottle, profit by this—the delicacy and 'length' will be a delight and surprise. A frequent reference to these wines as 'Breton' is because Cardinal Richelieu, when his property was made into a duchy, sent some Bordeaux vines up to his intendant at Richelieu; this man's name was Breton, hence the use of the term as applied to the quality wines of the region. There is some red wine also produced at Amboise and *rosé* is found in most areas that also make red wine; the other wines of Touraine, which are white, vary from being dry to slightly sweet, and may be still, *pétillant* or fully sparkling. The most famous is Vouvray. It may come as a surprise to some to find that it is also a still wine, about which opinions are very mixed. For a long while it was said that Vouvray did not travel; now it seems to be the thing to say that it may not taste the same when divorced from local cooking. It is probably fair to put it down as a 'holiday' wine that can sometimes be very good in Britain and that is always enjoyable on its home ground. Montlouis, on the bank of the river opposite Vouvray, is sometimes called 'the poor man's Vouvray'; it is light and pleasant. Other white wines, still, *pétillant* or sparkling, may be just given the name of Touraine, or have the village from which they come attached to this.

Up in the Sarthe the dry white wine of Jasnières merits attention; it is pleasantly full in the mouth and slightly fruity when of high quality. Then there are the Anjou wines, most of which are white or *rosé*, the *rosé* in particular having become very popular indeed recently; it is drunk in vast quantities with either fish or meat, and is usually not too palate-scrapingly dry for general appreciation. Any *rosé* described as 'Cabernet' will have been made from the Cabernet grape, one of the great claret grapes, and this should mean that the wine is superior in quality to the ordinary *rosé*. There is a little red wine made, Champigny being perhaps the best-known, but it lacks the charm of the Chinon and Bourgueil wines. The white Saumur, however, both still and sparkling, can be really good, full, flavoury and varying from fairly dry to slightly sweet. The place names of some quality still wines are Tigné, Parnay, Turquant, Montsoreau, Souzay and Dampierre (there is also a red wine made near Dampierre, at Aunis). The Coteaux de l'Aubance wines are medium dry, those of the Coteaux du Layon are golden in colour (whereas the others are rather pale silvery-gold) and all tend to be sweet; those called Quart de Chaume and Bonnezeaux are the best-known, delicious with fruit or by themselves, but usually too sweet for most people to drink with a meal. The Coteaux de la Loire produce some really fine white wines, the names to look for being Coulée de Serrant, La Roche aux Moines, Savennières, La Possonière and Ingrandes; these are exactly the sort of wines that, while being good, are not usually worth sending abroad in quantities, because their character demands that they should be bottled on the spot and this prices them out of their market. So, both because they are value for money and most interesting and enjoyable on the spot, they should not be missed.

Things to see and do

Museums As well as collections of interest mentioned separately, the following have interesting exhibits to do with food and drink:

La Porte Royale, at Loches, contains a folklore exhibition.

Maison de la Reine Bérengère, at Le Mans, contains a good collection of china and kitchen ware, and 'simarts', which are metal goblets in which the city offered a ceremonial drink to important visitors.

Musée de Sologne, in the Hôtel de Ville, Romorantin, shows the background to life in the Sologne district.

Musée de Berry, in the Hôtel Cujas, Bourges, contains furniture and kitchen utensils.

Musée Folklorique de l'Orléanais in the Château de Dunois, Beaugency, contains a poem to wine by Jules Lemaître.

Château de Plessis-les-Tours, outside Tours, includes the reconstruction of the interior of an old house, in a museum devoted to the silk industry.

Château de Gien, at Gien, has a collection of the local ware in a department of the Musée de la Chasse à Tir et de la Fauconnerie, and at the *Château de la Bussière* nearby there are important exhibits to do with fishing, including china decorated with fishes.

Musée du Vieux Chinon, at 81 Rue Voltaire, Chinon.

Wine museums, tasting rooms and cellars

For Anjou wines, the *Maison du Vin d'Anjou*, 21 Boulevard Foch, Angers, can provide full information for the region. Also in Angers, the *Hôpital Saint-Jean* has a museum of glasses and bottles, drinking vessels and holy wafer moulds—like waffle irons—and, in the old storehouse of the hospital, there is a twelfth-century cellar now made into a small wine museum.

The *Cointreau establishment,* in Angers, is very well organised for the reception of visitors.

Outside Tours, the *Musée d'Espelosin* or *Musée Tourangeau de la Vigne et du Vin* in the Château de Basses-Rivières houses a comprehensive collection of objects to do with wine production, including the remains of a Gallo-Roman press, many tasting cups, bottles and *dames jeannes* of the region (a type of large bottle; note the drawing of the Marie Jeanne on p. 63).

In Tours, the cellars of the *Église Saint-Julien* date from the twelfth century. A *son et lumière* performance about the wines of Touraine is held here.

Outside Saumur, the suburb of *St-Hilaire St-Florent* is the place where most of the wine firms of the region have their establishments and many of the larger ones can receive visitors. Rémy Pannier is the largest of the firms handling white and *rosé* wines, Ackerman Laurence (next door) the largest dealing with sparkling wines and the house that started the process in Saumur at the beginning of the nineteenth century. There are many tasting rooms to the east of Saumur, with cellars cut into the cliffs, which are used both as houses and storage space, but most of these belong to small dealers, restaurants or bars.

Bourgueil The *cave touristique*, a little distance outside the town, is open to visitors and contains a collection of very ancient presses, well worth seeing.

Brissac The Cave Co-Operative have taken over the kitchen at the side of the château and transformed it into a tasting room where one can sample any of their wines and give, though only if one wishes, a small payment. In addition to the kitchen well, there is an alcove for washing up, rather like a sink in an old-fashioned butler's pantry.

Châteaudun, in Dunois' castle   Visitors can see the cellars and kitchens of the fifteenth century.

Abbaye de Noirlac, near Saint Amand   Visitors can see the refectory and cellar, dating from the thirteenth century.

Beaulieu-sur-Layon   A small Caveau du Vin has been installed in a house on the D 55 road, with a collection of old bottles and glasses.

Vouvray   Many of the wine houses are able to receive visitors.

Other things of interest

Fontevrault l'Abbaye   The Romanesque kitchen is the most remarkable thing of its kind in France. It provided food for the five departments of the huge religious establishment and has five separate cooking places and twenty chimneys. Visitors can now also see the refectory.

Montreuil-Bellay   There is a Gothic kitchen in the château, modelled on that of Fontevrault.

Château de Villesavin, near Bracieux   There is a most interesting kitchen, with a separate pastry oven, and many ancient utensils, also a huge pigeoncote (*colombier*), still with its revolving ladder for gathering the eggs. The nobility were permitted two pigeons per section of land (a half hectare) and the pigeon house at Villesavin held 5,000 pigeons. In the carriage house there is a large German omnibus-type carriage, for ladies to use in following the hunt, decorated with bunches of grapes.

Ménars, north-east of Blois   Visitors can see the seventeenth-century kitchen of the property belonging to the brother of Madame de Pompadour.

Azay-le-Rideau   The kitchen is also on view, dating from the Renaissance.

Pontlevoy   The kitchen of the seventeenth-century abbey buildings is open to visitors.

Villandry   In addition to the Renaissance flower gardens, there is a kitchen garden reconstructed as it might have been when the castle was built.

Amboise   In the Clos Lucé, Leonardo da Vinci's house, the kitchen is on view.

La Devinière, Chinon, is the house where Rabelais lived as a young man, which now contains a museum of the man and his works.

Château de Talcy   Visitors can see a large dovecote of the sixteenth century and a 400-year-old wine press that is still in use.

Chartres   The cathedral windows show, among other occupations, those of coopers, vignerons and wine merchants. At 5 Rue Cardinal-Pie, the former cellar of the chapter may be seen.

Saint Benoît-sur-Loire   One of the capitals in the abbey church shows a monk cooking.

Château d'Angers   In the magnificent display of tapestries, there is a scene of the symbolic vintage in the series of the Apocalypse.

Château de Montgeoffroy   To the east of Angers, the Château, built in the eighteenth century for the Maréchal de Contades (whose chef evolved *foie gras truffé*, see pp. 153–155), still contains the furniture that was specially designed for it in the first place. The only exception to this is in the oval dining-room, where the large table dates only from the nineteenth century because, when the place was built, the family used small tables (as, for example, were used by the monarchs when dining in public though by themselves, or only with other royalty); when a banquet or large-scale meal was given a caterer (*traiteur*) would put up trestle tables. So there are no big eighteenth-century dining tables in France.

Montrichard   There are wine cellars open to the public in the hollowed-out caves in the rock, also galleries devoted to mushroom cultivation, which may be shown to visitors by arrangement.

Vernou-en-Sologne The establishment dealing with researches on fruits can be seen on application.

Orléans The rose gardens and nursery garden establishment can usually be visited on application.

Illiers in the valley of the Loir, was the birthplace of Dr Proust, father of Marcel, and the original of 'Combray'. The *Maison de Tante Léonie*, which is still furnished as it was in Proust's time, may be visited, and is the scene of the famous madeleine eating episode.

St Martin of Tours The saint who divided his cloak with a beggar is credited with being the man who discovered how to prune vines. This is said to have come about because, at his abbey of Marmoutier, the monks tethered their asses near a vineyard, and one spring the beasts escaped and devoured the young shoots. To everyone's surprise the vines that had been thought to have been partly destroyed yielded the best grapes in the forthcoming season.

Louis XIII is said to have enjoyed doing his own cooking when staying at Amboise, and to have specialised in an onion omelette. Amboise was also the place where the first incubator for chickens was installed in 1496.

Henri IV is reported as having praised the Chavignol wine as the best he had ever enjoyed, and **Louis XVI** is said to have drunk Sancerre in quantities.

The Sancerrois are very proud of the fact that the crottin was one of the cheeses served at the Coronation banquet of Queen Elizabeth II.

Marseille and the Riviera

Although this must be the part of France most familiar to hundreds of thousands of holiday-makers, it is that with which I am least acquainted, as I have a distaste for resorts and for any places where the inhabitants are outnumbered by the visitors. Generally the gastronomy of resorts tends to consist either of international cuisine in large hotels and restaurants or else becomes folksy in the worst sense in the smaller establishments, where straightforward local specialities are debased in the interests of tourism. Away from the Côte d'Azur, in the country, the real specialities are to be enjoyed—not perhaps any very outstanding creations, but the delicious raw materials of Provence and the Mediterranean combining to make superlative country fare in the magnificent countryside.

The influence of Italy and the mountains, as well as of the sea, are apparent in the regional dishes of this part of France. The country is actually not very rich, but local cooking is resourceful and inventive (for examples of what may be done even on a limited budget as well as very limited ingredients, see Stephen Lister's accounts of south of France home cooking as given in *Fit for a Bishop* and *More for a Bishop*). And it can be no accident that this is the country of many artists, for the simplest *hors d'œuvres* salads and stews are somehow arranged and presented with great taste, making pictures on the table. Those who love tableware find endless temptations in the local pottery and, nowadays, in the sophisticated creations of Vallauris, where Picasso has so greatly influenced the regional productions, and Biot, where Fernand Léger has done the same.

Food in general

Olive oil is the supreme cooking medium and although good Provençal oil does undeniably taste of olives, it has none of the rancidity or over-fatty flavour that some people associate with it (largely, one has to admit, because of the experiences they may have had in Portugal or Spain, where it may not be refined to suit our insular taste, or else because they are used to the horrors of inferior frying oil in Britain, or because their sole experiences of oil in cooking have been with so-called medicinal oils, which taste of nothing at all).

Fish in great variety is naturally plentiful along the coast. There are fresh sardines, *poulpes* (small octopus) and *supions* (another name for squid), small fry, often on menus as *petite friture de la rade*, a curious but excellent thing called *poutina et nounat*, which is a combination of very young fish and their roe. Anyone who has struggled with the vocabulary in the Marius-Fanny-César trilogy of Pagnol, will remember the *violets* (a type of shellfish tasting of iodine and named as 'sea anemones' in some dictionaries), *clovisses* (a large clam) and *praires* (a small clam) sold by Fanny at her fish-stall; there are also *oursins* (sea-urchins), which look just like prickly chestnuts, and taste rather like a snail that has been taken to the sea, and a number of fish regarded highly by the makers of bouillabaisse (see pp. 171) which appear to have no English language names—*rascasse*, *galinette*, *chapon*, *grondin* (rather like a red mullet, but uglier), *congre* (conger eel), *fiélas*, *sarran*, *orade*, and *pagel*. The *loup de mer* (sea bass) is usually served grilled over sprigs of fennel which may have been sprinkled with brandy. *Estocaficada* is dried salted stockfish, which is usually imported from Norway and transformed by southern magic into something delicious, and most restaurants make a *soupe aux poissons*, incorporating a variety of fish, though this, it is worth remembering, is not like bouillabaisse in which the fish are whole or at least solid, but in which they have been either reduced to pulp or else pounded—a soup, in short, and not a fish stew. Shellfish such as crabs, lobsters, and mussels are also plentiful. Anchovies feature in many dishes, and there is an eel stew called *la raïto* which is a Christmas dish. Grey snails, called *cantarèu*, are also found.

Because of the rather poor pasturage, meat is not always of very high quality in this region, although one may find *menon* (roast kid) on a special menu, but the vegetables and fruits certainly are. The Cavaillon melons, asparagus, peaches, figs, artichokes, are sent to the Paris markets and abroad; pumpkins, aubergines, water-melons, peppers and tomatoes, spinach and every kind of salad vegetable and herb make the menu varied and colourful. *Polente*, similar to Italian polenta (maize flour), and other pasta are featured. Garlic, of course, comes into many dishes, especially *aioli,* the Provençal version of mayonnaise, served with raw vegetables and shellfish, and *rouille,* a red pepper and garlic sauce sometimes stirred into soups and stews to give spice and flavour. *Pissala,* another cooking essence, containing anchovies, is also often used in this way. *Blète* is a vegetable rather like Swiss chard, the stems being slightly similar to asparagus and the leaves to spinach. A type of vegetable tart called a *tian* is made and so, of course, is *ratatouille* for which the local name is *ratatouia.* Black olives are another thing inseparable from the southern table, and radishes and *fèves* (small beans) are also usual as *hors d'œuvres. Basilic* (sweet basil) is frequently used for flavouring. Table grapes appear regularly at the ends of meals, and nuts are also abundant —Olivier de Serres planted his own Asian almond trees in his estate at Pradel. A *pâté* of quinces *(coings)* similar to *cotignac* of the Orléanais is often made.

Among sweet things, the little almond biscuits called *calissons d'Aix* are especially famous; Grasse makes *fleurs pralinées* (candied flowers) and Nice candied flowers and fruits of various kinds. *Chaudèus* are orange-flavoured biscuits.

Specialities and dishes

Bouillabaisse This is certainly the great dish of the south of France and it must immediately be admitted that, however good it is, I do not like it, just as I do not like any of the great fish stews—*pouchouse, cotriade, ttoron* and so on. If I have to concentrate on sorting out the edible from the inedible in a mixture of fish in liquid, I cannot enjoy the flavour of any and I detest getting anything into my mouth that I then have to take out. But *bouillabaisse* has been a favourite even before Thackeray wrote a ballade to it, though ideally it should be made specially for you (which disposes of the restaurants who keep a large pot simmering) as each fish must be cooked just to edibility and no longer, and the whole operation should not take hours anyway. It is often served in two plates, liquid in one, fishes in the other. There are endless arguments as to which combination of fishes make the best *bouillabaisse.* The dish is said to have been of Greek origin and even a favourite of the gods, for Venus is said to have given Vulcan a dish of fish and saffron (a supposed soporific) when she wanted to meet Mars; each town has its own recipe for *bouillabaisse,* the only point on which everyone seems to be agreed being that it should contain garlic, olive oil, tomatoes, saffron

271

and a hideous looking fish called the *rascasse*. Various other fishes are included, according to what recipe is followed, herbs, and a slice of bread over which the bouillon is poured. Sometimes grated cheese is served too. There are, however, seldom shellfish in *bouillabaisse* (useful for people with allergies to remember), although it is possible to find it made with lobster or mussels. *Bouillabaisse borgne* (literally 'one-eyed') is a vegetable soup made in the same way as the fish variety, with poached eggs in the bouillon; *bouillabaisse de sardines* contains only fresh sardines, *bouillabaisse d'epinards* is a bouillon of the same olive oil, saffron, garlic herb type, plus potatoes, poached eggs and spinach.

Bourride Also a fish soup, but generally consisting solely of white fish, and, according to some authorities, made without saffron—though saffron is often included, and possibly aïoli and egg yolks too.

Soupe au pistou A type of minestrone, special to the Nice region, which derives from the Genoese *pesto*, a sauce consisting of pounded basil, cheese, pine nuts, oil and garlic. This concentrated sauce is put into the vegetable soup, which usually includes tomatoes, beans, onions, and a little vermicelli, as well as other vegetables.

Aïgo Saou A fish and vegetable soup, with *la rouille* added to it. *Aïgo boulido* is a Provençal vegetable soup into which egg has been beaten.

Sou fassum Stuffed cabbage. A Grasse speciality.

La socca A huge, thin, flat pancake, made of chickpea flour, oil, water, salt and pepper.

Pissaladiera A Nice speciality, and a version of Italian pizza—an open tart with onions, anchovies and black olives, sometimes with tomatoes.

Pan bagna Another Nice speciality and a type of giant sandwich. A roll is sliced and filled with tomatoes, peppers, black olives, anchovies, and possibly hardboiled eggs, radishes and onions, the bread being well sprinkled with oil.

Anchoïade Anchovies pounded with garlic and oil.

Poutargue Grey mullet roe, with onions, hard boiled eggs and oil. A Martigues speciality.

Tautènes farcies Squid stuffed with onions and tomatoes, usually served au gratin with spinach.

Salade Niçoise An *hors d'oeuvres*, which varies but should contain black olives, anchovies, green pepper, tomatoes, olive oil and possibly hardboiled eggs. Additional vegetables and tunny fish are sometimes added.

Pieds et pacquets A Marseille speciality of tripe and sheep's trotters in rolls, cooked in a bouillon with vegetables.
Bléa tourte A vegetable tart of beet leaves, pine nuts and currants.
Esquinado Toulonais A type of gratin of crabmeat and mussels.

Cheeses

Brousses Ewe milk fresh cheese, sometimes served with sugar, but also with salt, pepper and chopped chives. *Brousse de rove* is a fresh goat cheese from the Bouches du Rhône.
Poivre d'âne A goat or goat and cow milk cheese, often flavoured with rosemary and the herb savory (*poivre d'âne*), which gives it its name.
Le cachat A strong ewe milk cheese, mixed with wine and brandy.
Bleu de Corse Sometimes found on the coast. Like Roquefort.
Banon A small round goat cheese, made in the Basses Alpes. The small cheeses are wrapped in savory leaves and then passed through a bath of *eau-de-vie* and marc and covered in chestnut leaves, then tied round with straw while being dried. Their flavour is fairly strong but delicate.

Wines

Vines abound in this part of France, but although a lot of pleasant white and *rosé* wine is made, and a little red, there is nothing very memorable. The white wine of Cassis is good with all fish dishes. Bandol makes both red and white wines and also a Muscat. Around Nice the red and white wines of Bellet are produced. The many different *rosés* of this part of Provence go well with both fish and meat and salad dishes and are excellent holiday wines. Ratafias of orange flowers, jasmine and other flowers are also found locally.

Things to see and do

Aix-en-Provence The Musée du Vieil Aix contains a collection of local objects relating to the region, including *santons*, the small figures carved for putting round Christmas cribs, which feature local crafts and trades. The Pavillion de Vendôme is a seventeenth-century house furnished in Provençal style.

Near Brignoles The abbey of Thoronet, built in the twelfth century, is open to visitors, who can see the refectory, cellar and an oil press.

Vallauris The Hall du Nérolium is open in summer with an exhibition of the local pottery.

Grasse The Musée Fragonard contains exhibits relating to the life of Lower Provence, including furniture and ceramics.

Marseilles The Musée Cantini contains an important collection of ceramics of the region. The establishment of Noilly Prat, the largest of French vermouth houses, is open to visitors.

Menton The Musée contains exhibits of local folklore and history. There is a Lemon Festival and fruit show, together with a 'Race of the Golden Fruits' held each February.

Moustiers The Musée des Faïences has an important collection of pottery, including exhibits showing how it was made.

Nice The Musée Masséna, as well as containing collections specially relating to the history of Nice and of the work of artists who worked in the region, also has exhibits of pottery and porcelain.

Roquebrune-Cap-Martin In the Donjon of the castle of this perched village, visitors can see the dining-room, kitchen with bread oven and furnished rooms of what is thought to be the oldest feudal castle in France—end of the tenth century.

Vence There are two oil presses which are still working, and the baronial mill of Boursac is open to the public.

Cagnes The Musée in the Château contains exhibits to do with history and a complete display dealing with the cultivation of olive trees and the production of the oil.

Bandol On the nearby Island of Bendor, M. Paul Ricard (of the pastis firm) has installed a museum of the world's wines and spirits.

Normandy, Picardy,
Artois and Flanders

Normandy is supremely the butter and cheese country, and the whole northern coastline has good fish and shellfish. Although the Normans, Picards and those who are either Flemish or who live near Flanders are all heavy eaters, there is not a very wide range of haute cuisine; the inhabitants prefer first-rate foodstuffs, either cooked simply or made into substantial dishes such as are always popular with people who either live and work outside in weather that can be often bad, or else those who are engaged in heavy industrial tasks. The richness of some of this superlative 'farmhouse fare' is sometimes responsible for tourists feeling overwhelmed by French food at the outset of a holiday. Only comparatively few vegetables are specially featured and towards the north an increasing range of sausages, blood sausage and pork products is available. Cream goes into a vast number of Norman dishes and so does butter.

Food in general

Among the fish and shellfish are the *demoiselles de Cherbourg*, which are either a small lobster or enormous shrimp. There are numerous *pâtés*, especially from Amiens, and plenty of game birds, such as woodcock and snipe.

Different kinds of herring are available in Flanders; these may be *harengs salés* (salt herring), *harengs fumés* (smoked), which may be colloquially known as *gendarmes*, and *harengs kippers*.

Among the vegetables that are widely available are chicory (*endive*) and salsifis (the same word). Butter and cream are good and plentiful and the *graisse normande* is also used in cooking. This is a mixture of pork fat and the fat from around a calf kidney, flavoured with vegetables.

Apples, cider and calvados are also featured in many dishes, and sweet things include *les chiques de Caen* (rather like our bulls' eyes), biscuits from Abbeville, aniseed biscuits from Honfleur, candied fruits from Beauvais, *sablés* (a rather dry biscuity cake) from St Quentin, *tuiles* from Amiens (thin chocolate and orange biscuits), *Duchesses de Rouen*, which are macaroons, and *mirlitons de Rouen*, which are a type of creampuff. *Citron confit* (candied lemon peel), and *falnes normandes* (flat cinnamon cakes) are also specialities. *Le gâteau de Trouville* is a cake filled with apples and cream, *le pain de pommes des Picards* a *compôte* of fried apples, *la bissade* a type of round brioche, *la rabote* or *un bourdelot*, apples baked in paste, and *douillons*, which are pears treated in the same way.

Specialities and dishes of Normandy

Andouille fumé de Viré Smoked chitterlings, served hot or cold.

Andouillettes grillées Small tripe sausages, special to Caen, Viré, Rouen and Pont-Audemer, but found throughout the region.

Sanguette An Orne speciality. Black pudding made with rabbit's blood.

Matelots Stews of freshwater fish of various kinds. *Matelote normande* is made with sea fish.

Omelettes The famous ones from Mont Saint Michel, evolved by Mère Poulard, are what we should call fluffy omelettes, with the yolks and whites beaten separately. They are large, light and spongy—not, frankly, to my taste, but definitely worth trying.

Soles There are three main ways in which they are served: *sole normande*, which is the smart restaurant way of describing a dish made with a *sauce normande*, of butter, flour and cream, but the *vraie sole à la normande* that may be featured in the country of its origin is the fish just simmered in plain cream in a covered dish. *Sole Dieppoise* is sole cooked in a white wine sauce with shrimps and mussels, and *sole Fécampoise* has soft roes in addition.

Tripes à la mode de Caen Tripe cooked slowly, covered with onions and carrots, herbs and apples, cider and a little Calvados.

Caneton Rouennaise Duckling of a kind special to the region, reared mostly at Yvetot. The bird is strangled, lightly roasted and then cooked with wine and brandy. It is a rich dish, but can be delicious.

Salade cauchoise A type of potato salad.

Poulet Vallée d'Auge The Pays d'Auge is one of the most picturesque and gastronomically rich regions. Chicken cooked in this way is done with cream, mushrooms and wine.

Specialities of Picardy, Artois and Flanders

La caqhuse   Cold leg of pork, with onions.
Le hoche pot   A northern type of *pot-au-feu* (hot pot)—a substantial meat stew.
Flamiche aux poireaux   Leek tart. *Flamiche à la citrouille* is pumpkin tart.
L'étouffée   Onion and potato pie.
Daussade à la crème   Onions, lettuce, cream, served on bread.
Le pain daussé   Onions mashed in cider, served on bread.
Le dius   Sliced potatoes cooked in the oven.
Bêtises de Cambrai   A mint sweet, evolved years ago by an apprentice who made a mistake (*bêtise*) that turned out well.
Faluche   A large round, flattish loaf.

Norman cheeses

Camembert   Made certainly from the beginning of the eighteenth century and possibly before then, but brought to fame by Madame Marie Harel, wife of a farmer at Vimoutiers, near Camembert, at the end of the eighteenth century. She transmitted the secret of the special excellence of her cheese to her daughter, who married a man called Paynel, whose name was attached to what many considered to be the best Camemberts. The original Harel recipe produced a cheese with a bluish tinge, but after the mould used was changed Camembert became pale lemon in colour. Another native of Vimoutiers, Monsieur Ridel, invented a little wooden box in which the cheese could be sent to other countries without deteriorating, although nowadays the boxes in which the round cheese is presented are usually cardboard. Before the war there was a statue of Marie Harel, erected at Vimoutiers by an American specialist who claimed that Camembert and Pilsen were responsible for many cures of stomach complaints in his clinic; this statue was destroyed in the war but a subscription from private individuals in the U.S. enabled another one to be presented to the town in 1956, when the Prefect presiding was actually a gentleman with the tactlessly rival cheese name of Gervais. *Gournay* is a small-sized Camembert, *Carentan* and *Quillebœuf* brands that are seldom seen nowadays. Camembert-like

277

cheeses are made in other parts of France, as well as in many other countries. The 'real thing' is a seasonal speciality, at its best at the beginning of the year and really only to be served from November to June. One gourmet, sniffing a fine specimen, said it smelled like 'the feet of God'.

Pont l'Évêque   Made in the Lisieux district and the Vallée d'Auge, a square cheese and, after Camembert, one of the great ones. *Trouville* is a type of Pont l'Évêque, and *Pavé de Moyaux*, seldom made now, is a large one.

Port du Salut and **Port Salut**   This is a little outside the strictly Norman cheeses, but is bound to be met with in the region. There are actually two sorts of cheese involved: *Port du Salut* is that made by the Trappist monks at Entrammes, near Laval, who only produce 200,000 cheeses a year. Other Trappists, however, and other cheese makers in France and throughout the world are able to make and market a cheese under the name of *Port Salut*, which, unlike Port du Salut, is not a trademark.

Livarot   A round, flattish cheese, occasionally referred to as a *Lisieux*. It is matured and ripened in cellars for about three months and is really strong in flavour. *Mignot*, a similar cheese, sometimes square, sometimes round, may be either fresh (*blanc*), or ripened (*passé*).

Neufchâtel   The name of the best cheese produced in the Pays de Bray. It may be eaten when it has only been kept for a few days, in which case it is creamy, soft and mild, and is called *Neufchâtel fleuri*; if allowed to ferment and ripen it is known as *Neufchâtel affiné*, and is fairly strong. It is always a small cheese, but may be of different shapes: those like little rolls may be simply called a *bonde, boudon* or *bondart*, those in a square *le carré*, a heart *le cœur*, *le Gournay, la briquette* and *le Malakoff. Bourgain* is a fresh Neufchâtel cheese, very soft and light, *ancien impérial* or *petit carré* other fresh cheese, and *carré affiné* a matured cheese. *Incheville, Rouennaise, Villedieu* and *Maromme* are local names for the same type of cheese.

Petit Suisse   A small, round, fresh cream cheese, evolved by a farmer's wife, Madame Hérould, at Auchy-en-Bray, near Gournay, about the middle of the nineteenth century. Her cheese won a great reputation because, instead of selling it locally, she sent is straight to the Paris markets. Her Swiss cowman suggested that it could be improved by adding a little cream to the fresh milk, and because of this it got its name. A clerk in the Paris offices of the purchasers of the cheeses saw the possibilities, and went into business with Madame Hérould; this Monsieur

Gervais persuaded her to start a cheese factory at Gerrières, and arranged the distribution of the cheese in Paris by means of cabs with yellow wheels, which naturally attracted great attention. There are two sizes of Petit Suisse. *Pommel* is another brand name for a similar type of cheese, and *demi sel* and *double crème* the general types of fresh cream cheese and richer cream cheese respectively. *Mesnil, Castel, Suprême, Excelsior, Parfait,* and *le Curé de Bonneville* are other types of fresh cream cheeses, all excellent when really freshly-made. In France they are often served with sugar and/or thick cream and eaten with a spoon.

La Bouille and **Monsieur Fromage** Bland, mild creamy cheeses.

Le Bricquebec or **Trappiste de Bricquebec** Cheese made by the monks at the abbey of Bricquebec, and *Providence* is another mild cheese also made there.

Mignot From the Calvados region, a soft cheese, rather like Livarot, and can be *blanc* (fresh) or *passé* (ripened). May be round or square.

Cheeses of Flanders, Artois and Picardy

Maroilles Brownish-yellow on the outside, deep yellow within, square and substantial, with a very pronounced, rather rich flavour, this cheese really comes from the edge of the Champagne region. It has been made at least since the twelfth century, when the Abbot of Maroilles decreed that the four villages nearby should make cheese from the St John's Day (24 June) milk and give it to their parish priests on St Rémi's Day (1 October), to be sent later to him. Even today, Maroilles is the cheese provided for the vintagers in the Champagne vineyards. It is a matured cheese, the flavour deriving partly from frequent brushing of the rind and washing it with beer. Maroilles is also sometimes referred to as *Manicamp*. Other types of Maroilles are: *Sorbais, Monceau, Mignon, Quart, Maroilles Gris* or *Gris de Lille, Fromage fort de Béthune, Vieux puant,* or *Vieux Lille,* which is a rindless cheese, very strong, *le Dauphin,* which is shaped like a crescent and is flavoured with tarragon and cloves and is said to have received its name after being presented to Louis XIV's son; *Boulette d'Avesne,* or *Boulette de Cambrai,* shaped like a pear, *Baguette de Thiérache,* like a little loaf, and *Losange de Thiérache. Le larron,* or *fromage d'Ours* is a skimmed milk cheese of the same type.

Fromage de Bergues A rather rare cheese, somewhat similar to a Dutch cheese.

Carré de l'Est Semi-hard and square, with a flavour like that of a mild Maroilles. There are two sorts, that described as *fleuri* and the other as *lavé*, meaning that the rind is washed. (Also in the Ardennes and Alsace.)

Mont des Cats Rather like a Saint Paulin and made by the Trappists at the monastery that gives it its name.

Mimolette A round cheese with a greyish rind and orange colour, sometimes also called *Vieux Hollande*. *Rollot*, which gets its name from a village on the Somme, is a small type of the same cheese, and so are *Guerbigny* and *Monchelet*. Louis XIV, during a campaign in Flanders, is said to have been presented with some Rollot cheeses by a farmer called Desbourges, and the king is supposed to have liked them so much that he made the donor *'fromager royal'*.

Drinks

There is no wine made in this northern region, but there are many types of cider, from very pale, almost greenish in colour, to very dark orange, sweet, dry, sparkling and still. The best is supposed to be that of the Vallée d'Auge, but there are many good ones.

Calvados, or apple brandy, is the great *eau-de-vie* of Normandy, and that of the Vallée d'Auge is entitled to an *Appellation Contrôlée*, though there are many good kinds. To be good, calvados should be matured in oak casks for at least ten years. It is mostly distilled by individual proprietors.

Bénédictine liqueur is made at the distillery at Fécamp (see below) and *Michelaine*, a herb-based liqueur from an ancient recipe, in the locality around Mont Saint Michel. The yellow kind is the most usual, but the green variety is stronger.

In the other northern regions beer is also widely consumed.

Things to see and do

Fécamp The famous liqueur Bénédictine was made in 1510 by a monk called Vincelli. The impressive distillery, in which the liqueur is produced today, and the magnificent museum, with its art treasures, and also the huge range of imitations of Bénédictine, are all worth a leisurely visit. In the Musée Municipal there are collections relating to domestic local life of former times.

Conches In the Church of Sainte Foy one of the windows, showing the 'mystic wine press' is the most famous of all.

Jumièges In the magnificent abbey ruins, visitors can see the twelfth-century cellar.

Villedieu-les-Poêles A picturesque little town, specialising in copperware.

Mont-Saint-Michel Guest reception rooms and adjacent kitchen fireplaces.

Museums with regional collections, reconstructions of rooms

Neufchâtel-en-Bray Musée Mathan, specialising in local Bray art.

Granville The museum in the Grande Porte shows local life of the past.

Bricquebec The Tour de l'Horloge in the Château.

Abbaye de la Lucerne Exhibitions of regional life and products in the *bailleverie* and Salle de Justice.

Other things to note

Madame Bovary's wedding feast 'at which they sat down forty-three to table and remained there sixteen hours; it was resumed next day, and in a lesser degree on the following days. . . . On the table were four sirloins, six dishes of hashed chicken, some stewed veal, three legs of mutton, and in the middle a pretty little roast sucking-pig, flanked by four pork sausages flavoured with sorrel. Flasks of brandy stood at the corners. A rich foam had frothed out round the corks of the cider bottles. Every glass had already been filled to the brim with wine. Yellow custard stood in big dishes. . . . For the tarts and sweets they had hired a pastry-cook from Yvetot.'

In the Pays du Caux the farms, which are still old-fashioned, employ a special method for grazing the animals, which are attached to stakes and crop the grass in a circle, being moved as soon as they have eaten uniformly of the rich pasture. The meat of such animals is found by many to have a slight flavour of parsley.

In Camembert, a woman who had been particularly fond of

Calvados, was commemorated by her husband with the following verse:

> *Ci-gît qui, dans son agonie,*
> *N'imagina rien de plus beau*
> *Que d'être mise en un tombeau*
> *Comme une prune à l'eau-de-vie*

(Here lies she who, at the end of her life, could imagine nothing better than being buried in a tomb just as a plum is buried in brandy.)

The Pyrenees

This mountain range presents some of the most appealingly beautiful and varied countryside in the whole of France— Atlantic and Mediterranean coast, high peaks, undulating foot-hills and the individual traditions of several ancient kingdoms. Like most frontier regions, each district has firmly clung to its own ways of food and drink, and although the nearness of Spain has certainly influenced the way in which certain things are cooked, and the availability of particular fishes and game adds to the repertoire, the regional dishes are definitely individual. The main regions, the names of which are often applied to dishes, are, from the Atlantic to the Mediterranean: the Pays Basque (there are seven Basque provinces, of which only three are in France, and which include the old Kingdom of Navarre), Le Béarn, La Bigorre, Le Comminges, Pays de Foix, Pays de Sault, La Cerdagne, Les Corbières, and Le Roussillon (at one time included in the kingdom of Majorca and where Catalan is still spoken by many of the inhabitants). In very general terms, it may be said that, in the districts to the west, goose fat is the cooking medium (it is said of Béarn cooking 'one gets elbow deep in fat', but in mountain regions fat usually forms an important part of the ordinary fare), in the central regions butter, and on the Mediter-ranean side oil.

Food in general

There is plenty of game, from the small birds called *bec-fins* or *bec-figues*, which are like plump larks and are a Landes speciality, ringdoves (*ramereaux*), and *ortolans* (wheat-ears) and *étourneaux* (starlings) in the Roussillon, to the *izard*, or Pyrenean chamois, often found in a *civet* (the sort of stew we should call a 'jug', as in jugged hare) and *perdreau* (partridge) which is also special to the Roussillon. Bear (*ours*) is sometimes mentioned as a Pyrenean speciality, but there cannot be any bears left to hunt today. Chickens are plentiful—remember Henry of Navarre's wish that everyone should have a *poule au pot*—and so are geese, and the *confits* of goose and pork, and various other pork products. Apart from the beans, sweet peppers and cabbage found in many dishes, vegetables are not a prominent feature of the cooking of this region, but fruits are abundant, especially in the Roussillon, and the mountainsides yield a variety of berries, such as *myrtilles* (bilberries). Chestnuts (*châtaignes*) appear as vegetables and accompany meat dishes, as well as in sweetened form.

Trout are found in the mountain streams, and *chipirones* (small squid or inkfish), sardines (the same word), and *thon* (tunny) or *bonites* (little tunny fish) on the Atlantic coast. On the Mediterranean coast there are all the fish of this sea, and especially *anchois* (anchovies). Snails, grilled and called *cargolade*, are a Catalan speciality, though '*En juillet, ni femme, ni escargot*', according to the local proverb.

Sweet things consist mostly of varieties of cake; there is the flat *gâteau Basque*, like a large maid of honour, but softer, with a dollop of jam inside it, a *confiture de myrtilles et de raisins* (jam made of bilberries and grapes), various forms of *pastis*, which are types of cake-cum-bun, flavoured with liqueur and *pâte de cédrat* (citron jelly) from Bayonne. *Rosquillas* are almond cakes, *bunyetes* a type of fritter, *crouquets*, almond biscuits, and *macarons*, which are made in Saint Jean de Luz, Orthez and Bayonne, in which last place chocolate has been featured since the Jews were driven out of Spain and Portugal in the sixteenth century and brought the tradition of chocolate drinking to France; it was then considered to be an exotic beverage, possibly because, originally popular with the Moors, it was mixed with cloves and cinnamon. Madame de Sévigné refers to its 'mortal fever', and to a friend, who drank so much chocolate during a pregnancy that she produced a chocolate-brown baby!

Specialities and dishes

Jambon de Bayonne Raw ham, cured by being rubbed with Bayonne salt and sometimes buried in the earth to develop a succulent and delicate flavour. Served in paper-thin slices as a first course.

Cousinette A vegetable soup, containing spinach and *cousine*, a type of mallow, sorrel, and lettuce, with shin of veal. A Béarn dish.

Ttoro A Basque fish soup, also containing peppers, garlic and tomatoes.

Bouillinade des pêcheurs A Roussillon fish soup.

Elzekaria A Basque soup containing onions, cabbage, beans and garlic.

Garbure One of the substantial soups of the region; the soup ladle must be able to stand up in a properly made garbure. It varies from place to place and according to what is available, but in general contains potatoes, beans, other vegetables according to the season, chestnuts occasionally, garlic, peppers, and some kind of meat (called *le trebuc*), either bacon or ham, or goose or pork or sausage. Garbure is made in an earthenware pot with a glazed interior called a *toupi*, and when a plateful is nearly finished, the eater may pour a little wine into the plate and eat this with the rest of the soup, a custom known as *'faire goudale'*.

Ouillade or **ouliat** A soup found in many parts of this region, but in the first form of its name a Catalan speciality. It is made in two *ouilles*, dishes which must never be washed or allowed to get cold. In one are cooked the vegetables (except for beans), cabbage and anything else that goes into the soup, and the beans, salt, pepper and garlic in the other, and the two are only combined when the ouillade is to be served. Eggs are sometimes added in the Roussillon, and if tomatoes are added the soup may be called *tourin*; if leeks, cheese and tomatoes are in it, it is often called *soupe du berger*. An onion soup made in the same sort of way in Bigorre is called *toulia*.

Braou bouffat A Cerdagne speciality, is a vegetable soup like the potée found in many parts of France.

Pâté aux anchois de Collioure A type of savoury doughnut containing anchovies.

Poule au pot dou nouste Henric This is the 'chicken in the pot' of Henry IV. The bird is stuffed with a mixture containing Bayonne ham, herbs, garlic and Armagnac, then poached in a bouillon of vegetables and giblets, some of the stuffing being cooked separately, wrapped in cabbage leaves. The traditional way of getting the chicken out of the broth is to pull it out by a string tied to one of its legs, hence the dish is sometimes known as *poulet à la ficelle*. *Poulet farci à l'ariégeoise* is the version made in the Ariège.

Estoufat or **daube de bœuf à la béarnaise** A stew of beef, vegetables and red wine, rich, substantial and delicious, often served with *broye*, a type of cornmeal mush, which is also called *pastet*, *paste* or *yerbilhou*.

Poitrine de mouton farcie à l'ariégeoise Breast of mutton stuffed with ham, garlic, eggs and seasoning, cooked with vegetables and served with stuffed cabbage and potatoes.

Pétéran A stew of mutton with veal and potatoes; a speciality of Luchon.

Loukinka A small garlic sausage; a Basque speciality.

Tripotchka A type of blood pudding made with veal. Also a Basque speciality.

Piperade A Basque omelette, with sweet peppers and tomatoes, so made as to be more of the consistency of scrambled eggs.

El pa y all Known as the breakfast dish of the Catalan peasant, this is hardly a thing the tourist is likely to be served, but it is good enough to try for a picnic. Simply a slice of country bread, rubbed well with garlic and sprinkled with salt and olive oil; delicious with a salad, but you must either make everyone in your company eat it or seclude yourself until the effects of the garlic wear off.

Poulet béarnais Chicken cooked over mounds of whole heads of garlic. Unexpectedly, this does not give a fierce flavour to the food, but it is definitely garlicky though delicious. Anyone who is hesitant about taking garlic in this way, however, should read the quotation from Ford Madox Ford in Elizabeth David's *French Country Cooking*, and be encouraged. It is indeed a fact that, whereas a clove of garlic lightly rubbed round a salad bowl, can waft the smell and intensify the taste throughout the meal, large quantities of garlic, cooked, are nothing like as pungent.

Perdreau à la catalane Partridge cooked with bitter oranges, a great delicacy.

Saucisse à la catalane A long, coiled-up sausage, cooked with lots of garlic, herbs and a little orange peel.

The term Basquaise as applied to dishes usually means that sweet peppers are involved. The small ones (*piments*) are not usually anything like as hot or as coarse as the large, bulbous red and green peppers (*poivrons*).

À la catalane Implies the use of a lot of garlic, as does the term *en pistache*. (*Aux pistaches* means with pistachio nuts.)

The term bayonnaise usually implies that *cèpes* are included in a fried dish.

Magret Duck cooked in its blood, with pepper, served with a hollandaise sauce.

Merguez A strongly-flavoured light-pink sausage.

Cheeses

Poustagnac   A fresh milk cheese, flavoured with sweet pepper.
Oustet   A similar cheese, from the Ariège.
Oloron   A cheese made from ewe milk, in the shape of a moderate sized cylinder. This cheese is also known as *Laruns* and is found in Béarn and the Basque country. It is moderately strong, the Basque variety slightly stronger, and the Béarn type rather creamier.

Drinks

There is a Basque cider, known as *pittara*, which is rather sharp, and the Basque liqueur, *Izarra* (the word means 'star' in Basque), which is made from Pyrenean herbs and flowers, and Armagnac. There are two kinds, yellow and green, the latter being slightly stronger. It is a good digestive and neither aggressively herby nor cloyingly sweet. As well as serving it at the end of a meal, the inhabitants, especially the smarter ones, drink it poured over crushed ice (*frappé*) and through a straw between meals, and this can be very good.

Armagnac is the great brandy of the region. It is not weaker than Cognac but some people find that it has a gentler quality than Cognac; it is not widely consumed in Britain, so the tourist will do well to try it on several occasions when in the region or indeed anywhere in France, for it is a quality drink and, although not cheap, tends to be cheaper than the Cognacs. The production is very much more a country affair than it is in the Charente, but visitors to Condom and Auch, as well as to the Distillerie de la Côte Basque in Bayonne, can see the Armagnac maturing in the oak casks and of course buy different kinds to try.

In the western part of the Pyrenees the wine of Jurançon has been famous since the time of Henry IV, as it is supposed to have been with this and a touch of garlic that the royal infant's lips were moistened after his birth. Jurançon until recently was a sweet white wine, but nowadays a dry wine is also made, pleasantly full and fragrant, and there is also a red wine but of this I have no knowledge at all. The ordinary red Béarn and the red wine of Irouléguy (and there are also *rosé* wines bearing these names) are pleasant everyday drinking, and the white wine of Tursan, in the Gers département, is also worth trying. From the area known as Pacherenc du Vic-Bilh, south of the Armagnac area, come Madiran and Portet, two curious wines which are still made but only in small quantities; Portet is a white wine, sweet and rather full, made only after the grapes have shrivelled on the vines, so that the juice is concentrated richness. Madiran is a red wine which is often allowed to remain in cask for several years before it is bottled. Both are well worth trying on the spot, as they are non-commercial wines as far as Britain is concerned and, even in the region, they are often only to be found on the lists of restaurants with close connections with the proprietors, or, indeed, in the cellars of private individuals. Banyuls, from the Roussillon, is a slightly fortified, sweetish wine, of the kind that the French like to drink as an *apéritif* or just in between meals. Ordinary red wines, which can be pleasant partners to the Catalan dishes, are produced in the valleys of the Tet and the Tech.

Recently, a sparkling *Vin Sauvage* has been produced in the Gers. This is used for topping up a distillate of Armagnac to make an *apéritif* called *Pousse rapière*—the drink to give the strength to a swordsman to withdraw his blade after he had spitted his opponent (who probably needed a drink even more). This contemporary *apéritif* is pleasant—and can be strong.

Things to see and do

Bayonne

The Musée Basque provides a complete picture of Basque history and life—it is one of the finest museums of its kind.

The Distillerie de la Côte Basque, which produces the Basque liqueur Izarra and Clés des Ducs Armagnac, is open to visitors.

The chocolate shops under the arcades (*sous les arceaux*) in the Rue du Port Neuf maintain the historic traditions of Bayonne's chocolate. My own favourite is Cazenove, where you can drink chocolate and eat cakes and pastries, as well as buying chocolates and sweets to take away or send to friends.

Good selections of Basque tablecloths and napkins are also in this street.

Biarritz

The Musée de la Mer is a well laid-out aquarium and vivarium and there is also a seal pool and aviary.

Lourdes

The Musée Pyrénéen in the Château Fort contains collections of objects portraying Pyrenean life.

Oloron Sainte Marie
The Église Sainte Marie, formerly a cathedral, has a remarkable doorway to the belfry porch, part of which represents local activities, work in vineyards, ham curing, cheese making, boar hunting and salmon fishing, and there is also a statue of a monster devouring a man.

Pau
In the Château there is the **Musée Régional Béarnaise,** showing, among other objects relating to Béarn life, cooking utensils and furniture.

Thuir
The Byrrh establishment is open to visitors, who may see the huge installations where the *apéritif* is made.

Tarbes
The small **Musée du Pays de Bigorre** shows a collection relating to local life.

Banyuls
There is an aquarium containing most Mediterranean fish.

The Rhône Valley and Provence

South of Lyon is where the holiday country starts for numerous tourists, and although the Midi does not really begin until south of Montélimar, I have included in this region the part of Provence that stretches to the Bouches du Rhône and Camargue, but not east of Marseille, and have also included the river banks up to Vienne, simply because this enables me to deal with the Rhône wines in a single section.

The Roman influence in the southern part of the region is supposed to have resulted in the cult of the olive and its oil, and the nearness of Italy today to the predominance of tomatoes in Provençal cooking—I think myself it is mainly because fruits and vegetables seem to flourish almost in a contradictory way in this often barren and stony soil, swept by the Mistral, the rivers either dried up or in ravening flood, and the sun baking all but the very stones to splitting point. There is much great cooking throughout, but I think that the charm of the regional food and the smaller restaurants in the heart of Provence is somehow a product both of the good simplicity of the ingredients and the atmosphere of a region that has attracted innumerable artists for everything; the most ordinary dishes of olives, radishes and *pâtés*, the most straightforward soup or salad are usually arranged and served with unconscious artistry, making each course a still-life.

It can be no mere chance that this countryside was one of the cradles of romance literature, with poetry and painting that are a continuing tradition today, nor that the women of a town such as Arles are not only supposed to be outstandingly beautiful, but are actually made even more so by one of the most becoming regional costumes in existence. It may be just 'the sun and old stones', but this is a countryside where even the most everyday things become enchanting.

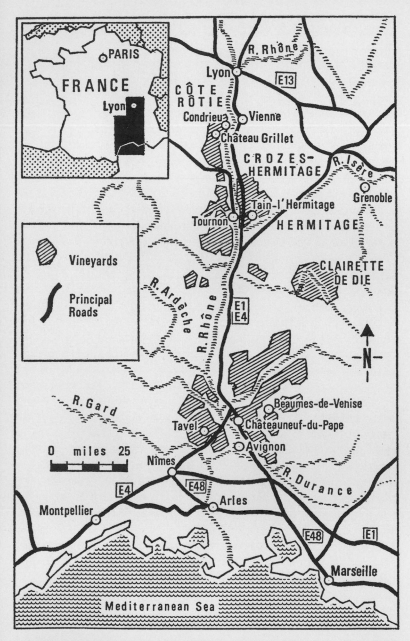

The Rhone: showing the principal wine areas, with some of the main vineyards. These have been, and are being, considerably extended. Detailed wine maps of the region will give the sub-divisions and main properties.

Food in general

The three great ingredients in Provençal cooking are olive oil ('a fish lives in water and dies in oil'), garlic—'the truffle of Provence'—and tomatoes; these last are the bulging irregularly shaped fruits seen in the markets, flavourful in a way surprising to anyone only accustomed to the smallish, dark red watery ones too often available in Britain. Artichokes, *courgettes* (the baby marrow-like vegetables), *aubergines* (the same word, though sometimes called eggplant), *cardons* (cardoons is the translation, but it is like large-scale celery), *poivrons* (peppers) are some of the vegetables that make the markets such a delight; among the fruits are *pastèque* (watermelon), the famous Cavaillon melons, figs, *grenades* (pomegranates), and even *kaki* (persimmon), as well as peaches, apricots and every kind of soft fruit. *Pois chiches* (chickpeas) are sometimes found in salads, but *asperges Vauclusienne* are a local joke name for artichokes. It will be interesting to see whether the cultivation of rice in the Camargue in the last twenty years will cause new types of dishes to be evolved in the region. The wonderful fragrance of the numerous herbs, blown off all the meadows, is put to excellent use in the way in which the Provençal cook scents the plainest dishes; the use of herbs can sometimes have unpleasant associations for the Briton—stews tasting of very old plants, dried in damp books. This has nothing in common with the delicate touch of *romarin* (rosemary) with lamb, or *basilic* (basil), or *fenouil* (fennel) with fish, or *frigolet*, the Provençal name for wild thyme. The fact that the pastures of Provence are not especially rich and the animals tend to develop muscles rather than fat flesh goes unnoticed, especially as dishes such as the *estouffade* and the *daube*, stews with red wines, mushrooms and onions—and, usually, garlic—are cooked so gently and for so long that the meat becomes tender. Hare and rabbit can be delicious cooked in Provençal style. *Grives* (thrushes) are spitted and roasted, sometimes an assortment of small birds being presented in this way—perfumed with the berries on which they have been feeding.

Pike and other river fish are found inland, and trout in the mountain streams of the Vaucluse. The tiny fish of the Rhône are presented in fried form as *friture*, or in a stew, as a *matelote*. Around Valence there is the curious *pogne suisse* described as a type of pike. On the coast there are the usual crabs, lobsters and langoustes; the mussels of Toulon are renowned, and there are also *palourdes* (clams), *patelles* or *arapèdes* (limpets), *poulpes* (octopus), *seiches* (cuttle fish, sometimes also called *supions*), *tautènes* (tiny inkfish or squid), *oursins* (sea urchins), *favouilles* (little crabs), sardines, and of course the *loup de mer*, that Mediterranean fish translated by the dictionaries as sea perch or sea bass. Snails are also often on menus and may be called *limaces* here.

Because of the abundance of fruits, there are delicious jams (*confitures*) in Provence, and Apt is especially known for its jams and preserves of whole fruits. Candied flowers are also made. As well as the nougat of Montélimar (see p. 298) and *berlingots* of Carpentras (see p. 298), there are various types of hard biscuits, often flavoured with nuts and/or honey.

Specialities and dishes

Aioli The great sauce of Provence, virtually garlic mayonnaise. Often served with raw or cooked vegetables as an *hors d'œuvres*.

Poutargue The roe of grey mullet, which appears as an *hors d'œuvres* or in salads.

Anchoïade Pounded anchovies, often served on a piece of toast—very salty.

Tapénade or **tapanda** Pounded black olives, served on toast or as an *hors d'œuvres*.

Limaces à la sucarelle Snails cooked with white wine, garlic, oil and tomatoes.

Catigau d'anguilles A type of eel stew, with the onions, tomatoes, oil and garlic that you would expect in this part of France.

Brandade de morue A *purée* of smoked cod, with cream, garlic and oil. The fact that, however well it is made, it inevitably reminds me of the worst kind of fish pie at boarding-school suppers should not deter the tourist from trying it.

Rastegais A type of fishcake.

Bourride An aioli to which the hot stock of a fish soup has been added, with the fish served separately.

Panisso or **panisse** A mush of chick peas or maize, cooked till solid and then fried.

Aïgo bouïdo A soup with garlic—there are several different kinds, but the prefatory word '*aïgo*' will give the clue to the predominating ingredient.

Aïgo sau A soup-cum-stew of fish, vegetables and garlic.

Pieds et paquets Although this is a Marseille speciality it is found elsewhere. Tripe and trotters are made into little bundles and poached with vegetables. It is far more delicious than it can possibly sound and is not at all greasy.

Cayettes de sanglier The liver of the wild boar compounded with bacon, boar's flesh, herbs and wine, put into a caul with chopped vegetables and baked, and usually served cold. A Provençal version of haggis might describe it, and it is as good as haggis but just as difficult to describe appetisingly.

Soupe d'épautre Stew made with beef or beef and veal, with herbs, vegetables and garlic.

Fassum Poached stuffed cabbage, flavoured with herbs.

Raïto A special sauce, usually accompanying smoked cod or eel at Christmas time, consisting of onions, red wine, tomatoes, herbs, garlic, pounded walnuts and sometimes including black olives.

Pastèque à la Provençale Water melon scooped out and filled with local red wine.

Gâteaux soufflés aux pignons Pastry puffs made with pine nuts.

Cheeses

Fromage de Banon A smallish, flattish goat cheese, usually wrapped in chestnut or other leaves.

Bossons macérés Goat cheese mixed with olive oil, herbs and wine or brandy.

Poivre d'âne A goat cheese, or goat and cow milk mixed, flavoured with savory (*sarriette*) and rosemary (see p. 273).

Cachat A very strong goat cheese.

Brousse or **brousse du rove** A fresh goat cheese, made in the Bouches du Rhône.

Drinks

The Rhône wines are not only interesting and very varied, but they present an attractive alternative to the other red wines, especially the Burgundies, that, in Britain, are rising in price beyond the everyday range of many people. They come from the départements of the Rhône, Loire, Drôme, Ardèche, Vaucluse and Gard. The red, white and *rosé* wines of this region are capable of great finesse and far more quality than many people expect; to taste the estate-bottled wines when you are in the region is an impressive experience.

The celebrated *apéritif* of the south is *pastis* (see p. 70), but as an occasional drink the various *vins doux naturels* (see p. 253) are taken. There is also a *muscat* of a particular kind made at Beaumes de Venise and named as such, which is especially well worth trying. It is slightly fortified to arrest the fermentation, is pinkish-gold in colour and has a very pleasant fragrance and flavour that is not at all cloying. Most people like it a great deal. *Rasteau* is another sweet *apéritif* wine which can be rather treacly but is capable of real quality when coming from a reputable house. Both wines are definitely for drinking in the sunshine and Muscat de Beaumes de Venise also goes very well with fruit.

The Côte Rôtie vineyards are across the Rhône from Vienne, their centre being Ampuis. They are divided into the *Côte Brune* and the *Côte Blonde*, the picturesque explanation for the names being that a lord had two daughters, blonde and brunette, to whom he gave the vineyards, but in fact the name probably refers to the difference in the colour of the soil. They are full-bodied red wines, made from the Serine or Syrah grapes, and the white Viognier. This last is used alone for the white wine of *Condrieu*, curious in flavour and so sparse in production that it is worth while for any wine lover to stop specially to taste it. Most famous of all the vineyards in this area is that of *Château Grillet*, about the size of an ordinary market garden, and the only single property in France to have an A.C. to itself. The wine is white, dryish and again quite unlike any other white wine. Many people consider it one of the great wines of the world and only a few casks are made each year. Because of their scarcity, none of these wines are very cheap.

The Côtes du Rhône produces both red and white wines, the whites being full-bodied but dry and crisp, the reds also full in character and capable of great roundness and fruitiness in flavour. Centre of this northern area is Tain l'Hermitage, with its twin town, Tournon, across the river. The vineyards of Crozes Hermitage and Hermitage are on the east bank, those of Saint Joseph, Cornas and Saint Péray (where sparkling wine is also made) a little further south on the west bank. The red wines are made with the Syrah grape, the whites with the Marsanne and Roussanne.

Châteauneuf du Pape was for a long time the only red wine of the southern Rhône region familiar outside France. The vineyards in this district are extraordinary, many being quite covered with gigantic orange stones, like baked potatoes, on which it is difficult to walk. It is the centre of large-scale and increasing production and it is well worth while to try the wines of several different houses and the few great properties of the region, and to see the quality of the great vintages. Curiously enough, where a fine wine is concerned, a variety of grapes are used in the production of Châteauneuf du Pape, the chief being Grenache, Clairette, Syrah, Mourvèdre, Picpoul, Terret Noir, Picardin, Cinsault and Roussanne. A little white wine is also made and can be very good. The wines of Gigondas (mostly red), Lirac (red, white and *rosé*), Cairanne and Vacqueyras, which at one time were sold as Châteauneuf du Pape, are excellent in their own right. Both red and *rosé* wines also are made in the Côtes de Ventoux, on the mountain slopes.

Vin rosé, of which the most famous of all is undoubtedly Tavel, is just the sort of wine to be lavishly quaffed in summer and with Provençal food. Tavel itself mostly consists of small estates, although there are a few large properties. The wine should be a clear, bright pink, with a distinctive flowery fragrance and definite character; the Grenache is the principal grape, but several others are used, and all good *rosé* in the region is made by leaving the skins of the black grapes for a few hours in the vats so as to colour the wine lightly. Good *rosé* is also made at Lirac, Chusclan and Gigondas—the last being one of the most picturesque villages in the whole region.

The Maison du Vin, 41 Cours Jean Jaurès, Avignon is very well organised to provide visitors with all information they may require about the regional wines. In addition there are the following tasting rooms and cellars open to visitors, though it should be borne in mind that some cellars may close on Saturday or public holidays.

Cellars
At Châteauneuf du Pape   Caves du Clos des Papes
Caves du Domaine du Mont Rédon
Caves 'Reflets du Châteauneuf' (a union of owners of selected properties)
Caves Bessac
Caves Saint Pierre
Caves Léon Couilon

The Establishment of Père Anselme can also usually receive visitors.

At Tavel   Domaine de Manissy
Caveau de Dégustation à Tavel

Gigondas	Cave Co-Opérative de Gigondas
	Caves Meffre et Cie
Also	Caveau des Dentelles à Vacqueyras
	Caveau de Dégustation à Cairanne
	Caveau de la Cave des Vignerons Le Rasteau
	Maison du Vin, Vaison la Romaine
	Caveau de Dégustation à Vinsobres
	Caveau des Vins de Lirac à Roquemaure

At Tain-Tournon the houses of Chapoutier and Jaboulet can usually receive visitors.

At Ampuis and **Condrieu** there are several houses who can receive visitors if application can be made in advance. **Château Grillet**, which is too small to receive large parties, may also usually be seen by appointment.

A *Foire Exposition des Vins des Côtes du Rhône et du Vaucluse* is held annually in July, August and September in the Grottes du Théâtre Antique at Orange.

Things to see and do

Ansouis The Provençal kitchen in the château is included in the tour for visitors.

Apt In the Hôpital-Hospice there is a fine collection of pharmacy jars.

Arles The Museon Arlaten is an especially fine museum, founded by Frédéric Mistral with the money he received for the Nobel Prize; some of the exhibits are labelled in his own handwriting. There are local exhibits of furniture, utensils, costumes and crafts, and the different-shaped loaves baked for special festivals, as well as the reconstruction of the hut of a guardian of the Camargue.

Avignon The Palais des Papes contains the private kitchen of the Pope, and also the kitchens of the rest of the household, the larder, butler's storeroom and pantry. On the front of the Mint, almost opposite the Palais des Papes, may be seen remarkably fine reliefs of fruit and flowers in swags.

Beaucaire The famous fair, held here in July in former times, in which merchants from many different countries took part, has been described by Stendhal in *Mémoires d'un Touriste*. In the Musée du Vieux Beaucaire visitors may see a number of exhibits relating to this fair, local furniture and utensils.

Bollène This is a very important centre for the market of fruit and vegetables, and the Co-operative may be seen if application is made in advance.

Carpentras This is the city of 'Berlingots', sweets like bulls' eyes, or satin cushions. There is a fine collection of china and pharmacy jars in the Hôtel Dieu. In the Musée Comtadin there are many regional exhibits.

Cavaillon The Musée du Vieux Cavaillon contains exhibits of local arts and crafts, furniture and equipment of former times.

l'Isle-sur-la-Sorgue In the Hôpital the pharmacy and its equipment may be seen, also seventeenth-century china.

Montélimar Almond trees were planted by Olivier de Serres (see p. 125) on his property at Pradel in the sixteenth century. Nougat began to be made with the increase in the cultivation of almonds, using local honey, and today Montélimar is a town apparently exclusively devoted to nougat. The main factories may be seen—the Chambre Syndicale des Fabricants de Nougat de Montélimar will direct visitors.

Pont Saint Esprit In the Hospice the sixteenth- and seventeenth-century pharmacy jars are well worth seeing. It was at Pont Saint Esprit that George Sand and Alfred de Musset stopped with Stendhal, while going to Italy, and where, in the evening, Stendhal got slightly drunk and danced wildly with the waitress, a scene of which de Musset made a sketch which still exists.

Saint Michel de Frigolet It was in the church here that Alphonse Daudet set the story of the elixir of Father Gaucher, in *Lettres de Mon Moulin*.

Salon-de-Provence In the Château de l'Empri there is a Musée du Vieux Salon, which includes regional exhibits.

Abbaye de Sénanque In the tour of the twelfth-century premises, visitors see the refectory.

Abbaye de Silvacane This is now in process of being restored. The refectory, rebuilt in the fifteenth century, is very large and of fine proportions.

Tarascon In the Hôpital Saint Jean there is a fine collection of china and pharmacy jars.

Tournon The sixteenth-century castle, which is open to visitors, provides from its terrace a fine view of the vineyards on the opposite bank of the river.

Vienne The Musée contains a very fine collection of china.

Savoie and Dauphiné

This is a most beautiful and unspoiled part of France, comparatively unknown to visitors from abroad, unless they go winter-sporting around Chamonix. For the purposes of this chapter, I have made the boundaries limited by the Rhône on the west, the Swiss and Italian borders on the east, and have arbitrarily drawn a line from Geneva to Bourg in the north and from Montélimar to the border in the south. Savoie (or Savoy) was only united with France in 1860, but the Dauphiné, which gave its name, rather as a sop, to the heir to the French throne, has been French since the fourteenth century. Italian and French influences are seen in the gastronomy, though the people are as independent as one expects those who live in mountain country to be.

The food is usually delicious both because of the high quality of such ingredients as the butter (the best butter I have ever had in my life was in the Vercors), cream, cheese, fish from the mountain lakes and meat from the high pastures, and because somehow the position of the region, a little apart but not remote from the richness of Burgundian and Lyonnais cooking and the spicy dishes of the south, has produced remarkable numbers of great chefs and thousands of first-rate cooks. The number of starred restaurants in the region is surprising. If it is possible at all to generalise, perhaps it might be said that the haute cuisine of the area combines the comforting quality of everyday, simple dishes with the lightness and inspired individuality of great cooking; it is the sort of French food that is immediately easy to like, even for people who are hesitant about strange things or who have delicate digestions as far as most elaborate recipes are concerned. It can be no mere chance that Brillat-Savarin, author of one of the most sensible and practical books on gastronomy and one of history's most considerate hosts, was born and lived here. Even the sensitive Ruskin brought back a recipe for soup from Chamonix. Elizabeth Ayrton's novel *The Cook's Tale* describes the life (and gives some recipes) of a restaurant in that part of France.

Food in general

Excellent dairy produce comes from the pastures and *fondue* appears on menus, though sometimes being more like a cheese pudding than the Swiss variety. The mountain lakes and streams yield fine fish, of which three anyway are unlikely to be found elsewhere—the *féra, lavaret* and *omble chevalier*; all are types of salmon, but the last looks more like a trout. Carp, eel, pike, perch, crayfish and burbot (*lotte*) are also plentiful. As in many mountainous and rather wild regions, the smoked pork products and sausages are abundant—husky fare for climbers and those engaged in ski-ing and outdoor sports; *cochonnailles* (assorted pork meats) feature as *hors d'œuvres*, smoked raw ham and smoked sausages, sausages called *longeoles*, flavoured with anis, and variations on the pig include *le caïon* (loin of pork in a marinade). Slightly exotic game, such as hedgehog (*hérisson*), squirrel (*écureuil*) and marmot (*marmotte*) are mentioned in books about the regional foods before the 1939 war, but they have not come my way, though I imagine one might find them on the menu of remote solitary village inns, or on demand in a private lodging house. The *chamois* (same word) gets featured, so do thrushes (*grives*) of which a variety of *pâtés* are made, and the *civet*, a term best translated by our culinary word 'jug', can include hare or pork in a rich sauce.

The chickens of Bourg-en-Bresse (this is just on the edge of the region and Franche-Comté) are famous throughout France, and in fact they have an *appellation contrôlée* guaranteeing their quality and are to be identified by a ring on the bird's foot. They are fed on corn and wander about the roads in the Bresse plain, plumpening visibly; when killed, they are bathed in milk and the flesh is very white. If you see them alive in the market, you will note their blue legs, wattles and combs. The flavour is delicate and therefore such a bird will usually be offered plainly roasted, when the skin turns a beautiful crisp golden-brown; the *poulet de Bresse* (*poularde* is the henbird, should a menu be that precise) will cost more than the ordinary *poulet de grain* (grain-fed chicken), but it should be worth the extra. However, the A.C. can be given to birds actually not of the original Bresse breed, which are either reared in the region or else brought in to be finally fattened in it, and then you may be in for a slight disappointment, though it is only fair to say that I have on occasions had a chicken that was as good as all but the finest of the Bresse type and only found it to be an outsider by inquiring. As with all things, the responsibility is that of the buyer of the bird.

Noodles (*nouilles*) are often featured in dishes as well as being served as vegetables, and there is a vegetable called the *cardon*, in fact an edible thistle, rather like celery. The potatoes are usually excellent, as they might be expected to be to feature in the numerous *gratins* (see below), and there are plenty of mushrooms of different kinds including one called a *mousseron*, in addition to *cèpes*, *morilles*, truffles, and even *épis de maïs* (sweetcorn), which elsewhere is considered—unless the cook is definitely advanced in his or her ideas—as really only fit for cattle food. Pumpkin (*courge*) is another vegetable not often seen much elsewhere. The nuts, both walnuts (*noix*) and chestnuts (*châtaignes*), from around Grenoble are famous and *huile de noix* (walnut oil) is often used for salads and seasoning as in the Dordogne (see p. 229).

A curious sweet dish is made with potatoes, called *le farçon* or *le farcement*, involving the potatoes being beaten up with eggs, sugar and butter, and sometimes even fruit and a liqueur, as well as salt, pepper and possibly chervil, and then being grilled. *Talmouses* are like small sweetened potato fritters. There are many other sweet things, the nougat of Montélimar being very well-known (the town is virtually one long nougat shop, see p. 298), *sucre d'orge* (sticks of barley sugar) from Evian, honey from Queyras, *pets de nonne* (small potato and sugar yeast buns) from Chamonix, *noix confits* (candied walnuts), from Grenoble, and all kinds of chocolates from Grenoble, including a type called *délices à la Chartreuse*, which are filled with the liqueur. *Biscuits de Savoie* are also well known.

Specialities and dishes

Le gratin This in various forms, is *the* local dish. The word actually means crust, hence the French slang term '*le gratin*' means 'the upper crust' of society, and in cooking gratin means anything on which a crust has been made to form, after the application of heat; thus it applies not only to things with a crisped surface of cheese, but dishes with crumbs on top, or even just milk or cream. Of the *gratin Dauphinois* the following rhyme has been written:

> *Non, tu n'es point un mets vulgaire,*
> *Savoureux gratin dauphinois,*
> *Blond chef d'œuvre d'art culinaire*
> *Qu'on mange en se léchant les doigts.*

Though why one should eat any gratin, except the famous one

with crayfish tails, with one's fingers, I cannot imagine. There are a whole range of gratins, including those made with millet, pumpkin, different fruits, thrushes and *bolets* (boletus mushrooms), but the two most famous are undoubtedly the *gratin de queues d'écrevisses* (crayfish tails), which are poached and served in a rich creamy sauce, and the two sorts of potato gratin. These last are really like the nursery dish, potato pie, but can achieve such delicacy of quality that I have known local gourmets argue for a considerable time as to the precise texture of the potatoes and the proportions of the cheese involved in a gratin. The *gratin Dauphinois*, in addition to thinly sliced potatoes, contains milk, eggs, butter and grated cheese, but the *gratin Savoyard* is made with bouillon instead of milk. Potatoes served as accompaniments to dishes are sometimes described as *à la savoyarde*, or *dauphinois* and will be cooked in these respective ways, and omelettes containing potatoes and cheese are also made with the same description applying to them.

Angurre de Belley   Pickled water melon.

Caillettes   Pig's liver chopped with spinach, herbs, rolled in a caul and baked and served hot or cold. *Caillettes triscabines*, a speciality of Pierrelate, also contain chopped white truffles.

Pain de lapin dauphinois   A type of quenelle (see pp. 196 and 210) or meat ball of pounded rabbit and cream, in a cream sauce.

Défarde Crestoise   A curious stew of tripe and lambs' feet, boiled with vegetables and herbs, and served in a sauce of white wine, tomatoes and stock. A speciality of Crest.

Pogne   This is a great sweet dish, but can vary considerably according to where you are. In north Dauphiné it is usually a deep, open fruit pie, with pumpkin filling or fruit, but towards the south it may be a sweet brioche or bun.

Cheeses

Bleu de Bresse   A blue-veined cheese, described as reminiscent of Gorgonzola, but much creamier, softer, and looser in texture.

Chèvrotins, or small goat cheeses, are usually found in the region.

St Marcellin   Formerly a mixture of cow and goat milk, it may now be all cow milk as well. It is soft and creamy. *Tomme de Romans* is similar. Both are round, flattish cheeses.

Tomme de Savoie   There are several *tommes* in the region and this is the most famous. It is large, round and quite tall, made entirely from cow milk.

Tomme au fenouil is fennel-flavoured, and *tomme au marc de raisins*, which recently became very popular in Britain, is the tomme which has been impressed with a coating of grape pips; it is sometimes also called *fondu*.

Picodon   A soft goat cheese, made in the Drôme.

Persillé des Aravis   A small cylindrical goat cheese.

Mont Cenis   A hard cheese, with a blue mould, usually a mixture of cow, ewe and goat milk.

Fromage de Tamié   A moderately soft, cow milk cheese, rather like Saint Paulin, made by the Trappists of the Abbey of Tamié, near Annecy.

Vacherin des Bauges   A round, thickish, fairly soft cheese, made from cow milk and rather like a Coulommiers when ripe.

Bleu de Sassenage   A cow milk cheese, with blue veining, moderately soft and cylindrical in shape.

Tignard   A cow milk cheese but the name *Tigne* is often given to blue goat or ewe-milk cheeses.

Gruyère and **Emmenthal** are both made in France in this region.

Beaufort   This, to me, is a very fine cheese, but seldom found. It is made up in the mountains and in several ways resembles Gruyère, but it should be quite 'blind', without any holes, and the big wheel shape to which it is moulded has curved-in sides. It has a fatter flavour than Gruyère.

Beaumont is similar to Beaufort.

Reblochon   Considered by many to be the great regional cheese. The name comes from a word in patois meaning the second milking of the cows—*rebloche*. It is yellow in colour, round and thick in shape, fairly soft in texture and is a little like Port Salut. *Beaupré de Roybon* and *Chambaraud* are similar.

Drinks

Ciders and beers are made in this region, as well as wine, but the drink that, in my opinion, best deserves wider knowledge is the vermouth of Chambéry, in which the herbs of the mountains are incorporated. Chambéry is very delicate, usually dry and rather fragrant and is mostly drunk by itself as an *apéritif*, chilled and sometimes with a twist of lemon. It is quite unlike the other French vermouths.

If you ask the sommelier for a fine red wine, he will probably recommend one from the Beaujolais or Côte Rôtie, in adjacent regions, but the red Savoy Montmélian, Saint Jean de la Porte and Côte Hyot should at least be tried when one is on the spot. The remainder of the wines are white and it is probably fair to say that none of them are really more than holiday drinks, which can be very pleasant but are unlikely to attain great subtlety or character. Seyssel is possibly the best known wine of Savoy, dry and pleasantly fresh, and there are in addition Chablais from the north of Savoie, Crépy on the borders of France and Switzerland, Frangy, Egignin, Aise and Roussette. In and around Chambéry a white wine called Apremont is to be had, also dry, and there is another called Marétel which is rather sweeter. All these wines go well with the fish and creamy dishes, such as the gratins. Seyssel is sometimes made into sparkling wine, but the best-known sparkling drink is Clairette de Die, which is perhaps the only really distinguished wine of the Dauphiné; it is made by the Champagne method, and is fragrant and not too dry, making a very pleasant *apéritif* indeed.

Fruit liqueurs are made, as they are in most mountain regions, and the slightly bitter *gentiane*, an excellent digestive, appears in various branded preparations. *China*, an odd name, is a liqueur made from wild cherries and is a speciality of Grenoble, which is also responsible for the violet coloured and scented *Parfait Amour*; camomile liqueur, different kinds of cherry brandy and kirsch, and fruit brandies made from *plosses* or *airelles*, berries variously translated as bilberries or barberries, are also found. *Genopy des Alpes* is a digestive from Grenoble and Voiron and *Vespétro* a sweetish digestive, also from Grenoble. Marc is made, as it is in most wine regions, but there is also a strange and very fierce liqueur called *la lie* which is distilled from all the residue of the grapes after the final pressings.

The great liqueur of the area is of course *Chartreuse*, named for the Carthusian order founded by Saint Bruno at Chartreuse near Grenoble in 1084. It was a group of French army officers, billeted in the abbey at Voiron in 1848 who spread the fame of the different liqueurs made—green, yellow and something known as *elixir de Chartreuse*, pure white. A distillery was built at Fourvoirie in 1860 and did good business until the Carthusians were expelled from France in 1903, when they took the secret of their liqueurs to Tarragona. They returned to France in 1931 and, after the Fourvoirie distillery was destroyed (see pp. 73 and 306) in 1935, another one was built at Voiron. Green Chartreuse is one of the strongest of all liqueurs, and is sometimes referred to as 'Chartreuse de santé'; the yellow is weaker. Both are excellent digestives.

Things to see and do

Albertville The Musée de la Maison Rouge contains exhibits and furniture of Savoyard life.

Annecy The Palais de l'Isle contains the Musée du Vieil Annecy, with the reconstruction of an old kitchen and equipment. The Hotel de Ville contains local china and glassware in its museum.

Belley The birthplace of Brillat-Savarin (1755–1826), author of *La Physiologie du Goût*, and containing a statue to him.

Bourg-en-Bresse Visitors to the church at Brou, a masterpiece of French art, should see the Cloître de Cuisines in which there is a reconstruction of a Bresse house with furniture and equipment.

Chambéry The Grande Distillerie Chambérienne is open to visitors and is of special interest because two quite different types of vermouth are made there—Gaudin and Dolin. The two other big vermouth establishments, Richard and Chambéry-Moulin, are also well worth seeing. The Musée Savoisien contains exhibits of popular life. It was in the part of the Château destroyed in 1798 that the famous feast was given by which a cake created a duchy. Count Amédée of Savoy was entertaining the Emperor Sigismond in the huge Imperial salon in 1416; no expense was spared, each course was presented by the local lords, each on horseback, magnificently caparisoned. A gigantic cake was finally brought in, in the shape of the Comté of Savoy and Amédée, proudly displaying it to his imperial guest, casually remarked, 'It would make a nice duchy, wouldn't it?' After which the Emperor took the hint, and Savoy did in fact become a duchy and Amédée a duke.

Grenoble The Musée Dauphinois contains exhibits relating to the region.

Thonon-les-Bains In the Château de Sonnaz a museum of the region has been set up. At the Établissement Domanial de Pisciculture there is an important series of exhibits of fishes and material to enable visitors to study their development, including the regional *omble chevalier*.

Château de Ripaille As well as the Château, the gardens and kitchens of the Carthusians who inherited the property from the last Duke of Savoy are open to visitors. The curious expression *'faire ripaille'* originally implied that a life of abstinence was lived, like that of Amédée VIII, who renounced his dukedom to live a monastic existence in 1439. Later on, however, the expression acquired a completely opposite meaning and, due chiefly to Voltaire, 'faire ripaille' came to mean 'to live a luxurious and self-indulgent life of feasts and parties'.

Bauges In this region 'argenterie des Bauges' means wooden tableware, a craft now on the decline, but of interest to anyone interested in handwork.

Die There are some local exhibits in the Musée.

Gap In the Musée Départemental there are exhibits of local furniture and furnishings and china.

Voiron The distillery where Chartreuse liqueur is now made, under supervision of the monks (the monastic buildings of La Grande Chartreuse are not open to visitors), may be visited. The former distillery built at Fourvoirie in 1860 was destroyed by a landslide in 1935, but the ruins may still be seen.

Evian-les-Bains Visitors may see the Source Cachat and bottling of the mineral waters. The guardroom of the Château de Larringes, from which there is a superb view over the Jura mountains and the Alps, is now a tea-room, worth a visit.

Genève The Musée Ariana is the international Academy of Ceramics, in which most interesting exhibits may be seen.

Annual wine occasions

Exact dates for these vary, but local tourist offices should have particulars and also provisional programmes. Otherwise, the French Government Tourist Office, by whose kind permission this table is reproduced, may have details of the regional events.

Ammerschwihr (Haut-Rhin) April: wine fair.

Arbois (Jura) September: *Fête du Biou*, or festival of the new wine.

Auvillars (Tarn-et-Garonne) May: *Fête de la Saint-Noë*, vignerons' festival.

Barr (Bas-Rhin) July: wine fair; October: vintage festival.

Beaune (Côte d'Or) November: *Les Trois Glorieuses*, culmination of the wine season; sale of wine at Hospice de Beaune.

Béziers (Hérault) October: vintage *corrida* in bull-ring.

Boulbon (Bouches-du-Rhône) June: procession of St. Marcellin, patron.

Brancion (Saône-et-Loire) January: wine fair, feast of St. Vincent, patron.

Brignoles (Var) March: exhibition of provincial wines.

Champagne region January: procession of St. Vincent, patron of vignerons.

SAVOIE AND DAUPHINÉ

Clos Vougeot (Côte d'Or) November: *Les Trois Glorieuses*.
Colmar (Haut-Rhin) August: Alsace wine fair.
Condom (Gers) September: Armagnac fair.
Dijon (Côte d'Or) September: wine festival; November: international food and wine fair.
Fontainebleau (Seine-et-Marne) October: sale of *treille du Roy* grapes.
Jurançon (Basses-Pyrénées) September: proclamation (*Ban*) of vintage.
Lesparre (Gironde) August: Médoc wine fair.
Mâcon (Saône-et-Loire) May: wine fair.
Metz (Moselle) October: vintage feast.
Meursault (Côte d'Or) November: *Les Trois Glorieuses*, wine banquet.
Molsheim (Bas-Rhin) May: wine fair; October: grape festival.
Montpellier (Hérault) October: international wine fair.
Nantes (Loire-Atlantique) November: wine fair.
Narbonne (Aude) September: vintage festival.
Nîmes (Gard) September: vintage *corrida*.
Nuits-Saint-Georges (Côte d'Or) November: *Les Trois Glorieuses*.
Obernai (Bas-Rhin) October: vintage festival.
Pauillac, Médoc (Gironde) June: festival of St. Vincent; September: *Ban des vendanges* proclaimed.
Peyrehorade (Landes) September: festival of the wine harvest.
Pomarez (Landes) October: *fête des vendanges*.
Ribeauvillé (Haut-Rhin) July: wine fair; September: *Pfiffertag* and wine tasting.
Saint-Emilion (Gironde) May: *Fete de la Jurade*; September: *Ban des vendanges* and *Jurade* of St. Emilion.
Saint-Pourçain-sur-Sioule (Allier) February: wine fair; August: wine fair.
Sancerre (Cher) April: wine fair.
Saumur (Maine-et-Loire) February: wine fair.
Thann (Haut-Rhin) July: wine tasting of wines of Alsace.
Toulouse (Haute-Garonne) June: wine fair.
Tours (Indre-et-Loire) January: wine fair.
Valbonne (Alpes-Maritimes) February: grape festival.
Villefranche-lès-Avignon (Gard) April: *Fête de St. Marc*, patron saint.
Villefranche-sur-Saône (Rhône) June: festival of wines of Beaujolais.

Suggestions for Further Reading

There are many books available on the gastronomic resources of France, but, except for the Michelin guides, I have omitted those written in French, presuming that those whose command of the language enables them to read it easily will be able to pick guide and reference books for themselves.

Recipe books and regional food

French Country Cooking
French Provincial Cooking
A Book of Mediterranean Food } Penguin
Summer Cooking

Elizabeth David, author of all these, is the individual most responsible for the post-war interest in cooking and her wise and delightful books, full of information and reminiscences, contain the sort of recipes truly intended for the cook to attempt at home.

Bouquet de France Samuel Chamberlain (Hamish Hamilton)
A handsome compendium of tourism and gastronomy, by an American gastronome and happy traveller.

La Belle France (Paul Hamlyn)
A translation of articles from the glossy publication *Réalités*, beautifully illustrated, with information and recipes.

The Cooking of Provincial France M. F. K. Fisher (*Time-Life*)
Very lavish, very American, but the pictures are excellent and the author is somebody who knows about food, not merely about recipes, which makes it worth studying.

The Food of France Waverley Root (Cassell)
A discursive account of the gastronomic background of the French provinces—strongly recommended.

Traditional Recipes of the Provinces of France selected by
Curnonsky (W. H. Allen)

A handsome book, with regional information as well as recipes.

The French at Table Raymond Oliver (International Wine &
Food Society)

An account of the history of French gastronomy, by the well-
known chef and television personality.

Wine books

The Penguin Book of Wines Allan Sichel, 2nd edition revised
by Peter Sichel

This covers all the world's wines on sale in the U.K., but the
author was a special authority on the wines of France, where he
was the owner of properties as well as a shipper.

A Guide to Good Wine (Chambers)

Essays on the classic wines by members of the wine trade, most of
them at least third generation of well-known wine dynasties.

Wines and Spirits L. W. Marrison (Penguin)

Rather heavy going but useful on technicalities.

Wines and Spirits of the World edited by Alec Gold (Virtue
Publishing Co.)

Comprehensive and authoritative, by members of the wine
trade.

Encyclopaedia of Wines & Spirits Alexis Lichine (Cassell)

Comprehensive and discursive, some of the features controversial.

Encyclopaedia of Wine Frank Schoonmaker, edited for the
U.K. by Hugh Johnson (Nelson)

Useful and less bulky than the two previous volumes, by a leading
American enthusiast and man of wine.

A Book of French Wines Morton Shand, edited by Cyril
Ray (Penguin)

An old classic, with much to interest the contemporary reader.

The French Vineyards Denis Morris (Eyre & Spottiswoode)

A personal account of visits in the wine regions. Now occasionally out of date.

Vineyards of France   J. D. Scott (Hodder & Stoughton)

Gracefully written, by someone who worked in several of the classic areas.

Alsace and Its Wine Gardens   S. F. O. Hallgarten (Wine & Spirit Publications)

Food as well as wine, and much guide book material.

The Noble Grapes and Great Wines of France   André L. Simon (McGraw-Hill)

Superb pictures of grapes and basic information.

The Wines of Bordeaux   J.-R. Roger (André Deutsch)

Translated from the French.

The Wines of Bordeaux   Edmund Penning-Rowsell (International Wine & Food Society)

Possibly the most detailed and authoritative book on the subject.

The Wines of Burgundy   H. W. Yoxall (International Wine & Food Society)

As well as wine, contains useful information for the traveller.

Champagne, the wine, the land and the people   Patrick Forbes (Gollancz)

A most scholarly and easy to read account of the whole subject.

Lafite and **Bollinger** both by Cyril Ray   (Peter Davies)

Very readable histories of two great wines.

Generalised books

Eating French   Spike & Charmain Hughes (Methuen)

Detailed directory of menu terms, with much helpful advice for travellers.

The Hungry Archaeologist in France   Glyn Daniel

Deals chiefly with Carnac and Lascaux, useful even for the non-archaeological.

Three Rivers of France, West of the Rhône, Ways of Aquitaine all by Freda White (Faber)

Excellent background guidebooks, and also especially useful on Romanesque architecture.

The Generous Earth (Penguin) and **Sons of the Generous Earth** (Cassell) both by Philip Oyler

The author lives and farms in France and makes many wish to do likewise.

Fastness of France Bryan Morgan (Cleaver Hume)

Deals with the Massif Central—and is often very critical of food and drink.

Blue Trout and Black truffles Joseph Wechsberg (Gollancz)

Includes an account of some of the greatest French restaurants.

On to Andorra P. Youngman Carter (Hamish Hamilton)

An account of eating and drinking en route.

The Oysters of Locmariaquer Eleanor Clark (Secker & Warburg)

Britanny oysters—in great detail, though a curious and often confused style clouds much of the fascinating information.

France, Paris and the Provinces, The Provinces of France, and The Paris We Love all edited by Doré Ogrizek (McGraw-Hill)

These are translations, very attractively presented, containing numerous articles by many distinguished writers, including sections on gastronomy.

Guidebooks

There are numerous books dealing with the history and architecture of France in general and of different regions. For basic background history, I recommend André Maurois' **History of France** (Jonathan Cape), **Modern France** by S. Roe (Longmans) and **The Gallic Land** by Len Ortzen (Phoenix), which I have found easy to read. But there are many others.

The **Guide Michelin** of the current year is, in my opinion, essential for any traveller in France. It is not necessary to be able to read French to make full use of it, for most of the essential information on towns, hotels, restaurants, garages and map references is given by means of figures or signs, a key to which (in English) is at the front of the book. There are, of course, plenty of good hotels and restaurants that may not yet be in Michelin, but it is invaluable when in doubt. A point that sometimes causes confusion is that of the grading of the restaurants and hotels, as compared with the grading of the food; the description often heard 'three star', or 'two star' refers solely to the category of comfort the hotel can provide, and is the description in use in hotel directories and tourist offices. In Michelin this is indicated by the sign alongside the name of the hotel, or, when a restaurant is concerned, by the number of knives and forks. It is, of course, unlikely that one would get a very poor meal in a luxury establishment, but it certainly can happen and the grading of such establishments according to stars is only indicative of, for example, the numbers of private baths and suites, the gardens or other resources, or the décor of the restaurant. The famous 'stars' of Michelin, which are indicated by rosettes in the guide book, refer *solely* to the standard of the food and drink and the accomplishment of the chef, though a three star restaurant (of which there were only 12 in France in 1971) will certainly be faultlessly appointed and usually luxurious in a most discreet way. But a two star restaurant and certainly a one star establishment may be comparatively simple—the Guide will indicate, by the knives and forks, whether it is elegant or informal and plain.

The **Green Guides** of the Michelin series in French are very thorough on various regions and useful for detailed accounts of towns and special tourist attractions.

The **Julliard Guide to Paris** (Studio Vista) is now in English, and contains a most comprehensive directory to hotels, restaurants, shops, clubs and goods and services in Paris that the tourist may require. The restaurants are described in practical terms, with enthusiasm but without gush. The shops include wine merchants and specialists in tea, cheese, coffee and caviare. Only criticism—and unfortunately it is a serious one—is that there is no map of any kind.

The **Guide des Logis de France et Auberges Rurales** is a most sensible directory of hotels that can provide good accommodation on a 'family' budget—in other words, where a standard of amenities is maintained without extravagance. The Auberges Rurales are establishments of a slightly humbler kind, that will nevertheless be perfectly adequate for travellers who seek good but simple places to stay.

The **Guide des Relais Routiers** is a directory of hotels, restaurants, service stations for drivers and installations for campers and caravanners, concentrating on good value at really low prices. Both these directories are in French, but, like the *Guide Michelin*, the bulk of the information is presented by means of figures and signs.

List of **Relais de Campagne**. This is a small directory, in the form of an attractive brochure, listing an association of hotels and restaurants now extended across Europe. The most modest will be very comfortable, all will have some special charm—gardens, isolation, unusual installation, such as in an old château—and the majority are undeniably luxurious and therefore expensive. Most, however, offer real value in the finest traditions of French hotel-keeping if you are able to treat yourself to a stay and they are exceptionally pleasant for people who do not want to make continual excursions, as each is delightful as a place of residence. The food in most is very good—a number of them have Michelin stars for cooking, and some more than one. (Brochure from Les Relais de Campagne, (Service des Échos), 'La Cardinale', Baix, Ardèche), or Chewton Glen Hotel, New Milton, Hants.

Châteaux-Hôtels de France et Vieilles Demeures are a smaller chain of old castles, manors and country houses transformed into hotels and restaurants. A few are in the Relais chain as well. Graded according to the degree of luxury or mere comfort, food usually good. (Brochure from M. Garnier, 11 Rue la Boëtie, Paris 8.)

Baedeker's France is nowadays designed exclusively for the motorist, and deals with different routes, though there are some notes on places off the roads. It is good, though brief, but the pre-war regional Baedekers, which can often be found in second-hand bookshops, are still excellent on history, geography and the meticulous accounts of works of art.

The **Nagel** guide and the **Blue Guides** are factual and detailed, somewhat similar to the early Baedekers, perhaps without their charm. Useful for conscientious coverage of the country and for up-to-date information.

The **Fodor France** is in a series primarily intended for American tourists. It is rather superficial, but it is amusingly and attractively written, with useful sections on food and drink and notes about regional specialities.

The **Companion Guides** to Paris and the South of France are, I think, the ideal of what guide books should be—informative but readable as well as useful for reference.

The **Observer Time Off** series, though short, are good on food, drink and hotels.

The **People's France**, a series in many volumes dealing with different regions, is useful and helpful, including references to food and drink as well as to places, by way of background.

The Penguin Guide to Travel in Europe is good on France with information about food and wine.

There are many others, but as it is usually easier to have one moderately substantial and authoritative guide book, rather than a lot of small booklets, I have included only such volumes as I myself have found constantly useful and reliable.

Index to Maps

Index of Foods

English and French foodstuffs (not dishes) and general catering terms not detailed on the contents page under the separate chapters. For specific French food and drink terms and phraseology see the vocabularies at the end of each general section.

Index of Cheeses

INDEX OF CHEESES

Index of Drinks

Wine regions, specific districts and types of wine are included but not individual properties or vineyards. These will be found under the appropriate region. For wine establishments, etc., open to the public see under *Things to see and do* for each region.

Index of Towns

Towns in which there is something of interest for the gourmet traveller.